FATAL WOMEN

FATAL WOMEN

LESBIAN SEXUALITY
AND THE MARK OF AGGRESSION

Lynda Hart

PRINCETON UNIVERSITY PRESS   PRINCETON, NEW JERSEY

Copyright © 1994 by Princeton University Press
Published by Princeton University Press, 41 William Street,
Princeton, New Jersey 08540
All Rights Reserved

Library of Congress Cataloging-in-Publication Data

Hart, Lynda, 1953–
Fatal women : lesbian sexuality and the mark of aggression / Lynda Hart.
p.   cm.
Includes bibliographical references (p.) and index.
ISBN 0-691-03379-X (cloth) — ISBN 0-691-00093-X (pbk.)
1. Lesbianism in motion pictures. 2. Women in motion pictures.
3. Feminism and theater. 4. Lesbianism in literature. I. Title.
PN1995.9.L48H27 1994   93-44908
791.43′65206643—dc20   CIP

This book has been composed in Sabon

Cover Illustration, "The Knife," © copyright Jan Saudek 1993
c/o Art Unlimited, Amsterdam. From the book *Love, Life,
Death & Other Such Trifles.*

Princeton University Press books are printed
on acid-free paper and meet the guidelines
for permanence and durability of the Committee
on Production Guidelines for Book Longevity
of the Council on Library Resources

Printed in the United States of America

10 9 8 7 6 5 4 3 2 1

10 9 8 7 6 5 4 3 2 1 (Pbk.)

FOR AILEEN WUORNOS

AND FOR ALL THE WOMEN WHO HAVE BEEN

VILIFIED, PATHOLOGIZED, AND MURDERED

FOR DEFENDING THEMSELVES

BY WHATEVER MEANS NECESSARY

Contents

Preface

Criminals come in handy.[1]
  (Michel Foucault)

THE PRODUCTIVE TEXT, Roland Barthes argues, is one that "needs its shadow . . . a *bit* of ideology, a *bit* of representation, a *bit* of subject: ghosts, pockets, traces, necessary clouds: subversion must produce its own chiaroscuro."[2] If such a thing as a nonproductive text existed, it would be purified of doubling, the interiorization of the other that is necessary to produce and maintain a fictive autonomy. It would be all surface or all depth, lacking the paradoxical hollow cipher that Lacan calls the *Real*—the element that eludes symbolization but is nonetheless integral to the texture of meaning and ideology.

As Diana Fuss has noted, lesbian and gay theory is infused with the rhetoric of "hauntings." Pointing to this striking, repetitive fascination "with the specter of abjection, a certain preoccupation with the figure of the homosexual as specter and phantom, as spirit and revenant, as abject and undead," Fuss identifies such preoccupations as signs of a symbolic order that reproduces itself through "indispensable interior exclusion[s]" and calls for "an insistent and intrepid disorganization of the very structures which produce this inescapable logic."[3]

Fatal Women tracks the invention and circulation of "lesbians" as a haunting secret. The prominent manifestation of lesbian sexuality as a "secret" derives not from some hidden, mysterious, or esoteric *content*, but is rather a discursive *act* performed by the hierarchical ideology that systematically reconstructs the hetero/homo binary. By tracing some of these "ghosts" as recurrent perseverations—pathological repetitions of a profoundly paranoid heterosexist/patriarchal culture that persistently and ostentatiously exhibits and produces its necessary other in order to keep it under erasure—I hope to expose the discursive/material violence of this system's effort to secrete (set apart, sift, distinguish) the hetero from the homo.

My specific focus is on representations of aggressive "women." Each chapter selects figures that both underwrite and undercut the rigid dimorphism of same/opposite sex desire. I argue that one ghost in the machine of heterosexual patriarchy is the lesbian who shadows the entrance into representation of women's aggression. I am not developing this nega-

tivity in the interest of making lesbians visible. Rather, I demonstrate
some discursive maneuvers in which the production of violent women in
representation depends on a dis-articulated threat of desire between
women. It is not a matter, then, of looking for the lesbian *behind* representations of violent women, but rather of understanding how the lesbian
functions in a structural dialectic of appearance/disappearance where the
aggressive woman is visible. The lesbian (dis)appears in the masculine
imaginary so that the violent woman can ascend to her place in the phallocratic symbolic. She is, in a sense, the silent escort of the violent woman.
By unlocking this coupling, I indicate one mechanism whereby "women"
are paradoxically constructed as both inherently violent and incapable of
aggression. Lesbians in mainstream representations have almost always
been depicted as predatory, dangerous, and pathological. This representational history is as banal as it is pervasive. My point, however, is to
show that the shadow of the lesbian is laminated to the representation of
women's violence, that indeed it is the lesbian's absent presence that both
permits women's aggression to enter the specular field and defuses the full
force of its threat.

Feminist theorists have found themselves up against a psychoanalytic
impasse: desire inevitably verifies masculinity, foreclosing women's desire
for women. Hence Judith Butler refers to the "epistemic regime of presumptive heterosexuality"[4] and Mary Ann Doane acknowledges the "obsessive, even hysterical, inscription of heterosexuality"[5] in the closure of
Hollywood films. Julia Kristeva describes the "double or triple twists of
what is commonly called female homosexuality, or lesbianism," indicating the impossibility of a voice that could speak other than heterosexu-
ally: " 'I'm looking, as a man would, for a woman'; or else, 'I submit
myself, as if I were a man who thought he was a woman, to a woman who
thinks she is a man.' "[6] Teresa de Lauretis neatly sums up this heterosexual imperative: "One may not be born a woman or a man, *but one can
only desire as a man*" (my emphasis).[7] Thus we are led to conclude that
the economy of desire, grounded in specularity, is either heterosexual or
male homosexual. Building on the insights of these theorists and others,
I approach this problem from a different angle. If desire inevitably confirms masculinity, so does crime. Masculinity is as much verified by active
desire as it is by aggression. The question that initiated this study concerned what the latter had to tell us about the former. Pursuing this question, I came to see that these two discourses were not discrete. On the
contrary, the desiring subject as confirmation of masculinity to some extent depends on the presupposition that women cannot perform acts of
aggression. Historically inscribed both as "not-woman" and as violent,
the lesbian occupies an ambivalent position in this symbolic order. She

"comes in handy" as a criminal, but she is also something of a Trojan horse. She operates within this system as a *necessary* placeholder to rein in and provide closure to a heterosexual imperative, but she also functions to expose that little bit of the *Real* that the Symbolic must exclude.

Inversion theory allows us to historicize the foreclosure of lesbian desire as an interdiction produced to insure the functioning of a specifically white, middle-class, Eurocentric patriarchy. Psychoanalytic models of desire and juridical interventions have together produced a legacy in which lesbians have been rendered in representation as overwhelmingly white and middle-class. The "secret" of lesbian sexuality is thus not only a sexual secreting, but also a distinction that has been made along race and class divisions. Given this historical legacy, the impossible object of this quest is one that always depends on a double displacement. If it is anxiety about "lesbians" that informs representations of violent women, these "lesbians" are always already the inverted others of a white, middle-class masculine imaginary.

In my introductory chapter, I trace the historical configuration of the "invert" as the paradoxical prohibition of something that was always already impossible. In conjunction with two other historical figures, the "female offender" of nineteenth-century criminology and the "narcissist" of psychoanalysis, the invert is part of a triadic construction. These three figures enter history in discourses that attempted to render them distinct. But it is in their overlap and the theoretical moments of failure that we can read the reality-effects they continue to inscribe.

Each subsequent chapter looks at the way this historical model continues to inform representations of "female offenders." Chapter 2 focuses on one remarkable text from the nineteenth century. As both a novel and a play, *Lady Audley's Secret* was a resounding success. An exemplary Victorian "villainess," Lady Audley is a touchstone for the analysis of the criminalized woman's function in the reproduction of a homosocial economy. The narrative compulsion of *Lady Audley's Secret* is to penetrate the mystery of women's capacity for violence; but this representation, I argue, takes place within the context of another secret located in the scene of the patriarchal unconscious.

The Countess Geschwitz in Frank Wedekind's Lulu plays marks the entrance of the invert onto the European stage. In chapter 3, I historicize the production of these plays in the context of the German "Uranian" movement, which deployed the sexologists' "congenital burden" theory to defend homosexuals against legal and moral persecution. I propose a reading of these plays in which the Countess (the invert) and Lulu (the narcissist) are doubles, the former a construction that functions structurally as a shadow haunting the spaces inhabited by the narcissist.

Chapter 4 isolates two films, *Thelma and Louise* and *Mortal Thoughts*, from among the recent proliferation of "killer women" films that have captured the imagination of a mass audience. These two films represent women acting *together* in retaliation against the dominant culture's gender expectations. Summoned through negation both within these films' "content" and extradiegetically in critical responses to them is a history of identification between the female outlaw and the lesbian. These representations carry with them, and work overtime to disavow, the unconscious weight of a culture that has made the lesbian and the female criminal synonomous by displacing women's aggression onto the sexual deviant.

Performance artist Karen Finley entered the spotlight as the cynosure of the "NEA Four," the four performance artists who were denied funding by the NEA after being recommended by their peer panels. Finley was the only heterosexual among the four artists, which seemed to derail the theory that homophobia was the fundamental factor in the NEA's decision. In chapter 5, I propose that homophobia is a much more pervasive psychic mechanism than can be attributed to the overt targeting of self-identified lesbians and gays. Reading Finley's performances as assaults on the seamless, nonporous body of humanistic discourse, I argue that reactions to Finley's work demonstrate that the hetero/homo binary is always already undone.

While empirical data unfailingly verify that women of color are much more likely to be marked as criminals than white women, in the particular representations I am interrogating the women are white. In part this can be accounted for by the obvious fact that women of color rarely appear at all in dominant cultural representations. However, there is more to this story than a simple absence. It is also a predictable outcome of the argument I make in my introductory chapter that the invert in sexological discourse was a construct designed to serve the interests of white European patriarchy. In a sense, then, the lesbian has entered representation *as* white, and this "whiteness" becomes further encoded in psychoanalytic theory. In chapter 6, I return to this problem to consider its ideological consequences through a close reading of the popular film *Single White Female*.

The film *Basic Instinct* became a center of controversy when lesbian and gay activists protested its depiction of lesbian and bisexual women as sick, predatory murderers. Attempting to ruin the film's box-office appeal, demonstrators launched the strategy of revealing the ending of this thriller. The campaign was ineffective; *Basic Instinct* was an enormous financial success. In chapter 7, I re-pose the question of the film's homophobia. Rather than taking a content-based, positivist approach to this representation, I consider it from the angle of the film's formal failures. *Basic Instinct* most remarkably fails to conclude, the queer activists' stance notwithstanding, that "Catherine *did* it." I argue that in failing to achieve the conventions of the classic "whodunit," *Basic Instinct* can be read as a film that subversively makes apparent how The Woman functions in the symbolic order as an always-doubled construct. This pairing has been latent in earlier representations I discuss. *Basic Instinct* is of interest to feminist and lesbian theorists precisely because it makes manifest a masculine imaginary's reproduction of itself.

Aileen Wuornos is on death row in a Florida prison for killing seven middle-aged white men, all of whom she claimed were attempting to rape her and threatening her with further physical harm. Wuornos was a hitchhiking prostitute when she killed these men. The media and the courts have labeled her the "first woman (lesbian) serial killer." Chapter 8 situates Wuornos in the context of the historical nexus of prostitution and lesbianism, the inheritance from sexology of the lesbian's propensity for violence, and the law's ironic use of psychoanalytic "trauma" to prosecute rather than defend the woman who kills. Uncannily, Wuornos is the masculine imaginary's "dream come true," her actions constituting a transgression of the boundary between the real and the phantasmatic. Having torn this barrier that preserves the phallocratic symbolic, Wuornos has become the "impossible-real" realized. And for that, I argue, she has been sentenced to death.

Inspired by Aileen Wuornos and the media coverage of her arrest and trial, Deb Margolin scripted *Lesbians Who Kill* for the New York–based lesbian feminist troupe Split Britches. The performance is a pastiche of memories, seductions, and identifications in which the controlling principle is a game the two lesbian characters play—"looks like/is like." This game functions as a commentary on the dominant culture's investment in resemblance, a mimetic/metaphorical structure that subsumes all difference into sameness. The world of this performance is one in which the "femme fatale" as a fantasy-projection of the masculine imaginary is held up for scrutiny and played for all of its subversive humor. While the Radicalesbians of the 1970s defined themselves as "the rage of all women condensed to the point of explosion,"[8] lesbian-feminism has tended to disassociate itself from this anger. *Lesbians Who Kill* dares to claim it by putting the historical displacement of violence onto lesbians into lesbians' own hands and keeping their guns loaded. A short sojourn with *Lesbians Who Kill* is my Afterword.

Acknowledgments

I HAVE many people to thank for making this work possible. Peggy Phelan read innumerable drafts of this book. Working with her taught me how to give and receive without accumulating debt. Her rich intellect is marked in precise passages of the book, but it is also invisibly inscribed in more ways than I can know or wish to tally.

Leslie Thrope's love and support has been immeasurable.

This book probably began when my sister, Kerry Hart, asked santa claus for a copy of *Infamous Murderers*. Together we have shared three decades of fascination with and respect for women who kill. Kerry also supplied me with endless information on serial killers.

Amy Robinson has been, from the start, more colleague than student. She has read and discussed this work with me from its inception, and I am grateful for her intellectual courage and honesty. Anne Cubilie has also read a good part of the manuscript, and I thank her for her sharp commentary. Sara Beasley rescued me one hot July when I was preparing the manuscript for initial submission. Liza Yukins assisted me in the final stages of preparation.

Among my colleagues at Penn, Betsy Erkkila, Phyllis Rackin, Rebecca Bushnell, David Boyd, Cary Mazer, Carroll Smith-Rosenberg, and Peter Stallybrass have been particularly generous with their time and support. Una Chaudhauri, Kate Davy, Elin Diamond, Jill Dolan, Mary DeShazer, Catherine Keller, Chris Straayer, and Janelle Reinelt have all given me crucial support at various stages in the process.

I thank Judith Stern for patiently helping me keep the faith. And Chera Finnis, for knowing why I dare more.

The Kentucky Foundation for Women provided me with a grant that gave me a semester off to begin this book. I am grateful to Sallie Bingham and her organization that funds women writers who are working on such projects. I am grateful to The Penn Trustees' Council of Women for a summer grant that gave me funds I needed to continue working without interruption.

Robert Brown and Lauren Lepow at Princeton University Press have been stellar editors. I thank them for the careful attention they have given this manuscript at every stage in the process.

A portion of chapter 4 appeared as " 'Til Death Do Us Part: Impossible Spaces in *Thelma and Louise*," in the *Journal of the History of Sexuality*,

© 1994 by The University of Chicago. All rights reserved. An earlier version of chapter 5 appeared as "Karen Finley's Dirty Work: Censorship, Homophobia, and the NEA," in *Genders* 14 (Fall 1992), published by the University of Texas Press. The Afterword, "Zero Degree Deviancy— *Lesbians Who Kill*," also appears as an essay in *Sexual Artifice: Persons, Images, Politics*, ed. Ann Kibbey, Kayann Short, Abouali Farmanfarmaian (New York: New York University Press, 1994).

FATAL WOMEN

1

Introduction: The Paradox of Prohibition

In 1921, the British director of public prosecutions, Lord Desart, opposed instituting legal sanctions against lesbianism through an act of Parliament. He reasoned:

> You are going to tell the whole world that there is such an offence, to bring it to the notice of women who have never heard of it, never thought of it, never dreamt of it. I think that is a very great mischief.[1]

The lord chancellor concurred: "I would be bold enough to say that of every thousand women, taken as a whole, 999 have never heard a whisper of these practices."[2] These British legislators thus found themselves confronting a rather odd predicament—should they formally prohibit something that virtually did not exist?

The director of public prosecutions, the lord chancellor, and his men presumed that the act would not flourish in the absence of a signifier. Naming the activity threatened to produce the category, and thereby to mark a site that could actively be assumed. Yet if these women, who were presumably the ones who would be "doing it," did not know that it could be done, then what was the danger that prompted such considerations of interdiction? If the act could not precede the signifier, then what was the content that necessitated concealment? The paradox of this situation was that the virtual content necessitating a concealment was precluded. Thus the lawmakers were prompted to perform the paradoxical double gesture of prohibiting "the impossible."

The dilemma faced by these British legislators might be accounted for in sexology's paradoxical construction of homosexuality as inversion. For Havelock Ellis, female homosexuality was a category primarily produced under "special" circumstances and contained within the "lower races," the working class, and the criminally deviant. In the extensive footnotes to "Sexual Inversion in Women," Ellis dutifully records his sources who claimed that homosexuality was a widespread practice among women in Brazil, Bali, Zanzibar, Egypt, French Creole countries, and India, among other "othered" worlds. For example, Ellis cites an Indian Medical Service officer who pointed out to him that the "Hindustani language has five words to denote the tribade."[3] And Ellis found cause to believe that in prisons and lunatic asylums homosexual practices between women might have been *more* pronounced than those between men. Furthermore, situational homosexuality was found to be particularly prevalent among working-class women, whose close proximity to each other under stressful conditions inclined them to engage in homosexual acts.

The invert in sexological discourse was not identified merely as a sexual subject, but was always also a race- and class-specific entity. Lillian Faderman has observed that lesbianism "was not, as Alfred Douglas said of male homosexuality later in the century, the love that dared not speak its name. It was the love that had no name";[4] however, this would seem to be true only from a Eurocentric perspective. Indeed if we were to make a composite of Ellis's "typical" invert, she might well appear as a working-class woman of color who was either a criminal or a lunatic.

If the historical entry of the lesbian into discourse was her identification as the "invert" of sexology, it was a historical construct that not only pathologized and criminalized her but that also displaced the threat of women's sexual "deviance" onto women of color and working-class women. It would seem to be precisely when the threat of lesbianism became an area of concern for white middle-class European men that lesbianism was construed as a *secret* that must be withheld from its potential practitioners. That is to say, when the objects of concern become white, middle- and upper-class women, lesbianism became *foreclosed*.

I want, then, to pursue not the secret of lesbian sexuality but lesbian sexuality's entry into discourse *as a secret*. That the "whole world" and the representative thousand women referred to by these British parliamentarians were in fact class-, nation-, and race-specific worlds and women is transparently acknowledged in the British lord chancellor's fearful commentary: "Among all these, *in the homes of this country . . .* the taint of this noxious and horrible suspicion is to be imparted" (my emphasis).[5] As an identity was created for "women" that was formulated on the principle of excluding women of color and working-class women, the "secret" of lesbianism as a mysterious or esoteric content was produced as a discursive effect, an *act* performed by the hierarchical structure of a dominant ideology that systematically maintains itself through secret(ing)—setting apart, distinguishing, sifting. The distinction that was being made between heterosexuality and homosexuality was thus built on a prior division between white, middle-class women and other(ed) women: women of color and working-class women. What the legislators feared was that the sexologists' displacement of deviant sexuality onto these "other" women would spread into the worlds where they desired to keep their white wives and daughters.

That lesbians have not been subjected to the same rigor of the law as gay men is a commonly held assumption among historians. For example, David Greenberg asks, "If the male sexual drive could not be contained without the help of the criminal law, why was similar reinforcement not needed to control female sexuality?"[6] Jeffrey Weeks also takes note of this phenomenon: "It is striking that it was male homosexuality that was chiefly subject to new regulation. Lesbianism continued to be ignored by criminal codes."[7] In the first rigorous historical essay on this question, Louis Crompton exposed the "myth of lesbian impunity" in a scrupulously researched study of prosecutions against lesbianism in criminal laws from 1270 to 1791.[8] Challenging earlier historians' unwarranted generalizations based on English laws, Crompton's research shows that the "sodomite" could be of either sex. Yet there was little debate about what constituted an act of sodomy between men, whereas in regard to sex between women there was much ambiguity. Thus legislators quarreled about whether women were capable of penetration or emission, whether lighter penalties should be imposed if the women did not use instruments, and whether the "passive" partner should be held as accountable as the "active" one. The extent to which such acts departed from nature and the question of women's agency underwrites these issues. In the case of the male sodomite, such nuances did not appear pertinent.

In the first full-length study of lesbianism and the law, Ruthann Robson further challenges the assumption that lesbians have been exempt from legal prosecution. Arguing that "lesbianism" has been misnamed in official records, Robson's research is most valuable for its attention to the profoundly race- and class-biased research of historians who assumed that European culture ignored female homosexuality. Robson points out that notions of the impossibility of lesbian desire often presupposed that a large clitoris was necessary to perform the act of penetration (a feature presumed to be prevalent only among "African women"); and she notes that working-class women were "routinely arrested for committing 'crimes against chastity' or 'lewd and lascivious behavior'" (prostitution thus becoming an "umbrella term for women's sexual transgressions").[9] Robson's invaluable study demands that we rethink the history of lesbians in relation to the legal field. Rather than no history or insignificant histories, what we seem to be looking at is a history in which "the danger of mentioning an act outweighs the danger of not criminalizing that act."[10]

Robson's and Crompton's work productively recovers much of this history. And yet the paradox is not really undone. Their research does not indicate that lesbians were equally subjected to legal prosecutions; rather, it shows that gay men and lesbians have not been prosecuted in the same way and for the same offenses. The historical relevance of this difference resides largely in the idea that lesbianism remained a *secret* that could be kept from "women"—white, middle- and upper-class wives and daughters of the legislators.

As I have already indicated, one reason for this discursive act was to maintain and construct a category of "women" that was purified, unmixed with racial and class differences. Because a visual economy based on recognition via resemblance was the basis of this division, the culture's indifference toward inversion in women made for some curious mise-en-scènes. Ellis attributes this indifference to three causes: the inability to detect homosexuality among women due to greater social acceptance of intimacy between women; women's own lack of awareness of "abnormal or even normal manifestations of their sexual li[ves]"; and women's unwillingness to reveal their sexual intimacies even when they are aware of them.[11] In all three cases, sexuality between women remains in the realm of the secret.

Scene one is the failed detection: the women may or may not be sexually active, and may or may not know it themselves, but the dominant spectator is unable to see them and thus know them. Scene two is the hysterical mise-en-scène: the women are not themselves aware; the scene requires reading by an analyst or detective. Scene three is the refusal to collaborate: the sexually active women deliberately withhold this information. In both scenes one and three, the dominant spectator's ocular powers are confounded by the women. Only in scene two is the male onlooker positioned with the privilege of the subject-supposed-to-know. In the other two scenes, the detective is disarmed, unable to uncover her; she does not make herself present to him.

These explanations were echoed in and supported by commonplace assumptions about women before and after Ellis—that women are more emotional than men, that women are basically all alike, and that women are inherently deceptive.[12] Despite Ellis's claim for indifference, it was precisely these enigmatic qualities of women that were obsessively subjected to scrutiny by his peers, predecessors, and followers. In particular, the popular theory of slight variation among women—they are mostly all alike—contributes substantially to the invert's unknowability. Still contemplating man's indifference, Ellis points out that "well-marked and fully-developed cases of inversion are rarer in women than in men," while nonetheless "a slight degree of homosexuality is commoner in women than in men."[13] Whereas male homosexuality was more clearly marked, the boundary between heterosexual women and inverts was much more permeable. What emerges is a sexual subjectivity that eludes detection, confounds discernment, and is dangerously fluid. Ellis must finally conclude that the invert's "masculine element," what marks her off from the normal woman, may consist "*only* in the fact that she makes advances to the woman to whom she is attracted and treats all men in a cool, indifferent manner."[14] Despite Ellis's efforts to capture the invert in the dominant culture's gaze, it is finally to her looking at other women that he concedes. It is *her* indifference that marks her as inverted.

I want to suggest that the foreclosure of desire between women can be productively historicized through a return to the trope of inversion, which marks the emergence of female homosexuality as a discursive identity. If, as Luce Irigaray provocatively argues, a woman, within the terms of psychoanalytic sexual difference, is "a man minus the possibility of (re)presenting [herself] as a man,"[15] the female invert was a woman minus the possibility of representing herself as a woman. Although the inversion model attempted to preserve active desire for masculinity and thereby to secure a psychic heterosexual model, there was something in it that opened a space for what Monique Wittig has seen as the "shadow of a victory." In the sexologists' agreement that the "true" invert was not really a woman at all, there was a negative "avowal by the oppressor that 'woman' is not something that goes without saying, since to be one, one has to be a 'real' one."[16] Although the woman seduced by the congenital invert retained her feminine gender identification, this was nonetheless a rather desperate measure to insure the heterosexual imperative. For the "masculinity" of the congenital invert had already upset sexual difference by wedging open the conflation of biological sex and gender. The positivity of the feminist assertion since Simone de Beauvoir's formulation (one is not born but rather becomes a woman) was preceded by the negativity of inversion theory, which ironically proclaimed that one who is born a woman might become a man.[17]

Early medical case histories that pursued exacting biological differences between inverts and normal women—the size of their sexual organs, the frequency and quantity of their menstrual flows—were underwritten by the assumption that, as George Chauncey points out, "persons who behaved as the female invert did simply could not be women."[18] Nevertheless, despite an occasional "radical" thinker like Luigi-Maria Sinistrari d'Ameno, who argued that "accusations of lesbian sodomy should be discountenanced *unless* such anatomical irregularities are found" (my emphasis),[19] rarely did it seem to matter if such anatomical differences could be discerned. On the contrary, women were certainly prosecuted for homosexual acts even and perhaps especially when they were discovered to be anatomically "normal." The sexologists' protest that female inverts were not "real" women relied on the "truth" of a specular economy that soldered genitality with gender, but produced a contradiction in which the former claim subverted the latter. Thus inversion theories contained within them the seeds of their own deconstruction of gender dimorphism. Pressing on this contradiction, one would be forced to admit that "heterosexuality" could be performed by members of the same sex.

Caught in its own logic of "indifference" (i.e., sameness, the male monopoly on desire), inversion theory at one and the same time reaffirmed desire as masculine and heterosexuality as the normative model, but it also surely was a perverse inscription. For if the "normal" woman was man's opposite, the invert as the opposite of the normal woman became man's double. Imagining the female invert as inhabiting *his* sexual subject position effected a rupture in sexual difference that also established her as a powerful threat to his exclusive claim to masculinity. If the female invert "becomes a man" in order to preserve the heterosexual imperative of desire belonging to men only, that economy pays a price for this construct. The paradox of inversion theory uncovers what is concealed in heteropatriarchy, what Irigaray has called "*the sexual indifference that underlies the truth of any science, the logic of every discourse*" (author's emphasis).[20] The female invert could thus be understood as a figure constructed to maintain the relationship between heterosexuality as a naturalized economy that is governed by the "invisible" logic of hom(m)o-sociality. The necessity of recuperating her as a "man" points to that "unseen other scene" and reverses the terms themselves, so that the hom(m)o-social becomes visible. She is thus both necessary to and disruptive of that economy, and would thus appear to operate precisely like the symptom.

The symptom is constitutively paradoxical, for it is an element at once necessary to any system's ability to constitute itself as a totality *and* the site that marks that system's instability. The symptom then both maintains and corrupts. It operates to produce the illusion of some hidden content, signifying that some presumptive whole exists behind or beneath it to which it is related as a part. The symptom, in other words, has a metonymic structure. It is a clue that seduces one to interpretation, making an appeal to a subject-supposed-to-know, just as the hysteric manifests her symptoms so that the therapist can read them. The symptom is what gives support to being; it is what allows a signifying system to appear consistent, and yet it is also always in excess in that system, for it cannot be fully circumscribed within it. The negativity of the symptom is not unlike the lesbian as Marilyn Frye sees her being (un)seen by the phallocratic spectator: "When one is suspected of seeing women, one is spat summarily out of reality, through the cognitive gap and into the negative semantic space."[21]

The Woman, according to Lacan, is a symptom of man, a necessary irritant. But "woman" is also "not-all"; there is something in "her" that exceeds the signifying system of the phallocratic symbolic.[22] Slavoj Žižek argues that if the symptom were to become unbound, it would mean "literally 'the end of the world' . . . the total destruction of the symbolic universe."[23] If the symptom is understood as a sign that signifies a concealed content, it would be difficult to see how the unbinding of "woman" as man's symptom would produce such a cataclysm. But if symptoms are understood as *forms* that "hide" only the fact that when the veil is lifted there is nothing to be seen, then Žižek's apocalyptic predictions make sense. The symptom, in other words, operates precisely like the commodity; it is not in the substantive content of the commodity that its value inheres, but in the form of its appearance.

To precipitate these fatal consequences something more drastic is at stake than women's ceasing to function as referents for "woman." It would seem that in the masculine imaginary there must already be some ideational content to the notion of an "unbound" woman to produce the category "Woman" which preserves the phallocratic symbolic. The Woman, I would agree with Lacan, does not exist. But the imaginary category nonetheless produces very real effects that are historically and culturally specific. And somewhere within this imaginary category there are no doubt historical "identities." Always produced retroactively, identities are belated. Constructed backwards from their structural effects, identities are rather like (after)effects; that is, they are the effects of effects, not the causes for which they are taken.

The female "invert" was one of those identities constructed after the fact of the sexologists' recognition of "homosexuality" in women. The inversion model of same-sex desire facilitated the entry of the lesbian into the visual field, by establishing a set of characteristics that could presumably be interpreted/read, while at the same time making it impossible for her to be seen *as* a woman.

Lesbian identity has served many functions, among them as a site where women's aggression has been displaced. It is commonly understood that the pathological model superseded the criminalization of homosexuality, that "sickness" replaced "sinfulness." But history is not so linear. Both models continue to operate. And what is particularly pertinent for lesbian historians and theorists to remember is that the female invert's *aggressiveness* was what marked her as deviant and therefore dangerous, *not* her object choice. As Chauncey has argued, it was the invert's usurpation of masculine privilege that defined her sexuality: the "polarization of masculine and feminine sexuality suggests that the perversion . . . was not so much in the object of the woman's sexual desire as in the masculine, aggressive form it took."[24] Havelock Ellis concluded that among all the characteristics he enumerated in seeking to isolate the female invert, it was finally only her *initiation* of the seduction that set her apart from "normal" women. Chauncey reminds us that a "homosexual" woman could have been defined as a woman who "often wants to possess the male and not to be possessed by him," or a woman for whom "orgasm is often only possible in the superior position."[25] Underwriting the distinction between female homosexuality and heterosexuality was, and I think has continued to be, the activity/masculinity passivity/femininity imperative. Lillian Faderman's research has shown that the majority of women prosecuted for lesbianism have been accused of usurping "male" privileges either by cross-dressing, using phallic prostheses, or otherwise initiating the sexual encounter.[26]

Although Ellis does not equate cross-dressing with homosexuality, he makes a strong connection between them as he looks for readable signs to fix the invert in the visual field. By establishing a congenital basis for homosexuality, Ellis may have believed that he was liberating homosexuality from legal sanctions,[27] yet many of his examples of female inversion were cases in which he emphasized the women's violence. Ellis effectively introduced the invert as a criminal, not against nature, but against society. This was especially pronounced in the female invert: "a considerable proportion of the number of cases in which inversion has led to crimes of violence . . . has been among women."[28] Without theorizing a causal relationship, Ellis extensively documents incidents in which lesbians kill or attempt to kill: the "Memphis" case, in which Alice Mitchell, thwarted in her plans to cross-dress, take a male name, and marry her lover Freda Ward, cut Freda's throat to seal their love pact; the "Tiller sisters," romantically involved at the urging of the "congenitally inverted" sister, who broke into a male rival's apartment and shot him; a nurse who shot the man for whom her lesbian lover left her after fourteen years. Ellis pauses after recounting each case to comment that there was no evidence of insanity in these women. Rather, they were "typical inverts." Ellis does not see their acts as crimes of passion committed by hysterics, who were otherwise "normal" women and susceptible to rehabilitation; on the contrary, he implicates inverts as inherently criminalistic. In each case, it is the invert who initiates desire—the "true" invert—who becomes inextricably bound to the perpetration of violence.

Lest we think this is a story of historical interest but of no continuing significance, we might look at contemporary sociological studies of women in prison. As recently as 1987 Robert Leger argued that incarcerated lesbians are more likely to be recidivists, more likely to be feminists, and more likely to be aggressive than heterosexual inmates. Ostensibly this researcher wants to determine whether homosexuality among female prisoners is due to "deprivation" or "importation." The underlying concern is to distinguish categories of "born" and "made" lesbians and to determine which is more likely to be violent. Not surprisingly, the "born" lesbian turns out to be the more criminalistic, feministic, and homosexually *active*. "Could it be," Leger then asks, "that this group contains a high proportion . . . [of] 'true' lesbians while the other group contains a high proportion of penitentiary turnouts?"[29] Like this researcher, Ellis would probably have insisted that he was not "implying that lesbianism is causative of female criminality."[30] Nonetheless, these negations have effectively displaced the threat of women's aggression onto the figure of the "true" lesbian, who has been the site of aggression in some of the most powerful discourses in Western history.

This entrance of the lesbian into representation as a *negation* is coupled with her carrying the mark of aggression. It is a paradox with a specific function and history. That which a culture negates is necessarily included within it. As Barbara Babcock points out, inversion, at least since the early Renaissance "used to mean 'a turning upside down' and 'a reversal of position, order, sequence, or relation' (OED: 1477)" is a topos "which grows out of stringing together *impossibilia*."[31] The major convention of symbolic inversion is paradox, "which demonstrate[s] that what is 'not' can be discussed, though in strictest logical sense it cannot."[32] That which is "not" is nominally impossible, but it is not therefore not "real." On the contrary, what is quite real about the negated entity is that it is produced *as* impossible within the ideological system of a certain "reality."

The inversion model for same-sex desire was a classification system, and like all classificatory models, it was structured on the principle of negation. In order to pursue the paradoxical production of lesbian desire as both prohibited and impossible, I want to turn now to the making of the female offender in nineteenth-century criminal anthropology to trace her interconnectedness with the congenital invert of sexology. If desire always verifies masculinity, so does crime. And it is the wedding of these two discourses that produces the paradoxical object—the "impossible" lesbian, who was always already a criminal.

Making the Female Offender Man

In collaboration with his brother-in-law William Ferrero, Caesar Lombroso, the "father" of criminal anthropology, produced the massive study *The Female Offender* in 1893. Havelock Ellis praised Lombroso's work in his own study *The Criminal* (1890), sharing the anthropologist's obsession with classifying and categorizing different types of individuals, offensive and not offensive. Both made huge contributions to the vast project of patrolling the borders of femininity by marking off the normal woman from her deviant sisters. Both also produced what they ostensibly set out to prohibit, and in doing so constructed "impossible objects" that defied the logic of their own classificatory schemes.

Lombroso wrote *The Female Offender* in order to rescue the theory of anomaly that his predecessors had "rashly abandoned" when, following the anatomicopathological method, they could find no salient differences between the skull of Charlotte Corday and the crania of certain assassins.[33] Following the disciplinary logic of distribution around a norm and along a scale, *The Female Offender* assumes an unarticulated "normal woman" and an irremedial "born offender" at the scale's limit. As Ann Jones points out, Lombroso seemed to be "haunted by the fear that an apparently good woman might, at any unexpected moment, turn out to be bad."[34] Hence the excruciating, painstaking calculation of his subjects' physical attributes; the obsessive measuring of their crania, anklebones, middle fingers; the scrutinizing of their handwriting; the registering of their voices; the counting of gray hairs, wrinkles, tattoos—all part of the project to render the female offender visible, and thus containable.

Exhausted by these efforts and weighed down with the mass of contradictory evidence, Lombroso finally admits, "It must be confessed that these accumulated figures do not amount to much, but this result is only natural."[35] Failing to keep his three fundamental categories—the normal woman, the occasional offender, and the born criminal—discrete, Lombroso falls back on his culture's naturalization of women's inherent sameness and concludes that there is really very little to distinguish the normal woman from her criminal sister since "external differentiations . . . [are] fewer in the female than in the male." Agreeing with his fellow naturalists that "for the type of a species one must look to the female rather than the male,"[36] Lombroso undercuts his own typology even as he attempts to underwrite it. Male offenders, he is quick to point out, display an amazing wealth of anomalies to distinguish them from normal men: "it is incontestable that female offenders seem almost normal when compared to the male criminal, with his wealth of anomalous features."[37]

The exemplary characteristics of his culture's idea of Victorian white womanhood—piety, maternity, absence of sexual desire, weakness, and underdeveloped intelligence—keep the "latent" criminality of *all* women in check. When any of these traits are in abeyance, "the innocuous semi-criminal present in the normal woman must be transformed into a born criminal *more terrible than any man*" (my emphasis).[38] And why is she more terrible than any man? Because she has *become* one. Despite Lombroso's desperate clinging to an absolute difference marked off by the born female offender, he is caught in the paradox of claiming that any woman might become one, and thus he admits that the born female offender *is* made as he *makes* her. His prohibition produces the product it sets out to preclude.

How to recuperate this "error"? Lombroso responds by arguing that the "born" female offender is really not a woman. Her propensity is to approximate the dress, behavior, appearance, and eroticism of the male. She is marked by an absence of maternal affection, indicating further that she "belongs more to the male than the female sex."[39] In fact, he argues, she is more like a man, even a normal man, than she is like a normal woman. She retains the sex of a female but acquires the gender attributes of masculinity. She is tyrannical, selfish; she wants only to satisfy her own passions. Love is replaced in her by an "insatiable egotism."[40] She is incapable of resignation and sacrifice, and her desire results in acts of tyranny "such as [are] more often found in the love of a man than of a woman."[41] She is, in fact, remarkably like Ellis's congenital invert. For Lombroso as for Ellis, a female was always a woman, "fallen" though she might be, unless she transgressed a certain sexual boundary or performed extraordinary acts of violence. These transgressions were not discrete but rather coupled in the cultural formation of categories that fell outside the bounds of "womanhood" altogether. The congenital invert and the born female offender marked the limits of cultural femininity. And they did so as a couple, not separately, but together.

This is a wedding that has continued well into the twentieth century. Because empirical analyses unfailingly report that males far outnumber females in the perpetration of violent crimes, criminology is an area in which gender dimorphism seems to be rigidly confirmed. However, modern criminologists have been remarkably resistant to taking into account the most basic tenet of feminist theory—that sex and gender are not synonymous. As Ngaire Naffine demonstrates in her feminist reappraisal of women and crime, nearly every conceptual tool used by empiricists assumes that crime is already gendered. She makes this point most lucidly in her chapter "Masculinity Theory," which comprises two ideas: "crime is symbolically masculine and masculinity supplies the motive for a good deal of crime."[42] Masculinity theory pursues its circular reasoning by arguing that women are less likely to engage in criminal activity because they are not men. Boys will be boys, say the masculinity theorists; and girls will be girls, unless they do become criminals, in which case they are likely to be masculinized women. Thus even quite recent criminological studies get stuck in the tautological trap of their father theorists. Along the way they find themselves reluctantly conceding that some women "become men." If desire always verifies masculinity, whatever the subject's sex, so does crime. And they are historically inextricably linked.

Because they were "disciplinary mechanisms" seeking to define and limit the "truth" of femininity, sexology and criminology were discourses whose theoretical failures produced paradoxical objects that were negated at the very moment they were produced. Foreclosure of desire between women was always an interdiction, and one moreover that was constructed in order to serve a specifically white, middle-class, Eurocentric patriarchy. The "impossibility" of this object, however, was made possible by the displacement of the categories' presumed "content" onto others who were not considered relevant to the juridical project of classification. Already outside these schemes were the women who served as models against which the scale could be constructed.

"Proper" foreclosure of desire between women would wait for psychoanalysis to theorize. But the inversion model already served its purpose and interests—the erasure of lesbianism for the maintenance of white, Eurocentric patriarchy. Lesbianism was already recognized as prevalent among women of color and working-class women; foreclosure would "properly" pathologize it in order to obviate the "contagion" of the white, middle-class, European female. Lesbians would become "not-women" through a phobic maneuver to contain the danger of contagion from women who were always already "not-women." Inversion theory would thus subversively allow "lesbians" to enter history as a negation, while women of color and working-class women retained the "positivity," which was of course a displacement of the cultural degradation of same-sex love between women.

Thus the double strategy that produced the paradox of prohibiting something that was already considered impossible is manifested in the history of the criminalization of desire between women. The prohibition is paradoxical *not* because the "impossible" *preceded* the prohibition, but because the prohibition *produced* the impossible. Inversion was not just the historical model that made foreclosure possible. Inversion *was* foreclosure. It was not sufficient to merely disavow the possibility of desire between women; it was also necessary to *criminalize* it. But in the achievement of the latter, the former was partially undone.

The notion of lesbianism as a secret practice that demanded prohibition *before* it had an opportunity to emerge operates as a kind of reversal of the fetishistic disavowal. Freud's model is the little boy, who sees that his mother is lacking the phallus but disavows its absence and imagines that she has one anyway. Hence the fetishistic formula disavows the absence of the object and hallucinates its (re)appearance.[43] The aforementioned legislation worked on precisely the opposite assumption: "We know very well that lesbians do exist, but let us proceed as if they do not." Here the disavowal aims at prohibiting the object that is known to be present. Presumably, however, the "object" (practice) was absent for the very people who would potentially perform it. Thus, rather than an absent object being hallucinated as present, the formula for the secreting of lesbian sexuality was to produce its presence *as a hallucination*.

The "secret" of lesbian sexuality in this way became more than even a mere *symptom*: "a formation whose very consistency implies a certain non-knowledge on the part of the subject."[44] Lesbianism necessitated a more radical erasure. For symptoms could be "read," and thus in the reading the hidden content might return to make an appearance in the subject's "history." Desire between women was not merely repressed but foreclosed; it became that which must never appear in the light of the Symbolic. Withdrawn from the possibility of language, lesbianism indeed had no name/meaning. And what is precluded from symbolization, as Freud would say, "returns from without"; that is, what is foreclosed from the Symbolic *"must logically appear in the Real."*[45]

Slavoj Žižek's contention that the prohibition of something already impossible invariably attests to the presence of the Real—that "pure nothing" that is *included* in the signifying texture and "constructed afterwards so that we can account for the distortions of the symbolic structure"[46]—is the very formula whereby "real" lesbians became "Real" lesbians. Barred from the Symbolic, which was always only *a* masculine imaginary, lesbians became the never-spoken words that signified the hole in the signifier of this masculine imaginary. The lesbian who was derived from inversion theory was not an "outlaw"; rather, she was a void around which white Eurocentric phallocrats maintained their patriarchal system. She was outlawed from the Law of the Father.

Apocalyptic Fantasies

Desire between women has persistently been represented as destructive of the social order. This is an assumption that is undoubtedly linked to the fear of any and all nonprocreative sexualities. George Chauncey describes the Victorian sexual order in which "sexual relations outside the heterosexual institution of marriage . . . represented not only a degeneration to an earlier, lower state of evolution, *but threatened civilization itself*" (my emphasis).[47] These apocalyptic predictions in the dominant culture's response to homosexuality tend to surpass the rationale of nonprocreative sex. Homophobia is a much more complicated psychic mechanism that exceeds such a simple explanation. As Marilyn Frye says, "This sounds extreme, of course, perhaps even hysterical . . . that feminists, whom [phallocrats] fairly reasonably judge to be lesbians, have the power to bring down civilization, to dissolve the social order as we know it, to cause the demise of the species, by [their] mere existence."[48]

And yet, as Eve Sedgwick rightly maintains, the homosexual "coming out" has attained a cultural potency that is unlike the revelation of any other secret—the "consciousness of a potential for serious injury that is likely to go in both directions."[49] Sedgwick refers to the commonly voiced fear among gays and lesbians that "in fantasy, though not in fantasy only, against the fear of being killed or wished dead . . . in such a revelation there is apt to recoil the often more intensely imagined possibility of its killing *them*" (author's emphasis).[50] The disclosure of a homosexual identity produces such intense fantasies of destruction because the knowledge that is imparted impacts on the subject to whom the information is directed. That is, it is not simply a disclosure of one's "self" that the homosexual coming out effects, but also always a shattering of the recipient's fantasy of a stable sexual identity. The disclosure violates the tacit pact between the addresser and the addressee, what Sedgwick has called the "open secret,"[51] which is structured as a fetishistic disavowal—"we both know that you are gay/lesbian, but we will proceed all the same as if we did not know."

Coming out is then not simply making an appearance as a sexual subject. The disclosure is not the revelation of a secret, but an implication of how the addressee's desire is constituted and maintained by the production and dis-appearance of its opposite/other. Homosexual disclosures thus reveal the paradox of sexual identities. For on the one hand, heterosexuality secures its ontology by constructing the homosexual as external and foreign, and hence implicitly hostile. On the other hand, the homosexual is intrinsic to the constitution of the heterosexual—the "other" *within*—the "perversion" always only comprehended as a deviation from "normality." Understood this way, coming out is a de-secreting, a rupture of the binary opposition. It instigates a crisis that undoes the distinguishing, the setting apart, the secession of the "one" from the "other." Hence, the cataclysm, the dissolve, the demise is directed at the coherency of *any* sexual identity. Within a cultural order that has been dependent on the notion of a structured self, the irony of the production of "selves" that have been defined as exclusively sexual subjects is in their assault on the inviolate cogito.[52] Sexual identities are at once necessary to the maintenance of the dominant cultural order and inherently disruptive of it. They are thus exemplary instances of what Lacan calls the "real-impossible."[53] That is, they are positions that are impossible to occupy, but their retroactive constructions are necessary to uphold the fictional coherency of a symbolic order.

The secret is thus not about the substance of something hidden, but rather it is a construct born in the desire of the one who proposes a narrative *of* secrecy. Like the Lacanian *objet petit a*, the secret is "the chimeri-cal object of fantasy, the object causing our [*sic*] desire and at the same time—this is its paradox—posed retroactively by this desire."[54] As long as the Law of the Symbolic (the Law of the Father in phallocratic reality) is functioning smoothly, we can predict that the force of other legislation is not particularly urgent. It is in historical moments when efforts to con-tain desire between women become pressing that we are keyed in to pro-ductive breaks in the Symbolic Order. When white European men at-tempted to check the contagious desire between women by laminating it to the body of the "true" invert, we are witnessing one of those breaks in the Symbolic Order. But like all typologies, the sexologists' model ulti-mately deconstructed itself. What inversion theory could not contain was the "true" invert's initiation of desire. Her seduction appropriated "mas-culine" subjectivity and her looking at other women disrupted the fiction of the gendered conflation of femininity with passivity. The actively desir-ing woman thus entered history as a "criminal," for in confirming her desire, she exceeded the terms that ratified masculinity. The very effort to authenticate her invalidated the gender dichotomy that it was intended to corroborate.

In pursuit of this paradoxical "real-impossible" desire between women, I want now to look at what happens to her when Freud takes on the enigma of woman. The woman with the "masculinity complex" in psychoanalysis carries the historical trace of the female offender in crimi-nological discourse and the congenital invert of sexology. I want to argue that the notion of a "female offender" is in some sense a redundancy. For the enigma of woman and the riddle of her capacity for violence are inter-dependent. The "violent" woman is not an exceptional figure. Rather, she is a handy construct that serves white patriarchal heterosexuality. She is essential to this discourse and functions most usefully as a specialized and hence containable category—The Lesbian—who, like The Woman, does not exist but most certainly has some useful properties for the patri-archal symbolic as well as some debilitating effects on it.

Reading Freud's theoretical detours, Sarah Kofman has provocatively ar-gued that "On Narcissism" presents a possibility that is quickly sealed over: the conceptualization of "the enigma of woman along the lines of the great criminal rather than the hysteric."[55] Kofman argues that the discourse of hysteria becomes a cover-up, a path constructed to evade a conclusion that Freud had nonetheless already reached. Like the panic that overcame him in the back alleys of Genoa when he fled from his accidental encounter with prostitutes, Freud, Kofman argues, fled from that which he thought he had overcome in himself—narcissism and femi-ninity. By following Freud, we are led down the path of hysteria rather

than confronting its alternative, the criminality of women. It was as if
Freud "(and men in general) 'knew,' dream-fashion, that women were
'great criminals' but nevertheless strove, by bringing about such a reversal as occurs in dreams, to pass them off as hysterics."[56] Underpinning
Kofman's reading are the traces of the female offender of criminological
discourse and the hysteric of sexological discourse, who are related to one
another historically. Kofman's insistence that women's criminality is suppressed in Freud's theory of narcissism highlights a negation that, when
developed, reveals a significant blind spot in psychoanalytic theory.

Jean Laplanche points out that "On Narcissism" confirms Freud's observations on perversions, homosexuality, and psychosis, while it also
"constitutes a veritable calling into question of the theory in its entirety."[57] Thus Freud came to consider his theory of narcissism "incomplete, if not monstrous."[58] Compellingly inspired by his observations of
"perverts and homosexuals," who were "plainly seeking *themselves* as a
love-object" (author's emphasis),[59] Freud's theory of narcissism might be
understood as "monstrous" because it inadvertently confirmed what
Lacan would later theorize: that the sexual *relation* is impossible.[60] For if
we follow the circuitous path of "On Narcissism," it leads to what Luce
Irigaray has called "the blind spot of an old dream of symmetry,"[61] in
which homosexuality is patently the prop for heterosexuality, and heterosexuality is always already hom(m)o-sexuality—the desire for the self/
same that necessitates the violent incorporation of the other.

In Freud's theory, narcissistic desire appears at first to be non-object-
directed. In an apparently rigidly gendered system, men love according to
the anaclitic (attachment) type, overvaluing their objects and thus impoverishing their egos. Women, on the other hand, at least the "purest and
truest" ones, do not form true object choices. Rather, they seek solely to
satisfy themselves and are indifferent to their objects. He is the lover; she
is the beloved. As the theory first unfolds, men are capable of recognizing
the different/other, whereas women can only desire the same/self. Initially
then, the paradigm of desire in "On Narcissism" situates men as heterosexual and women as autoerotic.

But the gendered asymmetry of this desire begins to break down as we
follow Freud's argument. First, men's desire for the different/other turns
into desire for the same, but for a psychically historical self, the "self" as
he *once was*, which he recognizes in the indifference of the narcissistic
woman who shares with great criminals an ego that wards off anything
that might diminish it. Men's desire for the narcissistic woman is manifested as envy for women's "blissful state of mind—an unassailable libidinal position,"[62] projected onto *her* image as something "we ourselves"
(Freud and other men) have since abandoned.[63] It is not the woman who
envies the man in "On Narcissism"; rather, it is "he who envies her for

her unassailable libidinal position, whereas he himself—one may wonder why—has been impoverished, has been emptied of this original narcissism in favor of the love object."[64]

Lacan points out that Freud does wonder why man suffers this impoverishment and "asks himself the question why does man get out of narcissism. Why is man dissatisfied?"[65] At this critical moment Freud responds by quoting the poet Heine: "God is speaking, and says, '*Illness is no doubt the final cause of the whole urge to create. By creating, I could recover. By creating, I became healthy.*'"[66] It is at this moment that we can understand Irigaray's claim that psychoanalysis is a *negative theology*.[67] God commands man to renounce the flesh and embrace the spirit. The narcissistic wound is a renunciation of eros, which is incorporated into logos. Man's ego becomes impoverished because it is in a state of being perpetually rejected by the object of his desire. But the paradox is, of course, that man constructs desire as the desire *for* desire, with Woman as symptom, holding the space around which his desire circulates but can never reach its object.

As Lacan has shown, the bipolar conception of the libido in Freud's *Three Essays*, which emerges from a "primitive auto-eroticism," begins to break down when "one generalises excessively the notion of libido, because, in doing so, one neutralises it."[68] Because it explains nothing about the "facts of neurosis if the libido functions roughly in the same way . . . [as the] function of the real," and since we must not fail to remember that Freud's observations on the libido's functions were based on the observations of neurotics (and specifically perverts and homosexuals in "On Narcissism"), then the "libido takes on its meaning by being *distinguished* from the real, or realisable, relations" (my emphasis).[69]

The formalization of this unrealizable desire is best expressed in courtly love, which Lacan explains as "an altogether refined way of making up for the absence of sexual relations by pretending that it is we who put an obstacle to it." For Lacan, courtly love was a ruse, a rationale "for the man, whose lady was entirely, in the most servile sense of the term, his female subject." Thus courtly love "is the only way of coming off elegantly from the absence of sexual relation." The formalization of courtly love is then, for Lacan, a "fraud" that needs to be exposed; for it is rooted in the "discourse of fealty, of fidelity to the person," but the person, the unattainable "lady" as object of desire, is in fact "always the discourse of the master," the "good old God" whom the theologians may be able to do without, but whom Lacan cannot dispense with because he is "dealing with the Other," which might be "one alone" but "must have some relation to what appears of the other sex."[70]

What is the Other's relation to the "other sex"? First, it is a relation of *appearance*, a specular relation. As Catherine Clément explains, the

Other may be "a person, a human being equipped like any other human being with powers of speech, thought, reflection." But more broadly, the Other "is that which lacks . . . a location, a place from which the human subject can draw what it needs to express its desire, desire notorious for its lacunae and always after what it does not have—what above all it does not want to have."[71] If the "lady" of the courtly love tradition is the "person" of the Other in the first instance, she becomes Woman as symptom in the second, broader, psychoanalytic formation of desire as the desire for desire, which is always predicated on a lacking. Lacan says it quite clearly: Woman is a symptom of man, for "when one is a man, one sees in one's partner what can serve, narcissistically, to act as one's own support."[72] Phallocratic desire is thus always a relation to the *objet a*, and "the whole of his realisation in the sexual relation comes down to fantasy."[73]

The desire for desire is a negative theology because it is a discourse of the spirit that deifies the Phallus as lacking. It subsumes eros into logos. Like courtly love, it is an ethic of renunciation that is sustained through the promise, and expectation, of attaining one's object (the master) in (an)other place—an (after)life. It is a sacrificial discourse that commands relinquishing the flesh to preserve one's soul. Lacan asks if the soul cannot be understood as "love's effect. In effect, as long as soul souls for soul . . . there is no sex in the affair. Sex does not count. The soul is conjured out of what is *hommosexual*, as is perfectly legible from history."[74]

As Richard Mackey brilliantly demonstrates, courtly love, perceived as a "rival religion" by medieval theologians, was parallel to what St. Augustine called lust[75]—the "inordinate love of created things from which [men] are urgently dissuaded and in which they experience nothing but misery and frustration," as opposed to the "ordinate love of God to which Christians are enjoined and by which they are beatified."[76] In the courtly love tradition, man's love was not aroused by its object "but by the mind's excessive meditation on what it sees." Thus sexual love was always narcissistic: "self-love—a fascination with one's own imaginings." Eros is subsumed by logos when the object of desire is not woman but "the representation of woman."[77] That is to say, man's representations of woman.

If, as Lacan says, "speaking of love is in itself a *jouissance*,"[78] phallocratic desire, like courtly love, is nothing but this speaking. As Mackey explains:

> The medium has become the message. The reality of sex is sublated and sublimated in the discourse of love. Eros is subsumed without remainder into logos. . . . love is spiritualized—made "courtly" or *honestus*—by its translation into language. Courtly love becomes thereby the inverse (and no doubt

perverse) counterpart of the heavenly love imagined in monastic commentaries on *The Song of Songs*. Each is a purified eros directed at an ideal object, in the one case God and in the other a lady, who, in her unapproachable remoteness, is the intentional (albeit not the actual) equivalent of God. Both the love of God and the love of woman are *meant* to produce a certain perfection in the lover: single-minded chaste devotion to the beloved.[79]

But courtly love (like inversion theory) threatens to deconstruct itself. Constructed "under the sign of paradox," as Mackey elaborates, courtly love's intentional design was to gratify desire; but it was constructed as an interminable postponement: "Without sexual desire, courtly love could not exist. But it cannot tolerate the satisfaction of the desire that sponsors it."[80] Andreas Capellanus, the primary spokesman for the rhetoric of courtly love, writes his text to his young friend Walter, whom he enjoins to "pass by all the vanities of the world, so that when the Bridegroom cometh to celebrate the greater nuptials, and the cry ariseth in the night, you may be prepared to go forth to meet Him with your lamps filled and to go in with Him to the divine marriage."[81]

The paradox of courtly rhetoric takes the shape of a failed incarnation—a dis-incarnation—in which the "flesh becomes word." And like phallocratic desire for desire, it is an ideology that interdicts the physical expression of desire between men, and at the same time an elaborate testimony to the value of hom(m)o-sexual love. Both proscribe homosexuality, prescribe hom(m)o-sexuality, and construct The Woman as the site where this paradoxical economy can maintain and reproduce itself. Desire in this masculine imaginary is, as Lacan unequivocally declares, "supported by the reflection of like to like."[82] Phallocratic desire thus presumes resemblance, which, as Foucault points out, itself "presumes a primary reference that prescribes and classes."[83]

Freud's association of narcissism with femininity exposes the construction of the feminine as a prop to maintain the Symbolic Order, which is always already a masculine imaginary. Narcissism is a negative ethic because it reveals the profoundly immoral nature of all sexual love. Phallocratic "reality" thus renders it under the sign of "Woman" who, as the always elusive object, permits the hom(m)o-social/sexual order to maintain itself. This desire, however, inevitably erupts into the social—in the "realisable" relations that are then designated as the "perversions."

Lacan explains that Freud's observations of perversions and neurosis gave way to the realization that they were in no way the same thing. "Neurosis is dream rather than perversion. Neurotics have none of the characteristics of the pervert. They simply dream that they have, which is natural, since how else could they *reach their sexual partner?*" (my emphasis).[84] The perversions thus exceed, or surpass, phallocratic desire. In the perversions there is "a subversion of conduct, based on a know-how, linked to a knowledge . . . which leads directly from sexual conduct to its truth, namely, its amorality."[85] Thus when Lacan writes, "Morality stops short at the level of the id," and this shows that "the sexual relation founders in nonsense,"[86] his reference is always heterosexuality. For the "perverts" do attain their objects, reach their sexual partners, though everyone, from Aristotle on, "has refused to recognize them at any price."[87] For the price one pays for recognizing the perversions is not only the recognition that sexual love is essentially amoral, but also that it is nonetheless *possible*. And it is this possibility that is so dangerous to the stability of a Symbolic Order that has constructed elaborate codes of desire to preserve itself from the anarchy of sexuality.

Jean Laplanche explains that narcissism has "nothing to borrow from the self-sufficient and closed form of an 'egg.'"[88] Rather, it is object-directed after all, but its "object" is displaced in order that homosexuality give way to the teleological narrative in which heterosexuality is the end point. Heterosexuality then becomes nothing more than displaced homosexuality, which is proscribed for men but returns through an uncanny projection onto women. If the male lover's anaclitic desire turns out to be a displaced narcissism, a desire for what he once was, then it would seem that he is in fact incapable of recognizing the object as truly other.

Women's incapacity for object-directed desire, following Freud's argument, is less complicated. They can achieve complete object love only by having a child, the road to salvation from their narcissism and the same program recommended for rehabilitating the female offender as well as anchoring the wandering womb of the hysteric. Nonetheless, there are certain exceptions that complicate this conception of women's desire. There are those women who do not have to wait for the birth of a child to achieve object-directed love. These are the women who "before puberty . . . feel masculine and develop some way along masculine lines; after this trend has been cut short on their reaching female maturity, they still retain the capacity of longing for a masculine ideal—an ideal which is in fact a survival of the boyish nature that *they themselves once possessed*" (my emphasis).[89] Thus these women, just like men, desire what they once were but were forced to abandon. In doing so, however, they become hystericized by the discourse of phallocentrism. That is, these special cases of women (Freud's "exceptions") are recuperated to what is for Lacan the "*ultimate* point . . . of hysteria . . . or of acting the man, . . . thereby becoming, they too, hommosexual or outsidesex" (my emphasis).[90]

What begins as a rigidly gendered asymmetrical relationship between the (male) lover and the (female) beloved in "On Narcissism" becomes an amazing symmetry when the displaced desire of men is traced back to its source and the repressed desire of women is lifted. Both men and women become narcissists. And narcissism collapses into homosexuality. Kofman argues that Freud's defensiveness in "On Narcissism" stems from the identification of narcissism with a regressive libidinal stage as well as its association with a negative ethic, "an egoism that has to be overcome."[91] However, Kofman skirts what Freud also "concludes" in "On Narcissism," that heterosexuality is only, at best, precariously achieved.

What Freud inherits from the sexologists is the historical inscription of the woman who seeks solely to satisfy herself as "inverted." As Ellis emphatically concludes, it is the invert who displays "absolute indifference toward men" as her determining feature. So too is the "born female offender" in Lombroso's typology a forerunner of the narcissistic woman. Unlike the occasional offender or the hysteric, the born female offender of criminal anthropology is also incapable of (object-directed) love. Her insatiable egotism and thus her desire presage the narcissist.

The Female Offender (1893), like *Studies in Hysteria* (1895), is a discourse of rehabilitation that is obsessed with transitional figures, "intermediate" types who defy classification. Lombroso marked off his "occasional offenders" from "normal" (nonviolent) women and "born" offenders. Occasional offenders were often hysterics, who differed almost imperceptibly from normal women. These intermediate types were "fallen," and from an almost hyperfemininity. Often they were excessively proficient in maternal love and chastity, and were seduced into crime by men to whom they were exceptionally devoted. Their crimes of passion could be attributed to an overabundance of love. In prison, they displayed undying devotion to the men they had wronged, and they avoided recidivism by recuperating in excess the qualities that typified the normal woman—piety, chastity, and maternal devotion. Their most remarkable characteristic, however, is their overbearing eroticism. Indeed "all the criminality of the hysterical subject has reference to sexual functions."[92] But unlike the "semi-masculine, tyrannical, and selfish" born criminal who wants only to satisfy her own passions, the occasional offender puts trust in her male protectors and regains confidence in men— especially her lawyer, and in some cases that Lombroso is fond of relating, her executioner.[93]

The criminal hysteric of Lombroso's typology is an obvious forerunner of Freud's hysteric, whom he refers to as an "accomplice" in the analysis. Like the criminologists, Freud emphasizes that the hysteric must divulge her secret willingly by overcoming her resistances. Her desire is to confess, although her resistances to confession mask this desire from herself. The "born criminal," on the other hand, is conscious of her secret and willfully conceals it. Kofman suggests that hysteria was such a vital and productive discourse because it provided a solution "more gratifying to men if not to women."[94] She argues that the "interests at stake [were] not at all 'theoretical': the task assigned to thought in both cases seems in fact to be that of warding off some formidable danger."[95]

But what constituted this danger? Citing Freud's "Taboo of Virginity," Kofman suggests it provides one answer in that men find women terrifying because their difference makes them "for ever incomprehensible and mysterious, strange and therefore apparently hostile."[96] She argues that Freud's fixed idea, penis envy, which all of his theorizing presupposed, allows men to solve the problem by conceiving of them as the "weaker sex," while at the same time it is paradoxically what "unleashes [women's] hostile bitterness."[97] If penis envy is the solution, which "effectively allows men to surrender to women's manipulations without danger,"[98] it is also the problem of women's potential aggression. Thus psychoanalysis produced women as paradoxical. First they were constructed as incomprehensibly different, and therefore apparently hostile in the first instance; then psychoanalysis was faced with constructing another theory that would mitigate the very danger it had made.

What we can infer from Kofman's analysis is that hysteria serves as a wedge to hold open a space for the achievement of femininity. Without the hysteric, Freud's theory risks collapsing into the assertion that all women are potential criminals, as did the criminal anthropologists. Hysteria becomes a site for the contest over the sexuality of women, and it is the therapist's (or magistrate's) task to facilitate her cure or rehabilitation. Although Freud attempted to erase it, Kofman's reading shows us that the "criminal" option haunts the hysterical path. That this hysterical space for controlling women's sexuality might be held open, stable terms had to be produced on either side of it. The hysteric could either be restored to the "wholeness" of normal femininity or "degenerate" into the perversity of the criminal. All three terms are necessary to the production of Woman.

In this sense, psychoanalysis was, like criminal anthropology, a differential typology. Like Foucault's "disciplines," it classified and categorized in order to effect the continual production of its terms, aiming not to answer the riddle, but to *reproduce* it. Solving the enigma is not the goal. On the contrary, reproducing The Woman as enigma is the solution to the reproduction of a specific form of desire. This desire for desire is male heterosexual desire in which the "object" is forever unattainable, elusive, because The Woman is a symptom. It reformulates, and thereby "confirms," a dynamic of desire that, like courtly love, is based on an interdiction of physical love between men and a foreclosure of desire between women.

Traceable in the constant preoccupation with the (im)morality of women and the ever-present paranoia that women possess an inferior sense of justice, psychoanalysis obsessively reproduces "women" as implicitly dangerous. The ideological enforcement of women's passivity, in concert with the theory of penis envy, makes this danger titillating without letting it become a serious threat. As a precaution to the potential chaos of this delicate balance, however, a particular historical "body" has been the site where women's aggression, when and if it is unleashed, can be contained by maintaining it *outside* the category of women. Due paradoxically to her *proximity* to men, who have constructed her as their intimate other/double, the lesbian body has been the site of the displacement of "women's" aggression. As Jonathan Dollimore argues, when relations between the dominant and the subordinate are considered in terms of their proximity rather than their differences, the "perverse dynamic" is born:

> First: those proximates will permanently remind the dominant of its actual instability . . . as well as produce a paranoid fear of impending subversion. So there will be both a justified fear as well as an excess of fear; second, that proximity will become the means enabling displacement and projection, while the justified/paranoid fears will be their motivation: *proximity becomes a condition of displacement*; which in turn marks the same/proximate as radically other.[99] (My emphasis)

We can see the displacement of women's aggression onto the sexually deviant woman operating as Freud's position on the ethical inferiority of women shifts subtly but significantly from "Some Psychical Consequences of the Anatomical Distinction between the Sexes" (1925) to "Femininity" (1933). In the first essay he writes, "I cannot evade the notion (though I hesitate to give it expression) that for women the level of what is ethically normal is *different* from what it is in men" (my emphasis).[100] Eight years later, Freud discovers the distinctly female Oedipal complex. Knowing then that women remained in the Oedipal complex longer than men, and that indeed they resolved it later *if at all*, he concludes that women's superego formation was not merely different, but unequivocally inferior: "[the woman's] formation of the super-ego must suffer; it cannot attain the strength and independence which give it its cultural signficance."[101]

Why does Freud become so emphatic after discovering the female Oedipal complex? It is of course this discovery that makes the achievement

of femininity (heterosexuality) particularly dubious. Difference has attained a more radical danger. Attempting to assuage his feminist colleagues, Freud throws them the bone of bisexuality: they can consider
themselves "exceptions" in this regard; that is, masculine. But what of
those other feminists, the ones he fears will be "anxious to force us to
regard the two sexes as completely equal in position and worth."[102] If
these were not the "masculine" feminists, then whom did he have in mind
and what kind of force were they prepared to use? Might these have been
the women who remained in the female Oedipal complex and were thus,
like the narcissist, forever incapable of object-directed (heterosexual)
love? Certainly the conflation of "militant" feminism with a propensity
toward homosexuality has been rife in medical and sociological literature
before and since Freud.[103]

Freud was confident that the inadequate formation of the superego
produces a "life-long insufficiency" that will displease the feminists. But
might it have been Freud's desire that the feminists would be displeased?
The superego functions to give "permanent expression to the influence of
the parents," and thus it "perpetuates the existence of the factors to
which it owes its origin."[104] It exercises moral censorship, produces a
sense of religious humility, and carries on the role of the father and other
figures of authority. Those "other" feminists, the ones who were not exceptional, were without a doubt proving the existence of their inferior
superegos as they agitated against certain forms of moral censorship, disrupted their prescribed social roles, and challenged the father and other
forms of authority. In "The Ego and the Super-Ego," Freud offers an
example of the superego's function as both prescriptive and prohibitive.
The compliant ego presumably submits to the superego's lesson: "You
ought to be like this (like your father)," but "you *may not be* like this (like
your father)—that is, you may not do all that he does; some things are his
prerogative."[105] If this is the dialogue between a fully functioning super-
ego and a compliant ego, then what would women's faulty superegos say
to their egos? They might not say anything at all, or they might even
invert the message: "You ought not to be like your father; but you can do
everything he does."

As the principal mechanism of the superego, guilt regulates "the tension between the demands of the conscience and the actual performances
of the ego."[106] Women's faulty superegos should render them less susceptible to guilt. In the short piece "Criminals from a Sense of Guilt," Freud
addresses the puzzle of people who are paradoxically guilty *before* a mis-
deed occurs, and thus commit crimes in order to assuage their guilt. Like
Nietzsche's "pale criminals," they offend in order to rationalize their
guilt. Although Freud makes no overt gender distinctions in this essay,

given his theory of women's inferior superegos they would seem to be more likely the "exceptions" in this essay: adult criminals who "have either developed no moral inhibitions or who, in their conflict with society, consider themselves justified in their actions."[107] Since Freud attributes this feeling of being guilty before the fact to memories of the Oedipal complex, men would seem to be more likely candidates as criminals from a sense of guilt.

The exceptions might be understood as "political criminals," a type adumbrated by Ellis in *The Criminal* (1890). Ellis describes these political criminals as "victim[s] of an attempt by a more or less despotic Government to preserve its own stability."[108] And Lombroso considered the political criminal "the true precursor of the progressive movement of humanity."[109] Ellis asserts that the word "criminal" in the political criminal's case is merely a "euphemism to express the suppression of a small minority by a majority," and considers the word "crime" in this context to be an "abuse of language," a conception "necessary to ensure the supremacy of a Government, just as the conception of heresy is necessary to ensure the supremacy of a Church."[110] When Lombroso picks up Ellis's typology of criminals and expands it in his work on the female offender, the "criminal of passion" and the "insane criminal" are fully elaborated. Yet glaringly absent from Lombroso's classification of female offenders is the political criminal. Only male criminals can be justified in their actions. Legitimately or illegitimately, crime is constantly a verification of masculinity.

The path briefly opened, then sealed over, in "On Narcissism" is a particularly charged moment in this history. For in the popular imagination narcissism and lesbianism had already been linked. Bram Dijkstra has traced nineteenth-century artistic transformations of the altruistic woman into the narcissist. The woman who ceased to be self-sacrificial became "destructive of the masculine ego"; the construction of the ideal woman was ironically revealed as the "ideal destroyer"; the woman's "kiss in the glass" became the century's "emblem of her enmity toward man, the iconic sign of her obstructive perversity."[111] At first, these "criminally self-absorbed" women were depicted as autoerotics, as was Zola's Nana who displayed "a passion for her body, an ecstatic admiration of her satin skin and the supple lines of her figure, [which] kept her serious, attentive and absorbed in the love of herself."[112] These "narcissists" were represented as increasingly dangerous as they "drew away from man's civilizing influence."[113]

Ellis found this self-absorbed autoerotic particularly "true-to-life" in a representation from a novel, *Genio y Figura* (1897). In this passage Rafaela's urge to make love to her own image is instigated by the admiring gaze of her maid as she bathes. She insists that "what I do is not out of gross sensuality but aesthetic platonism. I imitate Narcissus; and to the cold surface of the mirror I apply my lips and kiss my own image."[114] But what is clearly indicated here is that the admiring look of another woman instigates sexual desire. That Rafaela's desire could be expressed only through "self-love" is undoubtedly due not merely to a denial of same-sex desire, but also to the class difference between the women. That it is the *maid* who initiates the look that precipitates desire affirms Ellis's displacement of active homosexuality onto the "lower classes." The upper-class woman's response cannot be directed at the source of her pleasure; it is recuperated as autoeroticism/narcissism. Rafaela might imaginably, in seeing herself being seen, recognize that she might also be authorized to look and reciprocate her maid's desire; but this threat is contained so that the purity of the Woman whom she represents may be preserved. Despite these recuperative ploys, as the altruist became the egoist, so the narcissist nonetheless became the lesbian. It was an incarnation that contained—held together—the masculine imaginary *and* pointed to its inherent instability.

Criminal anthropology, sexology, and psychoanalysis shared in the complex historical construction of the female offender. Each in its own way linked criminality with deviant sexualities. These discourses overlapped and sometimes contradicted each other. If it is in their imbrications that we can read a hypostatization of the "lesbian" as criminal, it is in their internal disturbances that we can see a series of phobic displacements of criminality onto lesbianism. In the chapters that follow, I consider the ways in which the residue of this history has continued to inform representations of female offenders.

2

The Victorian Villainess
and the Patriarchal Unconscious

> Common sense and [Caesar] Lombroso's own
> experience told him that there were only . . .
> two kinds of women in the world—bad and
> good—but he seemed haunted by the fear that
> an apparently good woman might, at any unex-
> pected moment, turn out to be bad.[1]
> (Ann Jones, *Women Who Kill*)

IF VICTORIAN patriarchs shared this concern with the father of criminal
anthropology, the popular fare of the nineteenth-century melodramatic
stage frequently allayed this anxiety by reversing the formula. For the
most part, at their worst Victorian heroines were fallen but recuperable.
In Lombroso's typology of "female offenders," most Victorian villainesses would have been categorized as "occasional offenders," women
like the immensely popular Lady Isabel of *East Lynne* (1862) whose unrestrained passion meets unparalleled punishment. After the spectacle of
Isabel's abjection, the explicit warning—"Lady-wife-mother! should you
ever be tempted to abandon your home, so will you awake!"[2]—is almost
subversive in its superfluity. It would appear to serve not only to remind
female spectators of the shaky foundation upon which their own claims
to respectability had been erected, but also to blur the distinction between
"bad" and "good" women. The message that any woman might become
a Lady Isabel if she lost her footing may have struck terror in the hearts
of women, but it also might have provoked more anxiety in the eyes of
men. The trajectory of "normal" femininity and that of "fallen" womanhood were not two parallel lines incapable of meeting; on the contrary, a
slippery slope lay between the two states. This could not have failed to
disconcert the keepers of a social order who relied on a stable and circumscribed image of woman. Like Lombroso's troublesome occasional offenders, who were repentant and open to rehabilitation, fallen women
differed only in circumstances from normal women.

Lombroso and his fellow criminologists sought a distinct barrier to isolate the normal woman from the born offender, a boundary manufactured as rigidly gender-dimorphic. Women who were incapable of redemption simply were not women at all. The born offender, usually a murderess, was in the last analysis not even an aberration of femininity, but rather a man, albeit problematically in a woman's body, a close cousin to her newly constructed sister the invert. Thus the ultimate violation of the social instinct, murder, and the perversion of the sexual instinct, same-sex desire, were linked as limits that marked the boundaries of femininity. Crossing either one of those borders constituted a transgression from which there was no return. Women who killed, and women who loved other women, passed through the mirror of oppositional gender discourse and landed on the other side.

The unrestrained passion of a Lady Isabel was thus no match to the threat of a Lady Audley. For it was the woman who killed, and especially the woman who murdered to further her social interests and *not* in response to sexual passion, who most profoundly challenged the order of heterosexual patriarchy. The cool, calculating killers whom Mary Hartman documents in her study, *Victorian Murderesses*, may have inspired theatrical representations, but the stage versions were rarely the rational, self-conscious women of her observations. Like the nineteenth-century woman-who-wrote, the Victorian woman-who-killed more often than not did not really do it, or she did it only as an accomplice, or she did it but did not know what she was doing.[3] Even when she *did* do it, she was not really present to herself. The frontispiece of a playbill may have lured spectators with the titillation of female villainy, but sinister images like "Joanna preparing the poison for Sir John" in Lady Cavendish's *The Woman of the World* (1858) usually miscarried in the action. Joanna is one of those heroines who was controlled by the evil mesmerist Monti, and her meek and truthful nature is affirmed in the end by doting Uncle John, her erstwhile victim.

The female criminal of the melodramatic stage and the sensation novel from which many of these plays were adapted usually fit the specifications of the classic "femme fatale," who, as Mary Ann Doane points out, has power that is "not subject to her conscious will . . . she is not the subject of power but its *carrier*"; she is "evacuat[ed] of intention."[4] The nineteenth-century stage and the sensation novel would then seem to be most unlikely places to look for feminist subversions. We might at first simply agree with Elaine Showalter: "even as they recorded their disillusion, their frustration, their anger, indeed, their murderous feelings, the sensationalists could not bring themselves to undertake a radical inquiry into the role of women."[5] And yet, as Martha Vicinus compellingly argues, Victorian drama is not a minor art form without literary interest, but "a

vehicle for some of the most powerful fantasies and desires of the time."[6]
While Showalter rightly laments the absence of a conscious critique of
gender inequities in the sensation novel, Vicinus perceives a latent subver-
siveness in the surface conservatism of melodrama. I want to argue that if
we position ourselves on a slightly different axis in relation to these texts,
we can read a *patent* critique of heterosexual patriarchy by developing
the virtual image of these texts' unconscious. The picture that emerges
may be something like a hologram—an image that is produced through
the recording of interference patterns. But I contend that it is precisely
these "interferences" that can be reconstructed, not in order to get a
"true" print, but to introduce another angle to what can never be more
than a partial perspective.

As the most popular of Victorian villainesses, whose character was
drawn from a novel that was "one of the greatest successes in publishing
history,"[7] Lady Audley and her secrets might bear a closer look. Even
though Lady Audley badly bungled her principal crimes, and indeed did
not succeed in killing either her first husband or her prying stepnephew,
she is nonetheless a rare example of a Victorian woman who intends to
kill with calm, premeditative deliberation and fails to repent with any
sincerity. In the truncated stage adaptations of *Lady Audley's Secret*, her
hysteria at the end is introduced as the deus ex machina of madness, a
thoroughly predictable formal device for resolving a plot that would otherwise end with the evidently unseeable scene of a woman who attempted
two rational homicides. As Vicinus points out, "The central problem of
melodrama was that it raised serious issues and then could not resolve
them"—could not, that is, resolve them without posing a radical challenge to the social order that melodrama was designed to uphold.[8] This
melodramatic pattern of raising the issues only to recuperate them to the
status quo, however, risks the excesses of paradox, where that which is to
be warded off instead overtakes the *doxa*. If we return to Braddon's
novel, it is possible to read an excess that overflows this containment of
the female offender within a hysterical discourse. The obsessive presentation of the Victorian villainess speaks to a desire for the unveiling of her
secret, and thus to some corner of the "enigma" of woman at large. But
the narrative compulsion to penetrate the mystery of women's violence
takes place within the context of another secret, in the scene of the patriarchal unconscious.

Braddon is not nearly so concerned with the sensationalized woman as
she is with the character and investigative strategies of her hero, Robert
Audley, who develops both aim and passion in life in the pursuit of Lady
Audley's secrets. *Lady Audley's Secret* unfolds mystery after mystery as

Robert unflaggingly chases the truth that he believes lies hidden in Lucy Audley's past. But as each secret is unveiled—her bigamy, her change of identity, her attempted murders, and her mother's insanity—we find out less about Lady Audley, who is always both more and less than any information that can be held about or against her, and more about Robert. As he unveils her secrets, she paradoxically becomes *more* enigmatic and he becomes less and less puzzling. Braddon's "low" art form has something in common with her "high" foremother, George Eliot. In Jacqueline Rose's reading of Eliot, she isolates "a structure of fantasy which greatly exceeds the domain of the novel, in which the man and the woman are distributed between the two poles of spectacle and the tale of female sexuality becomes the ultimate story to be told because . . . she has already been made the cause of a crisis in the act of telling itself."[9] What Rose says of *Daniel Deronda*, in which the reader is implicated "in a panic about the meaning of the woman" and positioned "as spectator vis-à-vis a woman whose ultimate decipherment [is] the overriding objective of the book,"[10] could also be said of *Lady Audley's Secret*.

And yet Lady Audley is if anything *more* mysterious by the end of the novel, whereas Robert has become an easily recognizable romantic hero. It is the progress of the novel, however, to make him so. The narrative has two interlocking movements: the recovery of Lady Audley's past and the progress of Robert's "becoming." His self-realization depends on discovering who she is, or was. Robert Audley is introduced to the readers as a perplexing problem. Unlike the mysteries surrounding Lady Audley, Robert's problems are sympathetic and rather endearing. He is an idle bachelor and a nonpracticing barrister whose celibacy and lack of professionalism are constantly linked to a muted discourse of impotency. Robert represents both manhood and the law, but in name only. Here is how Braddon introduces us to him: "As a barrister was his name inscribed in the law-list; as a barrister he had chambers in Figtree Court, Temple; as a barrister he had eaten the allotted number of dinners. . . . If these things can make a man a barrister, Robert Audley decidedly was one."[11] Obviously however, Robert has not yet realized his title: "he had never either had a brief, or tried to get a brief, or even wished to have a brief."[12] What is immediately at issue here is Robert's identity; he lacks the requisite fit between his name and his actions, not only as a barrister, but as a man.

Robert's refusal to engage in manly pursuits is equally problematic. He spends the hunting season "quietly trot[ting] to covert upon a mild-tempered, stout-limbed bay hack, and keep[ing] at a very respectful distance from the hard riders; his horse knowing quite well as he did, that nothing was further from his thoughts than any desire to be in at the death."[13]

And as for his falling in love, his smitten cousin Alicia thinks "the idea is preposterous. If all the divinities on earth were ranged before him . . . he would only lift his eyebrows to the middle of his forehead, and tell them to scramble for it."[14] When Alicia's father—Lucy's new husband, Sir Michael—tries to offer some solace to a suitor Alicia has rejected, reminding him that there is a cousin waiting in the wings, Harry Towers is appalled rather than comforted: "Don't say that . . . I can get over anything but that." What Towers cannot bear is being bested by less than a man: "A fellow whose hand upon the curb weighs half a ton . . . a fellow who turns his collars down, and eats bread and marmalade! No, no . . . it's a queer world, but I can't think *that* of Miss Audley."[15] Sir Michael is left musing on this odd absence of passion in his nephew: "There's some mystery—there's some mystery!"[16]

Formally, this scene prepares for a complication in the narrative. Later Lucy will attempt to rid herself of Robert's prying presence by insinuating to Sir Michael that Robert has a love interest in her. So here Braddon technically establishes the occasion for Sir Michael to accept the accusation. Robert's mysteriousness would be cleared up by his secret desire for Lucy. But this formalistic reading presupposes a complication in the plot that has not only not yet occurred but that the reader also knows is merely one of Lucy's artful devices. Robert's mystery is unaccountably in excess of the narrative's formal demands. His lack of interest in his pretty cousin, his odd dislike for manly activities, his generalized absence of aim and purpose cannot be explained by exigencies of the plot. Braddon unmistakably *feminizes* her hero, down to the birds and flowers that decorate his bachelor apartments.

As the bachelor, Robert Audley thus approximates the character type that Eve Sedgwick locates in the nineteenth-century novel. Like James's, Du Maurier's, and Barrie's bachelors, Robert is selfish, bitchy, physically timid, and desexualized. But whereas "the bachelor is a distinctly circumscribed and often a marginalized figure in the books he inhabits,"[17] Robert begins in this mock-heroic mode while the thrust of the narrative is to reconstruct him as a full-fledged hero who occupies center stage.

Robert's rehabilitation is as much the subject of this novel as Lady Audley's past, and the two are intimately linked. Through his revealing the truth of her past and thus her real identity, we come to know the "real" Robert. In order for Robert to lay claim to his profession—the law—as well as to his masculinity, the path that he must follow is the excoriation of the duplicitous woman. The narrative promises to solve not only Lady Audley's mystery but also Robert's, and his will be resolved through his unveiling of her. By exposing her, Robert takes up his rightful place in society.

As we shall see, the secret of *Lady Audley's Secret* is the homosocial and homoerotic bond between men, *as secret*. For all of Robert's mysterious impotencies vanish only when George Talboys, Lucy's first husband, disappears. Robert is idle and (femininely) "impotent" in George's presence, but in his absence Robert is restored to all the conventional manly virtues while embodying the very image of the melancholic lover. Robert wonders at his own transformation:

> Who would have thought that I could have grown so fond of the fellow . . . or feel so lonely without him? I've a comfortable little fortune . . . ; I'm heir presumptive to my uncle's title; and I know of a certain dear little girl who . . . would do her best to make me happy; but I declare that I would freely give up all, and stand penniless in the world to-morrow, if this mystery could be satisfactorily cleared away, and George Talboys could stand by my side.[18]

If it is the secret of Lucy's past that the play exploits, the novel reveals a truth that arises from the narrative resistances. By so boldly *misrecognizing* Robert's desire for George, *Lady Audley's Secret* makes visible the homosocial/erotic economy within which the criminalized woman marks a necessary place.

In order to understand the fascination with the menacing woman, whose dangerously latent criminality erupts into the social, we have to see how she stands in for the disavowal of desire between men. Lucy Audley serves as both a catalyst to Robert's desire for George *and* an obstacle to be overcome. That is, by prohibiting the visibility of that desire she thereby permits it to proceed. The paradox of the criminal woman is thus her positioning as, at once, problem and solution to the homosocial economy. Lady Audley's real secret is, semiotically, the holding open of the se-creted space of the homosocial.

Luce Irigaray has given us a marxist-feminist analysis of the ways in which women serve as commodities in the hetero-sexual economy. Arguing that the "use of and traffic in women subtend[s] and uphold[s] the reign of masculine hom(m)o-sexuality, even while they maintain that hom(m)o-sexuality in speculations, mirror games, identifications, and . . . rivalrous appropriations, which defer its real practice,"[19] Irigaray's critique of heterosexuality as "alibi" operates quite transparently in *Lady Audley's Secret* through the figure of Clara Talboys, George's sister, who becomes Robert's wife in the novel. Clara appears as a deus ex machina to rescue endangered heterosexuality in much the same way that Shakespeare pulls Sebastian out of the hat to replace Viola as Olivia's husband in *Twelfth Night*. Clara is nothing more than a patent copy of her brother. When Robert first sees her, he is struck by her likeness to George, and he begins to love her when he perceives the depths of her "suppressed passion" for her brother.[20] In moments of despair, he wishes that George were sitting by his side, "or even George's sister—she's very like him."[21] Clara has Robert's "lost friend's face"[22] and "the dark brown eyes that were so like the eyes of his lost friend."[23] Clara occupies the classic position of exchange object as copy, the one who resembles "the one who is his representative."[24]

Lady Audley, however, as the representative of the woman-as-criminal, is not so patently an object of masculine commerce. On the contrary, she would seem to be only a problem to be overcome, a defect in the system that has to be eliminated. But before she is expelled from the social order, she serves a critical and necessary function in the symbolic. As I have indicated, Robert *needs* Lady Audley as an object to be investigated in order to "realize" himself—in order, that is, to take his place in the social order as a man-of-the-law, or as a lawful man.

Lady Audley's Secret might have been the story of Robert's paranoid delusions were it not for the "facts" of Lady Audley's duplicitous past. In moments of doubt, Robert fears that "this edifice of horror and suspicion is a mere collection of crotchets—the nervous fancies of a hypochondriacal bachelor."[25] In his dreams, Lady Audley appears as a "pale, starry face looking out of the silvery foam . . . my lady, transformed into a mermaid, beckoning his uncle to destruction."[26] In Nina Auerbach's analysis of the Victorian "myth of womanhood," the mermaid submerges herself in order to conceal her power: "the mermaid exemplified the secrecy and spiritual ambiguity of woman's ascribed powers. Fathomless and changing, she was an awesome threat to her credulous culture."[27] Lucy surfaces in Robert's dreams, but he is isolated in his efforts to expose her. In the waking world, she passes successfully as meek, self-sacrificial, angelic. Without anyone else to verify his suspicion that Lady Audley murdered George, Robert is plagued by the terror of his own imagination: "Oh, my God, if it should be in myself all this time that the misery lies. . . ."[28] He shivers with horror to think that "this woman's hellish power of dissimulation should be stronger than the truth, and crush him."[29] Thus the narrative contest is between proving the "truth" of his theory and exposing the "lie" of her pretense. On this level, the rivalry of the text could be understood as Platonic mimesis—Robert's "idea(l)s" as model (the real) versus Lady Audley's "copy."

However, as I have pointed out, the model to which Robert aspires comes into being only during the course of his exposure of the copy. The model exists neither prior to the copy nor without it. In order for Robert to be realized, Lady Audley must be verifiably fake. She must, in other words, assume the paradoxical position of a *real impostor*. Lady Audley does not pretend to be someone that she is not; she is that "not-some-one." She is not merely a defective copy of an idealized femininity; rather, she is wholly "other" to the feminine (absolute alterity). Simultaneously, as the narcissist, she is the "purest and truest" type of woman. It is thus in the figure of the irremediable woman-as-criminal that the essence of femininity meets the alterity of the feminine. And they turn out to be the *same thing*. Purified femininity becomes its own antithesis; zero meets zero and what is left is a functionary cipher with infinite capacity for multiplication. After Lady Audley, writes theater historian Michael Booth, "villainesses proliferated."[30]

In this proliferation of representations of the criminal woman, there is more at stake than the Victorian spectator's appetite for the lurid and sensational. The female offender is the locus of horror, the site where the inexplicable terrors of domesticity can be explained and surmounted. Lady Audley inhabits Audley Manor as the very figure of uncanniness in its contradictory logic. For what is "heimlich" is at once what is familiar, "homey," cozy, and comfortable, *and* its opposite—strange, foreign, haunting, menacing. The meaning of "heimlich," as Freud observes, "develops in the direction of ambivalence, until it finally coincides with its opposite, *unheimlich*."[31] The uncanny is thus produced when what is heimlich becomes unheimlich, or, more precisely, when the heimlich is revealed as always already *un*heimlich.

Recurrence is the primary mechanism of the uncanny; but is the repetition the return of the repressed, or the manifestation of something prior to repression, something that has been *foreclosed*? Schelling's definition of the uncanny, upon which Freud relies, is "something which ought to have remained hidden but has come to light."[32] The emphasis here is on "ought," an imperative that is ambiguous. If merely bringing anything to light that once was concealed constituted the uncanny, then almost any domestic drama or melodrama would arouse feelings of uncanniness. Doane points out that the femme fatale signals "a potential epistemological trauma," and that by "transforming the threat of the woman into a secret," her figure is "fully compatible with the epistemological drive of narrative, the hermeneutic structuration of the classical text."[33] It is thus *not* the exposure of Lady Audley's secrets that makes this work uncanny, for it is precisely the project of the work to reveal them. Uncanniness arises not from the something hidden that becomes visible (all mimesis works this way); rather, it is the revelation of the "something" which must be added to the movement from the concealed to the revealed that constitutes the uncanny. And that something, I suggest, is to be looked for in Schelling's "ought." To find what ought to remain hidden, we might turn to the psychic structure of fascination.

As Elizabeth Grosz explains, for Lacan fascination "is the consequence of an imaginary identification in which the self strives to incorporate the other in an act as aggressive as it is loving."[34] Such narcissistic identifications, Lacan insists, are prominently *social*. The paranoid delirium, as Mikkel Borch-Jacobsen points out, for Lacan "is a delirium of the hallway, the street, the forum."[35] The object of the paranoiac's knowledge is the secret of the other, a secret that for the narcissist is always already his *own*. And the ultimate act of aggressive incorporation is murder, a profoundly relational act.

In the manifest content of this text, Lady Audley is both the "murderer" and the narcissist. She occupies these positions in the place of another scene, as a sentinel at the gate of the invisible economy of hom(m)osexuality. Lady Audley is thus the keeper of *that* secret, but also, perhaps, a Trojan horse. Seemingly a figure of disorder, she violates the social contract through her attempted homicides and concomitantly breaches the fiction of womanhood. Her exclusive love for herself as well as her criminal "nature" would seem to locate her outside the social. Narcissism, understood as a failure of relationship with others, is presocial or asocial. Lady Audley is thus doubly abjected; she cannot take her place within the "proper" economy of gender, nor can she engage in the most fundamental of social relationships—the capacity for object-directed love and recognition. She can thus be accounted for only through the discourse of madness, which is precisely where the stage version(s) situates her. Her madness, however, is both the problem and the solution. It accounts for the woman's aggression *and* recuperates it.

Hazelwood's stage adaptation of the novel ends with the customary tableau of sympathy. Laughing wildly, Lady Audley lapses into madness: "Mad, mad, that is the word. I feel it here—here! [Places her hands on her temples]."[36] Hazelwood in no way prepares the spectator for this final tableau. His Lady Audley's motivations for the crimes are entirely rational—her fear of poverty, her anger at being abandoned by Talboys, her desire to retain the material comforts afforded by her second marriage. Hazelwood even omits the secret of her mother's insanity, which is the novel's final mystery to unfold, thus heightening his ending's implausibility by eliminating the "hereditary taint." Victorian audiences were by this time so accustomed to the spectacle of madness to recuperate the evil woman that they would perhaps have scarcely noticed one more use of this staple of melodrama.

And yet, returning again to the novel, we see Braddon twisting this device in some subversive maneuvers. Even though her Lady Audley has an insane mother, she is not herself insane, albeit she is locked up in an asylum. Even the doctor whom Robert brings in to examine her must declare that her motivations are altogether reasonable:

> She ran away from her home, because her home was not a pleasant one, and she left in the hope of finding a better. There is no madness in that. She committed the crime of bigamy, because by that crime she obtained fortune and position. There is no madness there. When she found herself in a desperate position, she did not grow desperate. She employed intelligent means, and she carried out a conspiracy which required coolness and deliberation in its execution. There is no madness in that.[37]

Following an interview with Lady Audley, the doctor concludes that "she has the cunning of madness, with the prudence of intelligence. I will tell you what she is, Mr. Audley. She is dangerous!"[38] And he agrees to sign the commitment papers. Robert justifies committing her to an asylum for life on the basis that it is more humane than the possible consequences of bringing her to trial; he also argues that she is likely to *become* insane, following her mother. Braddon's Lady Audley does confess to being mad, but in each instance she goes on to explain her behavior in terms of self-preservation. Only once do we see her breaking down: she becomes hysterical when she tries to explain Robert's accusations to her husband. Braddon describes this as "the one wild outcry, in which the woman's feebler nature got the better of the siren's art."[39] But even so, this "outburst of natural grief" ends up serving her better than any "artifice which she could have devised."[40] Even in her one moment of "authenticity," Lady Audley is a consummate dissembler.

What Braddon thus subtly accomplishes is the recognition that Lady Audley's violence and her narcissism are not asocial but, on the contrary, they are precisely constitutive of a particular social order, one based on homosocial bonds in which the woman occupies a place that is necessarily constructed as outside. From the perspective of Irigaray's postulation of a "hom(m)o-sexual" monopoly that makes possible the law of patriarchal societies, however, Lady Audley is fully *inside* the heterosexual economy. Indeed, she is the very site and symptom of a patriarchy that is "functioning in the mode of 'semblance.'"[41] Braddon's Lady Audley does not fall outside of the symbolic; rather, she demonstrates the necessity for an image of the "false" woman within a symbolic order that is produced by a masculine imaginary. Lady Audley's criminality is not an aberration within this order, nor is it external to it; it is a fiction that upholds the masculine imaginary's "reality." Hence she *is* a real impostor. Braddon makes no effort to show us a "real" Lucy behind the facade of Lady Audley, nor does she allow her detective-hero to uncover anything more than the straightforward man that presumably lurked in the shadows of his idle bachelorhood.

It remains to be explained, however, what precise function is accomplished when the woman's "latent" criminality becomes manifest in such representations. Is it a rupture in the phallocratic symbolic, a tear in the masculine imaginary? We should remember that these representations reached the peak of their popularity during a period in which the eruption of violence by women was perceived as a real threat to the social order. While on the one hand audiences were flocking to the courtrooms to witness the trials of real women who had performed acts of violence at least as heinous as those of their fictional counterparts, on the other hand reviewers were indicting the villainous heroines as inferior aesthetic creations on the basis of their incredibility. Reviewers did not find characters like Lady Audley merely revolting; they found them *impossible*.[42] What was then constantly disavowed was both the hom(m)o-sociality/sexuality of the purportedly hetero-social/sexual economy and the possibility of *real* acts of aggression perpetrated by women. What I want to pursue is the connection between these two kinds of denial. By understanding them together, I hope to show how the relation between them produces a discourse in which the criminalized woman is the object of a systemic paranoid knowledge.

Freud, Jung, and Ferenczi were "driven by experience to attribute to homosexual wishful phantasies an intimate (perhaps an invariable) relation to" paranoia.[43] Even though the sexual etiology of paranoid disorders is far from evident, Freud traces paranoid delusions (which are usually considered social) back to homosexual desires. Freud insists upon a libidinal development through four stages—autoeroticism, narcissism, homosexuality, and object-love (heterosexuality). We should keep in mind that women, at least the "purest and truest" ones, are fixated in the narcissistic stage:

> A different course is followed in the type of female most frequently met with, which is probably the purest and truest one. . . . Women, especially if they grow up with good looks, develop a certain self-contentment which compensates them for the social restrictions that are imposed upon them in the choice of object. Strictly speaking, it is only themselves that such women love with an intensity comparable to that of the man's love for them.[44]

Men, however, pass from narcissism into a homosexual phase, the logic of this passage being that the "object" of homosexual desire is a transitional object which bears a close resemblance to the subject's own "self," thus easing the way from narcissism to heterosexuality. Although Freud says that these differences are not universal, and accedes to the fact that some women love according to "the masculine type," the respective positions remain gendered, if not biologically wedded. As a number of theorists have indicated, "object-love" at any rate collapses into narcissistic identification. Borch-Jacobsen argues that Freud's struggle to maintain the fiction of anaclitic (attachment) love (masculine desire) necessitates the prior fiction of a purely non-object-oriented desire (narcissism). "Woman (womanly woman, child-woman, cat-woman), in this context, is such a fiction. She is the example. The exemplary figure of a narcissism that in principle ought to have remained without example, since it is inaccessible to direct observation."[45] If Freud "believes in woman's narcissism as he believes in a purely object-oriented love,"[46] then it would seem that in her *indifference* she ironically represents the possibility of "pure love"—that is, a love that escapes mimetic rivalry between men.

The homosexual phase is never simply left behind or surpassed; rather, the sexual aim is deflected and attached to the ego-instincts in order to constitute the social instincts. It is from this point that we can see how Lacan insists on the *sociality* of paranoia. For it is the *sublimation* of homosexuality that makes the social relation possible. Although Freud is unsure how large a contribution this sublimation makes to the social relation, he clearly finds it quite pronounced. It is on just this basis that Freud can make his claim that homosexuals—especially manifest ones who *resist* sexual indulgences—make particularly active contributions to culture.[47] The notion that homosexuals are superior artists (cultural makers and workers) that has entered popular mythology thus depends on a sacrifice of their sexual expression.

It is when this sublimation fails, when the social instincts become sexualized through a regressive return to narcissism, that paranoia emerges as an *"endeavour to protect themselves against any such sexualization of their social instinctual cathexes"* (author's emphasis).[48] For Freud, then, all of the principal forms of paranoia can "be represented as contradictions of the single proposition: 'I (a man) *love him* (a man).'"[49] Whether the contradiction is manifested as delusions of persecution, erotomania, jealousy, or megalomania, homosexual wishful fantasies can be found at the origin of the disorder. Freud does not explain, or even stop to question, why the ego *must* work so zealously to ward off homosexual desires. And yet clearly this particular form of libidinal regression signifies much more than an individual's "failed" psychic development. It is not only the paranoiac himself, like the famous case of Dr. Schreber, who experiences "end-of-the-world" fantasies. The internal catastrophe of the paranoiac also obtains external apocalyptic proportions. That is, there is nothing less at stake here than a collapse of the boundaries between the social (i.e., sublimated homosexuality) and the sexual (i.e., object-love, heterosexuality). As long as homosexual desires are deflected into the constitution of the social instincts, the boundaries between the social and the sexual remain impermeable, and the divide between homosexuality and heterosexuality stays impenetrable.

It is not, however, the failure to sublimate homosexual desire alone that produces the social catastrophe; rather, it is what occurs when the paranoiac withdraws his libido from the object and attaches it to the ego that produces the greater danger. In other words, it is the fixation at, or return to, narcissism that must be fought against. What does this mean for women who are always arrested at this stage of libidinal development? If men's "*step back from sublimated homosexuality to narcissism*" (author's emphasis)[50] produces paranoid delusions, women, it would seem, never even make that step forward. Then would not this male regression constitute a falling back into an already feminized space? In her analysis of paranoia and the specular economy of "gothic" films of the 1940s, Doane suggests that paranoia, because of its association with passive homosexuality, could be considered a "feminine" position whether it is adopted by males or by females.[51] But the female paranoiac would be inhabiting what can only be understood as a masculine subject position, if we follow Freud. For what could it mean for a woman to be positioned as a "passive homosexual," when that is where the feminine is always already located? It would seem that when paranoia is present, whether the subject is male or female, the economy that is evoked is necessarily hom(m)o-social.

Freud's essay on narcissism is perhaps the key text leading Lacan to his famous pronouncement that the sexual relation is impossible. For by accepting the popular distinction between ego-instincts and sexual instincts, the former aiming at self-preservation and the latter at the preservation of the species, and by locating the "true" woman in the domain of the former and men in the realm of the latter,[52] Freud locates his *gendered* subjects in an impossible double bind. Women's inveterate narcissism would preclude their participation in the preservation of the species; men's predilection for object-love would weaken their capacity for self-preservation. The entire edifice of this presumptive hetero-economy would crumble if men failed to sublimate their homosexuality and thus reentered the feminized space of narcissism. Men would thus "become" women. And social relations would degenerate into every woman for herself!

We are beginning to see why women are represented as dangerous, why the homosocial substructure of heterosexuality must be maintained through location of the paranoid object as "woman," and why our cultural representations are so fascinated with the recurrent spectacle of re-

cuperated feminized aggressivity. The criminalized woman points to the
profoundly *paranoid* nature of heterosexual patriarchy. In the Schreber
case, Freud argued that the paranoid delirium can be linked to the disavowal of homosexuality. It is the vehement rejection of the "homo" that
transforms love into hatred. "What begins in admiration ends in murder"[53]—narcissistic incorporation. If the paranoiac's fear and hatred is
attributable to the disavowal of homosexuality, would not also the reverse be true—that the disavowal of homosexuality produces paranoia?

Following Irigaray's argument that patriarchal heterosexuality is
grounded in a disavowal of "hom(m)o-sexuality," then this individual
psychic phenomena would also be manifest in the social field. Heterosexuality could then be understood as a paranoid discourse when read along-
side Borch-Jacobsen's argument that paranoia is "hypersocial," the paranoiac merely "exhibit[ing] in broad daylight the aggressivity inherent in
social relations."[54] Lacan makes the connection between aggressivity and
narcissism explicit: "Aggressivity is the correlative tendency of a mode of
identification that we call narcissistic," and it is this primary identification that "structures the subject as a rival with himself."[55] If the basic
objective of the paranoid mind is to dislodge the other (the other "myself") who is in "his" place, and if women serve as the figures that ground
the discourse of "hom(m)o-sexuality," thus permitting it to be perpetuated unimpeded with all the power of its invisibility, then would women
not come to *stand in for the beloved as persecutor?*

If this paranoid structure operated on the level of consciousness, then
the manifest content of Braddon's novel should position George Talboys
as the object of Robert's paranoid knowledge. That is, since Robert disavows his homosexual desire, George should be the beloved as persecutor. How is it, then, that Lady Audley becomes the hated object? The
woman-as-criminal solves the problem of masculine paranoid desire.
Through her, he can both *have* and *negate* the object of his desire. She is
thus the figure that allows hom(m)o-sexuality *as the secret*, but she is also
potentially the site where the logic of this discourse is forced to make its
appearance. I want to emphasize that it is *not* homosexual desire between
men that requires such a position for women; rather, it is the discourse of
compulsory patriarchal heterosexuality and its ever-present twin—homophobia—that at once prescribes homosocial and proscribes homosexual bonding between men. It is this persistent dualism of the social and
the sexual, which Freud insists upon while at the same time writing the
history of their inevitable imbrication, that marks the female offender as
a representation verifying heterosexual masculinity *and* undercutting it.

Within this phallocratic system, there seems to be no place for
women's sexual agency. As a few critics have noticed, Lady Audley is a

strangely desexualized character. Natalie Schroeder points out that this means that Lady Audley "is not sexually attracted to men."[56] She says as much to Sir Michael after he has had her past thrust upon him by his nephew Robert:

> "The common temptations that assail and shipwreck some women had no ter-
> ror for me. I would have been your true and pure wife to the end of time,
> though I had been surrounded by a legion of tempters. The mad folly that the
> world calls love had never been any part in my madness, and here at least
> extremes met, and the vice of heartlessness became the virtue of constancy."[57]

If Lady Audley were read after the "facts" of Freud's "On Narcissism," her incapacity for object-directed love, which is to say heterosexuality, would not make her any less "a woman." On the contrary, it positions her as, in her own words, "pure and true": the same words that Freud would later use, "the purest and truest," to describe the woman as narcissist. Braddon repeatedly emphasizes Lady Audley's vanity, her self-love, and her aggressiveness as a direct product of her will for self-preservation. Lady Audley is thus by no means an aberration; she is undistilled woman, the quintessence of "femininity."

It is not, then, the criminal woman as *deviant* that fascinates; rather, it is the inevitability of femininity collapsing into criminality. The fallen woman has not descended. She has ascended to the place that was already marked out for her by the patriarchal unconscious. This is the "truth" of pure womanhood that *ought* to have remained hidden. This is the truth that the criminal-as-woman holds motionless. The "heimlich" does not become "unheimlich" through some transformation; the uncanniness is always already there in the essence of femininity.

Lady Audley and her criminal sisters are thus already incorporated into the masculine imaginary. They serve as props to uphold that order, to render its fiction coherent. And yet, at the same time, they constitute a rupture in its invisible order. The women readers who voraciously consumed the narratives of criminal women, and the women spectators who packed both the popular theater and that other theatrical scene—the courtrooms where the real women were on trial—perhaps did indeed see "something like the truth,"[58] as Victorian critics feared. But what was on display was not likenesses of themselves, but the patriarchal unconscious paraded just visibly enough to perhaps *not* be misrecognized.

Negative reactions to the sensation novels and plays were legion. Often in the guise of an allegiance to high aesthetic values, these critics repeatedly expressed their fear that women would identify with the Victorian villainess and thus might follow her example mimetically. Similarly, men expressed horror at the spectacle of women crowding the courtrooms where real women were on trial for their lives. Hartman emphasizes the throngs of women who nearly unanimously supported the female murderers. When Marie Lafarge was tried for poisoning her husband with arsenic, women "waited for hours to catch a glimpse of the accused, and they fought for tickets for seats in court in the specially constructed ladies' gallery."[59] The scene of the crime, Le Glandier, became a pilgrimage site, and engravings of Marie were sold by hawkers on the street to satisfy her fans' idolatry. When Madeline Smith, the daughter of a wealthy architect, stood accused of poisoning her secret fiancé, female spectators' fascination with Smith's frank portrayal of her sexual passions produced an outcry among male commentators. Hartman speculates that the trials "supplied a vicarious outlet for [the women spectators'] frustrations. The accused young women had acted out what the female spectators, in their most secret thoughts, had hardly dared to imagine."[60]

Richard Altick finds this appetite for crime among otherwise "genteel" women one of "the most striking of the innumerable Victorian paradoxes."[61] Altick cites the assertion of a minor novelist of the period "that women of family and position, women who have been brought up in refined society, women who pride themselves upon the delicacy of their sensibilities, who would faint at the sight of a cut finger and go into hysterics if the drowning of a litter of kittens were mentioned in their hearing—such women can sit for hours listening to the details of a cold-blooded murder."[62] Men's complaints about the women's behavior implied concern *for* the women or simply bewilderment in the face of the women's desire to watch the drama, but as Hartman points out, "the men's remarks often display that they understood precisely what was happening, namely, that the 'female element' was showing a supportive identification with women accused of adultery and murder."[63]

Similarly, the critics who execrated the sensation novelists for producing inferior literature betrayed their anxieties about mimetic identifications between the female readers and the fictive characters. "Into uncontaminated minds they will instil false views of human conduct," writes one reviewer, who regarded Braddon's novels "as one of the abominations of the age."[64] He found *Lady Audley's Secret* "one of the most noxious books of modern times" for its lack of verisimilitude: "in drawing [Lady Audley], the authoress may have intended to portray a female Mephistopheles; but, if so, she should have known that a woman cannot fill such a part."[65]

Whereas the pleasures and terrors of narcissistic identification were made possible for men through an intermediary—the displaced figure of the evil woman—the possibility that women might engage in such narcissistic identifications was terrifying because there was no such safety valve in the social order. Homosocial bonding between women was doubly perilous. Not only would it remove women from their function as objects of exchange to facilitate heterosexuality, but it would also constitute a pairing, a *doubling* that would lack a third term, an intermediary figure, on which to displace the violence of mimetic rivalry.

Braddon conjures the menacing potential of homosociality between women through Lady Audley's relationship with her former peer turned lady's maid, Phoebe. A few critics have noticed that the only expression of tenderness and eroticism of which Lady Audley is capable occurs in relation to Phoebe: "Lady Audley smoothed her maid's neutral-tinted hair with her plump, white, and bejeweled hand. . . . Kiss me Phoebe, she said as the girl arranged the curtains."[66] Phoebe is part lady's maid and part companion to Lucy. She is privy to Lucy's secrets and they spend an unusual amount of time together. Alicia wonders at their companionship but concludes that since Sir Michael is frequently away, "it was perhaps natural that my lady . . . should find herself thrown a good deal upon her white-eyelashed maid for society."[67] Schroeder rightly perceives intimations of autoeroticism and homoeroticism in Lady Audley's behavior, but it is principally the intermediate phase between them, narcissism, that characterizes Lady Audley. Her relationship with Phoebe is depicted as that of a model to a faint copy; Phoebe is the washed-out image of Lady Audley: "[Phoebe] might have been pretty . . . but for the one fault in her small oval face. This fault was an absence of color. Not one tinge of crimson flushed the waxen whiteness of her cheeks; not one shadow of brown redeemed the pale insipidity of her eyebrows and eyelashes; not one glimmer of gold or auburn relieved the dull flaxen of her hair."[68] And yet Phoebe is the pale shadow of Lucy's splendid beauty: "you *are* like me, and your features are very nice; it is only color that you want."[69] The narrator explains that the women's "likeness" is due to the sympathy between them, but this likeness, like Robert's peculiarities, exceeds any demands of the plot. Phoebe is enlisted to serve Lucy's machinations through her own desire for self-advancement, through monetary rewards, and through the threat of violence from her husband Luke, who is blackmailing Lucy with Phoebe's assistance. There are ample reasons to justify Phoebe's alliance with Lady Audley.

Phoebe's haunting presence remains a curious excess. Passages such as this seem to be only atmospheric: "There were certain dim and shadowy lights in which, meeting Phoebe Marks gliding softly through the dark oak passages of the Court, or under the shrouded avenues in the garden, you might easily have mistaken her for my lady."[70] Unlike the doubling of Anne Catherick and Laura Fairlie in Collins's *The Woman in White*, which is crucial to the plot when their identities are switched by Laura's scheming husband, the doubling of Phoebe and Lucy reflects no authorial formal plan. Nonetheless, it is more than a casual note that might have been carelessly introduced. When Phoebe marries Luke, she appears momentarily, "in the obscure light of the foggy November morning," as "the ghost of some other bride, dead and buried in the vault below the church."[71] The allusion is clearly to Helen Talboys, Lady Audley's former identity. Phoebe represents what Lucy *once was*, a form of narcissistic identification. The novel stops short of representing the two women as a diabolical couple by pitting them against each other, first when Phoebe submits to Luke's desire to blackmail Lucy, and again when Phoebe cannot follow Lucy's plan to burn down the inn in which Robert and Luke are sleeping. For the women the homosocial bond must simply be broken. There is no solution for them through exchanging a man, and no figure on which to displace their paranoia.

The secret of *Lady Audley's Secret* is perhaps better understood as the pathological repetition of a profoundly paranoid culture that ironically displays what it suppresses. The homosocial structure of patriarchal heterosexuality is not invisible. On the contrary, it is persistently, conspicuously, and ostentatiously exhibited. If it appears most prominently as a secret, it is not as some hidden, mysterious, or esoteric *content*, but as an active verb: to set apart, sift, distinguish. Homosociality is not the ghost in the machine of heterosexuality. The semblance has more materiality than the body it purportedly shadows. And it is there—in the systematic effort to secret the hetero from the homo—that the violence is.

3

Enter the Invert: Frank Wedekind's Lulu Plays

WHEN G. W. PABST'S film adaptation of Frank Wedekind's *Pandora's Box* opened in Berlin in 1929, the censors rushed in to condemn "its open treatment of lasciviousness and prostitution—Lulu's sexuality, Geschwitz's lesbianism, Schigolch's pimping."[1] Following the judicial ban of the play in 1906, Wedekind appended a foreword that contested its characterization as "an incompetent piece of work devoid of any moral or artistic merits"[2] largely on the grounds that the censors had misunderstood the moving force behind his work:

> The tragic central figure of the play is not Lulu, as the justices mistakenly assumed, but Countess Geschwitz. Apart from an intrigue here and there, Lulu plays an entirely passive role in all three acts; Countess Geschwitz on the other hand in the first act furnishes an example of what one can justifiably describe as super-human self-sacrifice. In the second act the progress of the plot forces her to summon all her spiritual resources in the attempt to conquer the terrible destiny of abnormality with which she is burdened; after which, in the third act, having borne the most fearful torments of soul with stoical composure, she sacrifices her life in defence of her friend.[3]

No one has taken Wedekind's claim seriously. The Countess tends to be lightly passed over in critical commentaries of the play. Tragic or otherwise, Lulu is emphatically at the play's center.

It might seem an odd ploy by Wedekind to justify the moral and artistic qualities of the work by claiming that the "invert" is the play's true heroine. Perhaps it was because all three courts failed to pronounce "the fate of a human being burdened with the curse of abnormality"[4] inadmissible that Wedekind chose this route of justification. Nevertheless, Wedekind elaborates on his intentions with conviction: "When I published this play . . . I was permeated to the depths of my soul by the conviction that I was . . . satisfying a claim of the highest human morality."[5] Not seeking to sensationalize the appearance of the invert, but rather to handle "this affliction" as tragedy, Wedekind's avowed purpose was "to rescue the powerful human tragedy of exceptional but wholly fruitless spiritual struggles from its fate of ridicule and bring it home to . . . sympathy and compassion."[6]

Written between the years 1892 and 1901, the Lulu plays emerged just as the sexologists were prospering in western Europe, and especially in Germany. The Uranian movement was promoting a nascent identity politics for German lesbians; and organizations such as the Scientific Humanitarian Committee were using the sexologists' congenital burden theory to defend homosexuals against legal and moral persecution. From 1899 to 1923, the SHC's publications concerning lesbians in *The Yearbook of Intermediate Sexual Types* set out to demonstrate that women too could be born into the "third sex," thus initiating the essentialist argument for political expediency that to a large extent pertains even today. Although Wedekind's novel *Mine-haha* joined other fiction of the period in presenting lesbians as sick and sinister, his defense of the Countess in his foreword to the Lulu plays seems to follow the SHC's party line.[7]

By the time the American actress Louise Brooks arrived in Berlin in 1928 to play the part of the German Lulu, sex, she recollected, "was the business of the town"; and Wedekind's turn-of-the-century fiction was the reality on the streets:

> At the Eden Hotel . . . the café bar was lined with the higher-priced trollops. The economy girls walked the street outside. On the corner stood the girls in boots, advertising flagellation. . . . The nightclub Eldorado displayed an enticing line of homosexuals dressed as women. At the Maly, there was a choice of feminine or collar-and-tie lesbians. Collective lust roared unashamed at the theatre. . . . it was precisely as Lulu's stage entrance was described by Wedekind: "They rage there as in a menagerie when the meat appears in the cage."[8]

Nonetheless, Wedekind's elevation of the Countess to the position of tragic heroine, his insistence that she is the center of the play, and his desire to mark her as a figure of near sublimity have seemed to exceed the credibility of both his contemporary judges and later critical readers of the play. Even in recent critical commentaries, the Countess is tactfully referred to as Lulu's friend, Geschwitz the artist, or simply the Countess. With all due lack of respect for the author's intentions, I want to consider what a reading of this play would look like if we were to take Wedekind's stated purposes seriously.

The Countess Geschwitz is the first representation of a homosexual woman on the European stage. The time and place were ripe for her appearance. Not only was Wedekind's Germany the home of many of the major sexologists, but also western European artists, by the 1880s, were exhibiting work in which the motif of the autoerotic, mirror-gazing, self-sufficient narcissist was beginning to give way to more explicit sexual images of women together. Bram Dijkstra argues that lesbianism did not become a popular theme for artists until around 1900, after the cultural assumption that women were largely undifferentiated beings had been firmly established. Hence even when love between women did enter representation overtly, it retained the traces of its historical lineage from autoeroticism and narcissism. Where lesbianism was presented as an extension of autoeroticism, the threat was somewhat alleviated and an avenue was opened for "nonthreatening voyeuristic involvement on the part of the male."[9]

Although Dijkstra's assumption that voyeurism is nonthreatening is challenged by a psychoanalytic understanding of the voyeur's position,[10] his reading of late nineteenth-century artists indicates their historical prefiguration of the psychosexual trajectory later developed by Freud—from autoeroticism to narcissism to homosexuality to heterosexuality. The idea that masturbation led to lesbianism was a commonplace assumption inherited from the sexologists; and concomitant with this near conflation of autoeroticism and lesbianism was the "problem" of lesbianism's undetectability. Together these two assumptions produced the paradox of women's same-sex desire. On the one hand, the threat of lesbianism was alleviated by its perpetual reproduction as autoeroticism; on the other hand, this very maneuver produced the constant fear of a desire that exceeded the visual (and thus "knowable") economy. The slide between autoeroticism and lesbianism is articulated bluntly by Bernard Talmey: "The female masturbator becomes excessively prudish, despises and hates the opposite sex, and forms passionate attachments for other women."[11] And in the same treatise, he expresses the ubiquitous concern of his culture that homosexuality among women, unlike sex between men, eludes the juridical system: "The reason for this defect in our criminal laws may be ascribed to the ignorance of the law-making power of the existence of this anomaly."[12] Thus when Talmey restates the sexologists' construction of female homosexuality, he further betrays Ellis's assertion of the dominant culture's "indifference" toward same-sex desire between women by revealing the anxiety produced by the "solution" of its always only partial erasure.[13] The motif of resemblance that permeates this work (and to a large extent continues today in representations of homoeroticism) fully exploited what Sarah Kofman calls the "apotropaic function of the double which makes it possible to bear that which, in nature, produces disgust and horror."[14]

Also recurrent in these representations is the motif of sleep. The women are almost always depicted in a state of repose, if not actual somnolence, as in Georges Callot's and Ida Teichmann's works both entitled *Sleep*, or St. George Hare's *The Victory of Faith*. Visconti's *In Summertime* represents one of the women sleeping and the other peering dreamily over the footboard; and the women in Pierre-Georges Jeanniot's *After the*

Bath are reclining in the grass as if preparing to nap. The dream motif abets an eroticized voyeurism; but once again this is not finally as nonthreatening as it may appear. For the association between the desire to sleep and narcissism further extended the link between the narcissist and the lesbian.[15]

What we find, then, in both the art and literature of the late nineteenth century is sometimes a conflation, almost always at least an imbrication, of autoeroticism and narcissism, with lesbianism rarely if ever emerging as a distinct object-oriented love, but nearly always appearing as what we might think of as the unconscious of these texts. The sexologists had paved the way for these associations by theorizing a latent homosexuality and a persistent "femininity" in narcissists of either sex.

Havelock Ellis credits himself with the first coinage of the term "narcissism," which developed out of his earlier paper on autoeroticism. In 1898 he wrote:

> To complete this summary of the main phenomenon of auto-eroticism, I may briefly mention that tendency which is sometimes found, more especially perhaps in women, for the sexual emotions to be absorbed, and often entirely lost, in self-admiration. This Narcissus-like tendency, of which the normal germ in women is symbolized by the mirror, is found in minor degree in some feminine-minded men, but seems to be rarely found in men apart from sexual attraction for other persons, to which attraction it is, of course, normally subservient.[16]

Ellis's findings were published in the German *Archiv für Psychiatrie* in 1899. In this text he tracks the continuing associations of autoeroticism, narcissism, and homosexuality, as well as the preponderance of the phenomenon in women: Otto Rank's interpretation of a woman's narcissistic dreams as evidence of a "latent homosexuality of which the subject was not herself conscious"; Sadger's belief that women are arrested in the narcissistic phase and that homosexuality "is the Narcissistic perversion *par excellence*"; Rohleder's subsumption of narcissism under "auto-monosexualism"; Lowenfeld's inclination that narcissism favors homosexuality. Ellis cites the women psychologists Voigtlander and Spielrein to bolster his contention that women are particularly susceptible to narcissistic love. "The part of Narcissism in the girl and woman," Ellis authoritatively states, "has scarcely been disputed."[17] Even for those who argued that narcissism must be understood as a kind of object-directed love, the cultural assumption that women were undifferentiated beings rendered love between women virtually autoerotic anyway.

The legend of Narcissus and Echo itself contains the germs of these associations. In one version, the origin of masturbation is linked to Echo who insistently rejects Pan's love. Pan's father, Hermes, teaches his son to masturbate to relieve his suffering.[18] Narcissus was himself a feminine young man, an ephebe, who had not yet attained the "maturity" of object-directed love. But as Ellis points out, Narcissus was known for his skill with the "olisbos . . . an instrument for the sexual gratification of women" but also recognized as a device that could have a "masculine use *per anum*."[19] Thus it seems that even the mythical couple was associated with homosexual proclivities.

Given the historical conjunction of such theories, it is not surprising that when Wedekind constructs Lulu as the quintessential narcissist, he makes for her an invert as a constant companion and a figure who haunts the spaces that Lulu inhabits. What I want to argue is that the Countess Geschwitz can be placed at the center of the Lulu plays if we read her structurally as a shadow of Lulu. Quite literally, Geschwitz is a figure that haunts the plays, always lurking in dark corners, watching unobtrusively from the sidelines, hiding in closets or behind drapery. As the unconscious of these texts, Wedekind's Countess is a crucial figure of the plays' concern with social degeneration manifested in sexual rivalry. If Lulu is femininity as essence, her "presentness" is sustained by Geschwitz's absence. The invert is thus what must disappear in order that the fiction of the narcissist as woman may retain its substantiality. The Countess Geschwitz, as we shall see, also "comes and goes" with Lulu. Wedekind could not have made his Lulu without the Countess. They are a study of the sameness that lurks in evidential difference within a phallocratic exchange economy.

When Milton's Eve first awakens, she looks into the smooth lake and is startled by her own reflection. Yet she returns for those "answering looks" and would have "pined with vain desire," but for a voice that warns her:

> What there thou seest, fair creature, is thyself;
> With thee it came and goes: but follow me,
> And I will bring thee where no shadow stays
> Thy coming, and thy soft embraces; he
> Whose image thou art, him thou shalt enjoy
> Inseparably thine: to him shalt bear
> Multitudes like thyself, and thence be called
> Mother of human race.

Eve relinquishes control over the appearance and disappearance of her seductive image—"What could I do, / But follow straight, invisibly thus led?"—even though she finds Adam "less fair, / Less winning soft, less amiably mild, / Than that smooth watery image."[20] Much the same voice has led women to abandon their "narcissism" for an image less fair and a duty to "mother the human race." The injunction to reproduce is repeated in the repetition of the other woman as the same. Representational returns of the lesbian as the narcissist enable the ideology of reproductive heterosexuality. Wedekind's drama makes manifest the dominant culture's necessary construction of the invert as the disappearing term—the other woman.

> LULU: When I looked at myself in the mirror
>   I wished I were a man . . . my own
>   husband!
> ALWA: You seem to envy your husband the
>   happiness you give him.[21]

By virtual critical consensus Lulu is the "femme fatale," a preeminent narcissist. Gail Finney describes her as "a beautiful surface without substance."[22] Bram Dijkstra finds Lulu the "very personification of the narcissistic woman" and cites her intoxication "with her own beauty," with which she "seems to be idolatrously in love."[23] In a recent reading of G. W. Pabst's 1929 film adaptation of *Pandora's Box*, Mary Ann Doane states that "the fatality, the morbid sexuality associated with Lulu, together with the fact that what she generally provokes are catastrophes, would seem to suggest that she occupies the position of the classic femme fatale." Geschwitz, as Doane observes, "consistently occupies the margins of a masculine scenario structured around Lulu."[24] Contrary to Wedekind's claim, Geschwitz appears to be merely one of the entourage of Lulu's suitors that includes Dr. Schön, his son Alwa, the painter Schwartz, Dr. Goll, Rodrigo the acrobat, and Prince Escerny, an African explorer. Including an invert among such varied company would seem to be no more than a rounding out of the masculine group; and locating Geschwitz on the fringe of this group is perhaps a way of commenting on her marginal masculinization.

According to Wedekind, however, Geschwitz's heroic stature is attained through her transcendence of this scenario. He sets her apart from the rest of the company both spatially and rhetorically. The latter strategy is best exemplified in Geschwitz's monologue:

> These people don't know themselves, don't know what they are like. Only someone who is not human himself can really know them. . . . I wonder if there have ever been people who were made happy by love. Their happiness after all consists of nothing more than being able to sleep better and forget everything. Lord God, I thank thee that I am not as other men are. I am not a human being

at all—my body has nothing in common with other human bodies. But I have a human soul! The tormented have narrow shrivelled souls within them; but I know it is no merit on my part if I give up everything, sacrifice everything . . .[25]

Geschwitz's monologue is interrupted at this moment by Lulu who opens the door to admit her third trick of the night, Dr. Hilti. Unnoticed by either of them, Geschwitz watches passively as Lulu prostitutes herself to earn the few shillings necessary to maintain herself, Alwa, and Schigolch, who first sent her out to prostitute twenty years before. The juxtaposition of Lulu's degradation and Geschwitz's speech about transcendence suggests a coupling contrast between the two women: Lulu has never been more on display as the "flesh"; Geschwitz has become increasingly invisible as she attains a "spirituality." Both are images of abjection, but Wedekind attempts to ennoble the Countess by removing her from the social world in the brothel. Having arrived armed to protect Lulu from this final degradation, she finds herself helpless to rescue her as she had done previously. Now she can only sit passively and watch as Lulu descends to the streets and returns with one trick after another, up to the final one, Jack the Ripper.

What Geschwitz cannot do in these scenes, as she had done previously to save Lulu, is *substitute* herself for Lulu. Before, when Lulu was in prison for the murder of Dr. Schön, Geschwitz arranged for her escape by taking her place. She took a nurse's training course, arranged to attend cholera victims, put on the underclothing of one of the dying patients, came to the prison, and exchanged underclothes with Lulu. Both of them fell sick simultaneously, and while they were in the isolation wing Geschwitz "employed all her arts to make [their] faces as alike as possible."[26] When Geschwitz was discharged as cured, she came back to the prison and exchanged clothes with Lulu, and Lulu walked away from the prison. In the final scene, there is one more substitution. Geschwitz pushes Lulu behind her and fires a shot from her revolver through the door that Jack pulls open from the inside. He plunges his knife into the Countess's stomach. Geschwitz dies in Lulu's stead, just moments before Lulu is herself murdered by Jack. Geschwitz, who has promised Lulu that she will go with her wherever she goes, follows her unto death.

These comings and goings are substitutions suggesting a way of reading the relationship between Lulu and Geschwitz that links them as a couple on a level other than the masculinized woman and the essentially feminine—that is, other than as female replacements for a heterosexual scenario. It is possible to reconcile Wedekind's rather incredible claim that Geschwitz, not Lulu, is the center of the play when we begin to see the invert and the narcissist as an eternal couple, something like Genet's "criminal and the saint."[27] In this reading, the Countess and Lulu are not separate individuals, but rather two halves of a psychical splitting that reflect the masculine imaginary. From this perspective, it is also possible to better understand the structure of violence that orders the apparent chaos of the social in the Lulu plays.

> COUNTESS GESCHWITZ: Are you going because
> I'm coming?
> LULU: Good heavens, no!
> But when you come I
> go.[28]

When Geschwitz and Lulu change places the first time, both of them almost die as a result of this substitution. In the final scene, they are once more symbolically exchanged, and both are murdered. Geschwitz's sacrificial substitutions operate in a different economy of desire from that of Lulu's male suitors. Whereas the men function in a market economy where Lulu can be purchased and thus passed from one to the other, Geschwitz, who as the invert only resembles the masculine subject position without being able to "realize" it, lacks the necessary currency to obtain the gift. Pan-dora's Box etymologically signifies "gift for everyone," but this "everyone" is necessarily male. If the etiology of sexual desire is identification—putting oneself in the place of the other—it is a relation that is "ambivalent from the very first; it can turn into an expression of tenderness as easily as into a wish for someone's removal."[29]

In Geschwitz's case, her identification with Lulu leads to compassion, not rivalry and hatred. Jacqueline Rose equates Freud's three forms of identification with Lacan's Real, Imaginary, and Symbolic:

(a) privation (demand directed to a lost object);
(b) frustration (demand which cannot be given its object);
(c) castration (demand for which there is no object).[30]

According to Rose, the second form of identification—the Imaginary identification—is "the prototype for the girl's identification with the lost primordial object (the mother)" and "a pivotal point for identification based on sexual identity."[31] Because the lesbian has been historically constructed as a sexual identity whose object of desire is presumed to be the mother, we might expect to find her desire representing and reproducing this imaginary relation that can only end in frustration. And indeed Geschwitz is the very image of frustrated desire. She is capable of making the identification, but it is the exchange economy of phallocratic desire that renders her outside the market.

Sartre observes that the sexual act, in its manifest aspect, is a "festival of submission"; but it is also a representation of the "passion and ritual murder of the beloved."[32] The final act of *Pandora's Box* represents both the manifest and latent aspects of this sexual act. Lulu's submission to prostitution is her own worst fear realized. When Casti-Pianti proposes selling her to an Egyptian for five hundred francs, she refuses to go, even if it means returning to prison: "I'll go to America with you, or to China, but I can't sell myself. That is worse than prison. . . . I cannot sell the one thing I've ever owned."[33] The last act also manifests the content of her dream: "Every few nights I used to dream that I'd fallen into the hands of a sex-maniac."[34]

Geschwitz cannot follow Lulu into her "festival of submission": "I'll sit by the door. I'll watch it all without flinching."[35] But she accompanies Lulu in the ritual murder of the beloved. The last words of the play belong to the Countess: "Lulu!—My angel!—Let me see you once more!—I am near you—will stay near you—in eternity!"[36] The coupling of the narcissist and the lesbian is here made literal. But this final merger of the Countess and Lulu is an informing concept throughout the play.

However, the Countess and Lulu can form a couple—two who become one—only through death or near-death identifications. It is only when they are mis-taken for each other, when someone misrecognizes them or when they are in one another's place, that they are united. For most of the play, Lulu occupies the position of the eternal feminine, or essential femininity, and the Countess is in the place of the typical male lover. Lulu is the unattainable beloved, the narcissist with an unassailable libido, and the Countess is the impoverished lover. Ironically, it is this classic heterosexual scenario that makes intercourse between them impossible.

As the invert, Geschwitz approximates the male lover's position vis-à-vis the woman as beloved object of desire. When Freud analyzes a case of homosexuality in a woman, he understands his analysand in terms that precisely describe Geschwitz: "she displayed the humility and the sublime overvaluation of the sexual object so characteristic of the male lover, the renunciation of all narcissistic satisfaction, and the preference for being the lover rather than the beloved. She had thus not only chosen a feminine love-object, but had also developed a masculine attitude towards that object."[37]

Geschwitz plays this male lover's part with much more sincerity than

any of the male suitors. Wedekind's praise of Geschwitz's sublime sacri-
fices would seem to be a valorization of the paradigmatic male lover. At
the same time, he portrays her as so exaggerated in this role, so melodramatic, that she could also be seen as almost a parody of the male lover. It
is possible that by making the female invert more "manly" than the men,
Wedekind has constructed a wonderfully comedic commentary on the
heterosexual relationship. Setting Lulu and Geschwitz up as the essential
beloved and lover mimics the gendered division of the narcissistic woman
and the anaclitic man, and subtly demonstrates the impossibility of this
Freudian scenario. Instead of the lesbian-criminal and the "normal" (hysterical) woman, what Wedekind's Lulu represents is the already criminalized—the always already guilty—*normal* woman. If Lulu could be said to
develop at all in this play, it is in the sadistic narrative within which she
is frequently posed as the iconic fetishized spectacle.

Finney uses Laura Mulvey's psychoanalytic theory to read Lulu as a
representative figure of both possible reactions of the male spectator to
castration: devaluation, which produces the criminal, and overvaluation,
which produces the star as fetishized spectacle, the latter giving way to the
former when Lulu murders Schön at the end of *Earth Spirit*. In other
words, Lulu, as fetishized spectacle, *is* the phallus, the location for the
hallucinatory return of that which is lacking. Similarly, Doane refers to
her as an "eroticized ontological problem."[38] The issue is not to ascertain
Lulu's guilt or innocence legalistically, for as Doane writes, "guilt does
not necessarily attach itself to the woman through intentionality or motivation. Her sheer existence . . . is cause of disaster."[39] The question is not
whether she did it, but how she could have done otherwise. It is thus
femininity itself, essentialized in the narcissistic woman, that must be
eradicated. Like Lady Audley's, Lulu's femininity is not aberrant; on the
contrary, she is Woman at her "purest and truest." To put it differently,
what *is* an aberration is femininity *as* essence. When this impossible-real
is manifested, it is inexorably murderous.

Thus Lulu's criminality is represented as indistinguishable from her
narcissism. She is responsible for the deaths of all three of her husbands.
Earth Spirit, the first part of the Lulu plays, is primarily a narrative of
these deaths. Dr. Goll, Lulu's first husband and victim, dies of a stroke
when he discovers Lulu making love to the painter Schwarz. Schwarz
anticipates his own fate when he speaks to Goll's corpse: "I'd like to
change places with you, you corpse. I'd be glad to give her back to you."[40]
Schwarz cuts his throat with a razor when he discovers the alliance between Lulu and Schön; and this in turn prefigures Schön's death by Lulu's
hands. As she is passed from husband to husband, Lulu always represents
death. Schön calls her an "avenging angel," his "inexorable fate," a

"hangman's noose."[41] Alwa finds her, despite her "big brown childlike eyes," to be "the most designing bitch that ever brought a man to ruin."[42] In the final act Alwa nonchalantly expresses the opinion that it is a woman's "natural destiny" to "blossom for us precisely at the right moment to plunge a man into everlasting ruin."[43] Geschwitz charges her with "tormenting the helpless victims which inscrutable destiny has delivered into [her] power."[44] Here is the familiar formula: Narcissism = Death.

It is precisely because Lulu conforms so minutely to the patriarchal construct of Woman that she is represented as a catastrophe. For women, Kofman writes, " 'normality' consists in never settling down, in remaining changeable and capricious."[45] Lulu's protean ability is strongly marked. She is shown endlessly changing (usually her clothes, of course), and she quickly adapts to every new situation. After the death of each lover, she takes on a new costume. As she is shown to be all surface, Lulu is well equipped to make difficult transformations, as are girls called upon to perform changing their erogenous zones, changing their love objects, transforming their hostility into desire. And yet it is for *fulfilling* the roles imposed on her as a "normal" woman that Lulu must be dispensed with. First the idea of her must be produced; then she is coerced into embodying it; then she must be annihilated for having fulfilled this destiny.

In the opening scene, Schwarz is concerned to paint an unidentified female model who resists his efforts to isolate her image: "I was hardly able to fix a single feature."[46] When Schön watches him painting Lulu, he offers this advice: "Treat her as a still-life."[47] Lulu, however, resists becoming a "still-life": she tells Schwarz to paint her with her mouth open; she pulls her trouser leg up while he is painting. She cannot be captured. Containing the woman's image is ultimately accomplished by killing her, thus eliminating the threat that she poses. "Psychoanalysis," writes Kofman, "can never touch a woman except to make a dead body of her. To make a dead body of woman is to try one last time to overcome her enigmatic and ungraspable character, to fix in a definitive and immovable position instability and mobility themselves."[48]

The narrative pressure of the play moves toward the inevitability of stilling Lulu's life; and yet the image of her changeability must be constantly reproduced for it serves its function of shoring up the fiction of masculine wholeness/coherency. Lulu's function for the men who desire her is metonymic. The structure of subjectivity that Lacan reads through the mirror stage is a basic relation "between a fragmented or inco-ordinate subject and its totalizing image."[49] That image must be *fixed* in order for the alienated subject to capture its own sense of permanency and identity. Hence Lulu's portrait as Pierrot, a stock figure from pantomime (the

wordlessness of spectacle) who remains essentially the same in every appearance, is as much a desired object as she is. Whoever "has" Lulu also
owns the portrait, which is prominently displayed at every significant exchange: Schwarz hangs it over the mantel in a brocade frame; Schön displays it on an ornamental easel; Alwa reclaims it after Lulu leaves prison;
it is set into the wall in the salon in Paris when she is a fugitive; and
Geschwitz brings it to the London garret where she has become a prostitute. Lulu has been delighted by her portrait in all of its previous incarnations, but at this last appearance she is horrified by it: "Take that picture
out of my sight! Throw it out of the window!"[50] Alwa insists, however,
on nailing it to the garret wall: "In face of that portrait I regain my self-
respect. It makes my destiny comprehensible." Schigolch agrees that "it
will make an excellent impression on our clientele."[51]

It is not what Lulu is, or has become, that has meaning; rather, it is
what she once was, her timeless image, that has currency. Schön says to
her, "I know only too well that you're indestructible," and she replies,
"So you do know that?"[52] Castration anxiety produces a recurring pattern in which the woman's image is produced and destroyed, and then
inevitably reappears—a pattern that partakes of the compulsion to repeat
in these texts.

The question of the meaning of the compulsion to repeat leads us into
the murky concept of the death instinct—the "beyond" of "beyond the
pleasure principle." Lacan's famous pronouncement that the "unconscious is the discourse of the other"[53] must be understood in conjunction
with repetition. The "need for repetition," Lacan says, "such as it con-
cretely manifests itself in the subject," can be conceived of "as the form of
behaviour staged in the past and reproduced in the present in a way
which doesn't conform much with vital adaptation." The "discourse of
the other" is the discourse that one is "absolutely condemned to reproduce."[54] It is, then, the need for repetition that constitutes the beyond of
the pleasure principle, not the repetition itself, the content of what is repeated, but the inevitable necessity of repetition. And why this need? Because it is only from there that the human being who is "in part outside
life" can "engage in the register of life."[55] The principle of the pleasure
principle, following Lacan, is that "pleasure should cease."[56] If the death
instinct is what lies beyond the pleasure principle, this beyond is not in
opposition to or other than the pleasure principle, but rather its logical
extension. If homeostasis, constancy, equilibrium are the aims of the pleasure principle, it would seem to be only a matter of distance that would
regulate the pleasure principle carried to its logical conclusion—a return
to inanimacy. The perpetuation of pleasure requires a distance achieved
by the intervention of the reality principle that makes "the game last . . .

ensuring that pleasure is renewed, so that the fight doesn't end for lack of combatants."[57] This distance is not unlike the distance required in the love relationship: too much distance and what occurs is suppressed hatred; too little distance effects an identificatory merger. Both produce aggressions carried to their logical ends in the annihilation of the other. But this other is always fundamentally the other "oneself." It all begins, and perhaps ends, in narcissistic identifications.

Since historically and psychoanalytically narcissism has come to rest on the image of the woman, women bear the mark of this telos. Narcissism is fundamental to the development of the ego. It is not a phase in psychic development, but rather an ongoing dialectical process of the ego's relationship to the world. Fixing narcissism on the figure of the woman is thus a product of a particular sociosymbolic order. It is not the "reality" of the narcissistic woman that requires analysis, but rather the effects of this historical lamination, which at once establishes woman as the site for the ever-threatening potentiality of aggression *and* establishes the impossibility of women's actually acting this aggression out. If Woman is always "armed," women are persistently disarmed precisely because they are always already armed. This dialectic is crucial to the functioning of a phallocratic symbolic order.

The terrible power that Lulu holds emanates from her ability to lure, to fascinate her suitors while remaining indifferent to them. They are dispensable, replaceable, for as the narcissistic woman Lulu aims not to love but to be loved. She becomes, then, the "beloved as persecutor," the object that inspires love without returning it, hence impoverishing the male "ego as regards libido in favour of the love-object."[58] According to Freud, the reverse side of the narcissistic woman's charm is the dissatisfaction of the lover who "doubts . . . the woman's love," and "complaints of her enigmatic nature" are attributed to "this incongruity between types of object-choice."[59] Reciprocity in love is impossible in the narcissistic relationship: men love women; women love only themselves. As we have seen, historically this incongruity in object-choices, the woman's indifference toward men, is potentially a choice *for* women. Although Freud states explicitly that something *must be added* to autoeroticism to produce narcissism, there remains a historical residue of autoeroticism in representations of the narcissist.

Sarah Kofman argues that female masturbation must be understood as the trace of women's repressed masculinity, and that it is the prohibition against masturbation (rather than the narcissistic wound or penis envy) that is fundamental to the explanation of women's giving up a pleasure that they have no rational reason to renounce. This autoerotic pleasure "will continue to tempt and haunt her even after it has been 'suppressed.'"[60] Following Kofman, if it is the prohibition of masturbation that is fundamental to women's assumption of femininity, the fear that women can give pleasure to themselves is just one step away from homosexuality, and the intermediate step is narcissism. Arresting women in the narcissistic phase prevents their advancement into the next stage—homosexuality—where they are likely to remain since there is no compelling reason for femininity to be achieved successfully. Boys, who have a superior capacity for sublimation and are presumably afraid of "passivity" because it is feminizing, may pass easily through the homosexual "phase," but girls would seem to have nothing to press them beyond it.

Even so, historically the progression through these phases was less a linear movement than a palimpsestic structure. At least the threat of homosexuality is *already there* in the earlier phases of autoeroticism and narcissism, especially in the case of women. Therefore, when women are checked in the narcissistic phase, what is really at stake is their inability to achieve heterosexuality. According to Freud, the supreme achievement of femininity is the maternal; but Kofman points out that since the child is a penis-substitute, even maternal love is a "masculine" desire. Indeed the "norm of femininity itself . . . corresponds with . . . [women's repressed] masculinity."[61] Freudian desire itself then becomes a "vestige of woman's 'masculine' sexuality."[62] Kofman's nuanced argument supports what so many feminist psychoanalytic theorists see quite clearly: psychoanalytic desire confirms masculinity whatever the sex of the one who desires. If this desire is what must *disappear* to make way for femininity, it is also what must *appear* in order to reassuringly display the phallus to men.

But why is it masturbation that "plunges Freud into an aporia, an impasse, a violent inner conflict"[63] if it is not that the return of women's repressed autoeroticism is what threatens the assumption of femininity (heterosexual reproduction)? And what of the woman who refuses to give up her active desire, the women who refuse repression? These women, as inverts, are the paradox in the economy of the same. Unlike the "normal woman," who, as Irigaray points out, is simply "a man minus the possibility of (re)presenting oneself as a man,"[64] the invert cannot quite represent masculinity, but she does represent something else in her "not quite" status.

Lesbianism's historical derivation from autoeroticism has produced the still-common notion that lesbian sexuality is something like mutual masturbation. Understood as the primacy of clitoral stimulation, masturbation must still be relinquished for normal femininity to be achieved. The lesbian is thus a haunting figure not because she is the return of the repressed, but because she is the manifestation of that pleasure which women have no reason to renounce. She is the possibility of refusing to accede to femininity. Like Geschwitz, she inhabits the dark corners, peers out from behind the draperies, stalking the narcissist whom she captures in her gaze.

There is always the threat that the woman being watched will see herself being seen, and look back, thus exceeding the terms of Woman as specularity. The fearful power of this gaze's reciprocity is reflected in an anecdote about the making of Pabst's film. Alice Roberts, a heterosexual actress who was cast as the Countess, became terrified when Pabst explained to her "that she was to touch, to embrace, to make love to another woman." Pabst had to position her in her shots with Brooks so that she would be looking at *him* in the scenes where Lulu and Geschwitz exchange gazes: "Pabst positioned himself so that she could 'cheat' her look past Louise and look longingly at [him], who was returning her loving gaze from behind the camera."[65] What is it that Roberts thought she might see if she looked at the woman looking back at her?

Despite Freud's early point that choice of an object for both men and women is made independently of its sex, he still found in "inverted types" an *essential* "coming into operation of narcissistic object-choice."[66] And even though his later gender division of men as (anaclitic) lovers and women as (narcissistic) beloveds is qualified within the essay "On Narcissism" and seriously compromised by subsequent rereadings, these subtle theoretical reappraisals of Freud have not had a decided impact on cultural assumptions that continue to associate autoeroticism with narcissism and homosexuality. The *stamp* of narcissism continues to adhere to women and homosexuals. We can thus see why the theorization of women as narcissists was perceived as so dangerous to the social order of patriarchy. And we must also understand these historical and theoretical laminations to appreciate why women and homosexuals continue to be among the criminal class.

The woman-as-narcissist poses an immediate danger since she wants only to be loved without returning love—there is nothing to guarantee her fidelity. It is, in fact, Lulu's infidelities that lead directly to the deaths of all her husbands: Goll when he finds her with Schwarz; Schwarz when he discovers her alliance with Schön; Schön when he hears her making love to his son Alwa. In the most obvious sense, then, the rigidly gendered narcissistic/anaclitic relationship—the paradigmatic heterosexual dyad—would inevitably produce paranoid jealousy on the part of the (male) lover, who would always also be positioned to expend his libido without supplementing it with the woman's return. Taken to its logical end, the lover's desire would lead him inexorably to the beyond of the pleasure

principle, the paranoid delirium being a symptom of this anticipated
course.

Lulu's lovers manifest this paranoia. Schwarz, who is "afraid of
women," is consumed with apocalyptic dread after he marries Lulu.
"Terrified of what the news may be," he lives in fear that the world is
coming to an end.[67] Having acquired Lulu, he has "utterly lost" himself.
When Schwarz cuts his throat, Schön suggests that they attribute the suicide to "persecution mania." Schön then marries Lulu and suffers the
same fate: "So this is the evening of my life. I'd like to be shown a corner
that is still uncontaminated. The plague is in the house. . . . Either madness has already taken possession of my reason, or—exceptions prove the
rule!"[68] Schön carries a revolver, which Lulu will use to kill him, and
becomes obsessed with the fear that he is being watched. As he is dying he
warns his son Alwa not to let Lulu escape because he is certain to become
her next victim.

In its insistent repetitiveness, *Earth Spirit* takes the shape of an obses-
sional narrative. The pleasure of this text is not so much a matter of ascertaining Lulu's guilt, for as Doane observes, she is already the guilty one.
Rather, the text's pleasure would seem to be simply its display of her as
the guilty one. The plot of the play moves relentlessly toward Lulu's ritu-
alized extinction, thus confirming the sadism of narrative that Mulvey
articulates: "Sadism demands a story, depends on making something
happen, forcing a change in another person, a battle of will and strength,
victory/defeat, all occurring in linear time with a beginning and an
end."[69] The voyeurism of the film, however, operates much more ambigu-
ously. Rose points out that "the voyeur is not . . . in a position of pure
manipulation of an object . . . but is always threatened by the potential
exteriorisation of his own function."[70]

Pabst's film demonstrates the danger to the one who tries to isolate the
other in his gaze in a scene that uses a series of shot-reverse-shots to show
us Lulu dancing in Alwa's revue while Schön and his fiancée watch her
from offstage. When Lulu realizes that Schön's fiancée is present, she refuses to perform and throws a tantrum that lures Schön into her dressing
room. As she lies on the bed kicking and screaming, he sits in front of her.
The camera is positioned so that we see her body blocked by his, hers in
fragments with a focus on her scissors-kicking legs, his body in full view.
Lulu is incoherent, emotionally and physically. Schön appears fully present, frustrated but rational. As he looks toward the camera, appealing to
the sympathy of the viewer, she steals glances at him to gauge the effect of
her performance. When he finally turns to look at her, he is lured into her
embrace. Then Schön becomes the object caught in the gaze of his son and
fiancée as they open Lulu's dressing room door to discover him kissing

her. Schön becomes the guilty one as Lulu triumphantly resumes her dance. "This is my execution," he says. And in the next scene he marries her.

Whereas Finney reads the two parts of the Lulu plays as Lulu's rise and fall, the former her buildup as a fetish in the scopophilic economy, the latter her descent and the triumph of retributive justice, I would argue that Lulu, like the "fallen women" of Victorian melodrama, has already arrived at her end point from the moment she is displayed by the circus tamer in the prologue: "She was created for every abuse / To allure and to poison and seduce / To murder without leaving any trace."[71] And, of course, to be murdered without leaving a trace.

The compulsiveness of the text is not about what Lulu will do, or even what will happen to her. Her actions and her destiny are a fait accompli. Rather, what is articulated is the suitors' desire as a problem of unpleasure. The Lulu plays take place in the beyond of the pleasure principle in what Borch-Jacobsen calls the "space of adversity" that is opened up by the spectacle.[72] Lulu is the representation of narcissism, but this is a narcissism that is acted out in the mimetic rivalry between her suitors. Within this homosocial rivalry, Lulu serves as the object of exchange, each suitor needing her image in order to believe in his own sovereignty. They attempt to tame Lulu's improprieties by making her proper(ty). It is when she places herself on the market outside of their control, in the garret in London, that the narrative demands a mythical intervention in the figure of Jack the Ripper—the archetypal "sex killer" and the fulfillment of Lulu's recurrent dream.

Wedekind was the first to use the Ripper as a fictional character, but the killer had already become a mythical figure. The Ripper murders seem to have been eminently suitable to dramatic displays. As Judith Walkowitz points out, the London dailies that reported the crimes followed the conventions of sensationalist melodrama in their narratives.[73] One broadsheet even used a stock woodcut of a murder scene from Victorian melodrama in lieu of an original graphic.[74] While there certainly had been sexually motivated murder prior to the 1888 killings in Whitechapel, Jane Caputi's argument is that Jack the Ripper was the prototype for a particular kind of sex murderer—the serial sex killer who follows a conventionalized formula: he acts alone, preys on victims who possess a common feature, leaves a "signature" at the scene, becomes involved with the media, identifies murder and mutilation with sex.[75]

Jack the Ripper, and many of the killers who have since followed this formula, also had a penchant for displaying the bodies. The spectacle of the dead women appears to be almost as important as the murders themselves. Jack left his victims on display in the open streets; the Boston

Strangler posed his victims in what has been described as "a parody of the gynecological exam."[76] The Hillside Stranglers left the bodies of the women they mutilated and murdered on a hillside in Los Angeles, posing the corpses with their legs spread open and their hands upturned. The pleasure of having their work thus seen, the obsession with display, and the spectacle of the woman as body characterize the ultimate scene of to-be-looked-at-ness.

Jack the Ripper is the consummate actor to annihilate Lulu's dangerous specularity. Lulu becomes the "still-life" that in a sense she already was, despite her resistances. In her death she arrives at the end point of the teleology of normal femininity. And Geschwitz dies with her. Of course they must go together into eternity, transported by the hands of a "sexmaniac." For the Countess and Lulu *are* the perfect couple, the lover and the beloved who can never meet except in the vanishing point of an eternal symmetry. This is the "blind spot" of the *dream* of symmetry that Luce Irigaray articulates: Geschwitz, the invert, the straight man's double, a projection that can emanate only from an imaginary that cannot conceive of desire outside of masculinity; Lulu, the narcissist, the eternally unattainable woman, the enigma without an answer. Both nothing more—or less—than hallucinations emanating from the masculine imaginary, Lulu and the Countess are the perfect heterosexual couple.

4

Chloe Liked Olivia: Death, Desire, and Detection in the Female Buddy Film

> Men have committed the greatest crime against
> women. Insidiously, violently, they have led
> them to hate women, to be their own enemies,
> to mobilize their immense strength against
> themselves, to be the executants of their virile
> needs. They have made for women an antinar-
> cissism![1]
>
> (Hélène Cixous, *The Laugh of the Medusa*)

IN PURSUIT of her topic—women and fiction—Virginia Woolf randomly selects Mary Carmichael's pulp novel, *Life's Adventure*, from the stacks in the British Museum. Carmichael, she suspects, is playing a trick on us, "tampering with the expected sequence." Does her terseness mean that she is afraid of something, "being called 'sentimental' perhaps . . . ?" Will she, Woolf wonders, face the situation, make the jump? As she turns the page, Woolf abruptly cautions: "Are there no men present? Do you promise me that behind that red curtain over there the figure of Sir Char-tres Biron is not concealed? We are all women, you assure me?" Only then can she discover Carmichael's illicit sentence: "Chloe liked Olivia."[2]

Woolf is only half mocking when she admonishes us not to start or blush at the revelation that "these things sometimes happen."[3] Car-michael's Chloe and Olivia inhabit a "vast chamber where nobody has yet been," a room of "half lights and profound shadows" that the writer can inscribe only "in words hardly syllabled yet," noting it as if she were talking about something else.[4] This "thing itself," like the face of Medusa, cannot be looked at directly. Woolf's caustic exaggeration of the erasure of women's relationships achieves its tension by teasing the reader with connotations that are relieved by the banality of the denotation: Chloe and Olivia are *just* good friends. Chloe and Olivia work together in a laboratory; we are not told what else they might share. Could Woolf *not* have been self-consciously employing this language of the forbidden, the prohibited, to evoke the specter of same-sex desire?

"Until recently," D. A. Miller writes, "homosexuality offered not just the most prominent—it offered the only subject matter whose representation . . . appertained exclusively to the shadow kingdom of connotation, where insinuations could be at once developed and denied."[5] Consigned to the realm of connotation, homosexuality is constitutively dubious. Roland Barthes points out that "connotation has not had a good press." Those who believe in the text's one true meaning (Barthes's "philologists") insist on the primacy of denotation. Those whom Barthes names the semiologists challenge the elevation of the denotative over the connotative, pointing out that the former is merely a system like any other. Barthes wants to rescue connotation from both sets of criticism, retaining it as a "computable trace of a *certain* plural of the text (that limited plural of the classic text)."[6] The illusion that denotation and connotation are two different systems "enables the text to operate like a game," a game that affords the classic text the ideological advantage of "*innocence*."[7] According to the game, denotation gets to play the part of the original, though ultimately it is "no more than the *last* of the connotations." To play this game, we have to keep denotation—"the old deity, watchful, cunning, theatrical, foreordained to *represent* the collective innocence of language" (author's emphasis).[8]

Returning to Miller's argument, if the referent we are seeking can be located *only* in the province of connotation, support for its existence can be achieved only through an inexhaustible accumulation of connotations, never proven but perhaps made more or less probable. Once in motion, connotation is promiscuous, insatiable, and aggressive. Miller describes it: "Pushing its way through the Text, exploit[ing] the remotest contacts, enter[ing] into the most shameless liaisons, betray[ing] all canons of integrity—like an arriviste who hasn't arrived, it simply can't stop networking."[9]

Homosexuality is thus most prominently represented when it is virtually under erasure. We are still, as it appears, in the musty archives of the British Museum with Chloe and Olivia and their ambiguous desire. But is it not precisely in the undecidability, the un(remark)ability of women's relationships that much of the pleasure lies *between* women? The continuum of desire, the absence of discernment, is what makes lesbianism a "writerly" text. Why would we choose to be fixed in the signified, contained in the static realm of Meaning and Truth where "readerly" texts repeat their "merely polysemous" plurality when we can—and do, it would seem, by historical and symbolic mandate—exist as a "galaxy of signifiers"?[10] The problem is that in the material world, the endless play of signifiers does come to rest, even if only momentarily. And when the last connotation creates the illusion of closure, the pleasures of holding in suspense are expended, the enigma is disclosed, and the hermeneutical voice calls out some name.

Recently, a new genre of "killer women" films has captured the imagination of a mass audience. *Thelma and Louise* and *Terminator II* were the hits of the summer of 1991. *Sleeping with the Enemy* and *Silence of the Lambs* were top box-office sellers in the fall of that year. The less-acclaimed but generically related *La Femme Nikita*, *Mortal Thoughts*, *Drowning by Numbers*, *Rage in Harlem*, all of them spoken of together loosely as films about women who kill, have heralded the arrival of the "bad" girl. Perhaps it was the wildly successful film *Fatal Attraction* that spurred this ubiquitous resurgence of the bad girl/good girl phenomenon. "What is important," writes Julie Baumgold, "is that these warrior women . . . have been released."[11] Feminist critics will surely respond that what is more important is to interrogate the production and reception of these representations. The crude typology "killer women" overlooks the not-so-subtle difference between the majority of these films and two that I want to isolate for consideration—*Thelma and Louise* and *Mortal Thoughts*. Both of these films assume the primacy of emotional bonds between women as a test case for intelligibility. What these two films share is the representation of women *who act together* in indifference to or retaliation against the culture's heterosexual expectations. And one or more of the main characters is not just a murderer, but a woman who kills *for* another woman. I will be arguing that for these and other reasons the female protagonists of these films make "shameless liaisons," which expose the dominant culture's underwriting of lesbianism when the violence of women enters representation.

'Til Death Do Us Part: *Thelma and Louise*

Unlike the typical male heroes of road movies, Thelma and Louise do not die in the proverbial blaze of glory as they triumphantly shoot it out with the enemy. Remember the final freeze-frame of *Butch Cassidy and the Sundance Kid* (1969), perhaps the paradigmatic "buddy" film? These two heroes die running *toward* the camera, an image Cynthia J. Fuchs has characterized as "disastrous ejaculatory excess."[12] *Thelma and Louise*, by contrast, ends in a dreamlike sequence, the camera's eye caressing them as their Thunderbird gently floats above the canyon, then is arrested in midair, forever poised to penetrate the space that they are visually barred from entering. Their deaths are thus rendered as virtual but unrepresentable. This iconic ending might be read as the apotheosis of these uniquely female outlaws—together forever, forever unbound. It may also, however, function as a metonymic representation of the way in which the female "outsider" is already *inside* the circle of phallocratic desire.

In conjunction with the slow-motion movement of the final sequence, this scene might appeal to the common dream experience of falling without touching ground, inviting a spectatorial identification that crosses over any number of specific sociohistorical positionalities. On the other hand, there is nothing more pervasive and hetero-sex-gendered as the scene of a male subject in pursuit of a female object. Thelma and Louise run away from the camera, not toward it, and they are pursued by the "good cop" (Harvey Keitel) who is also shot in slow motion as he makes one last attempt to rescue them. While it is somewhat unusual in mainstream cinema for the male subject to fail to attain his female object, it is almost unheard of for the female object(s) of his quest to elude him by choosing to depart *together*. Thelma and Louise's suicide pact is a familiar device for recapturing and containing the woman who strays too far from the law of the fathers. But bracketing this diegetic containment, we could also read this film's final sequence as a commentary on the Lacanian subject's impossible relationship to the object of his desire.

Famous for some, infamous for others, Lacan's contention that the "sexual *relation* is impossible" is based on a theory of desire that presumes desire's aim is to *reproduce* desire, not to attain its object.[13] The detective running after the car in slow motion is a continuous approach toward an object that maintains a constant distance. Shot in slow motion, this sequence is suggestive of a fantasy space where the satisfaction of desire is impossible, an activity that never reaches an end point. Furthermore, these final moments are metonymic in that they recapitulate the film's narrative in its entirety: a chase in which the male detectives pursue the "lost objects" that continually elude them. In the dialectic of this film's desire, we can thus read the familiar trajectory of the woman as object-cause of man's desire. The Woman, who must be constantly produced *as* elusive in order to reproduce masculine desire, is certainly a master narrative in Western phallocratic libidinal economies. When Thelma says, "Let's not get caught," signaling Louise to drive over the cliff, her remark could be an ironic compliance with this tradition. And yet it may be possible to rescue *Thelma and Louise* from the containment that seems to overtake any subversion in poststructuralist readings of popular culture's representations. If, as Mary Ann Doane has argued, the desire *to* desire was the operative mode in the woman's film of the 1940s,[14] this "women's" film ends with a sequence that makes visible the economy of masculine desire as adamantly reproductive but nongenerative. That is, it makes a patent comment on masculine desire's aim to reproduce *itself* as its *own object*(ive).

With the exception of the ending, *Thelma and Louise* conforms point for point with the formula for the classic road movie/buddy film that Robin Wood has outlined.[15] Structured as a journey that has either no goal or an illusory one, *Thelma and Louise* marginalizes and/or grossly caricatures men, focusing instead on the female-female relationship as the film's emotional center. Furthermore, elements that Wood isolates as the ideological heart of the buddy film—the absence of a home that would signify the security of "normality," and the death of the protagonists as the most effective impediment to consummation of the same-sex relationship—are integral to *Thelma and Louise*. The only element missing according to Wood's paradigm is a recognizable homosexual character who stands in sharp contrast to the male heroes and thus functions as a disclaimer.[16] However, the heroines' heterosexuality is guaranteed by the production of male lovers even in the most unlikely circumstances. Wood's structural analysis of the buddy film's repressed homoeroticism is seconded by Tania Modleski: she comments on these films' insistent, sometimes explicit, more often latent, "censored 'subtext' " of homosexuality, and she wonders how audiences could ignore this dimension.[17] Since *Thelma and Louise* seems to do little more than substitute female characters in the conventional male roles, we might expect that the censored subtext of the film is lesbian desire. I will return to this point at length later. For now, however, I want to stay with my earlier suggestion that the film enacts, and possibly subverts, the conception of desire as a masculine pursuit and production of a lost female object.

Standing at the Crossroads

Reviewers could not have missed the preponderance of phallic images in the landscape of director Ridley Scott's imagination. The middle of this film traces the trajectory of Thelma and Louise's attempted escape from a symbolic order that is rife with images of the phallus. The women's origin and end point, however, are characterized by absent spaces that resist symbolization. The originary absence that sets the narrative in motion is Louise's "trauma," a space that she refuses to fill up with content. She exteriorizes this space, however, by giving it a local habitation and a name—Texas. This refusal to disclose the content of her traumatic past has troubled reviewers on both sides of the debate: those who find it a feminist manifesto and those who declare it a male-bashing exposé. Alice Cross, for example, argues that the keeping of this secret ruins spectators' ability to empathize: "Everything that happens in the movie is a consequence of [Louise's] earlier experience, but because it is a hole, a blank, we are left detached where we ought to be most moved, angered, sympathetic."[18] Similarly, Richard Schickel suggests that Louise's "cold-blooded" murder might be more palatable if that "something dark, something that the film never fully explains, in her past" had been articulated.[19]

The inarticulation of Louise's trauma is associated with consternation about the film's incoherent geography. Thus one critic faults director Ridley Scott for desiring to make "pretty pictures" at the expense of working out a realistic geography,[20] and another finds the women's escape plans to be the film's "running joke."[21] Just as Louise refuses to articulate the particulars of her past, she attempts to avoid literally traversing that history. Handing Thelma the map, she asks her to find all the secondary roads to Mexico from Oklahoma City. Thelma suggests taking Route 81 through Dallas, but Louise will not go that way:

> THELMA: We're running for our lives. I mean, can't you make an exception? Look at this map, the only thing between Oklahoma and Mexico is Texas. Look.
> LOUISE: I'm not going to talk about this. Now you either find another way or give me the goddam map and I will!

What Louise needs is an imaginary landscape, a map with another route to follow than the one preordained for her in the symbolic order. Thelma has to learn that reality is a ruse, a lure. But Louise already knows that "we don't live in that kind of world," that what passes for reality contains within it the void of the Real, that traumatic space which resists symbolization.[22] Filling in the empty space of her trauma might facilitate her reintegration into the symbolic order, but Louise is not disposed to collaborate with "justice"; she will not become an accomplice to the detective because she knows that the rescue is a trap.

Sarah Kofman's distinction between the criminal and the hysteric is apropos of Louise's dilemma. Kofman's "criminal" is the woman who knows her own secret and refuses to share it, because she is, or thinks she is, self-sufficient. By submitting to the "cure," the hysteric, on the other hand, becomes complicit with the analyst's desire.[23] That is, the transference constitutes the analyst as the subject-supposed-to-know. By resisting divulging her secret, Louise becomes the "criminal," and it is thus just as much what she refuses to *say* as what she has *done* that criminalizes her.

If there is one thing that narratives and their consumers cannot tolerate, it is a woman with a secret. Women are supposed to *be* secrets, not *have* them. Shoshana Felman neatly describes Freud's question of desire as the desire *for* a question. Since women are the objects of desire, they in effect "*are* the question" and hence "cannot *enunciate* the question."[24] So it is that women are the enigma, the place where the secret is embodied, not the agents that withhold it. In this reproductive libidinal economy, questions produce questions, desire produces desire. The enigma of woman is not a riddle with an answer to be found or a truth to be told, but the placeholder of a lack that is necessary to reproduce man.

The woman *with* a secret menaces this reproductive economy, and the aim of narrative is to render her fully exposed. Figured within the narrative as an interiorized space, a memory that she will not narrate, "Texas" could be read as a hysterical symptom demanding the interpretive intervention of a subject-supposed-to-know, an analyst. But unlike the hysteric, Louise does not try to overcome her resistances and allow the sympathetic detective, who in fact *does know* her history, to "save" her. On the contrary, she thoroughly mistrusts the mechanisms that would reintegrate her into the symbolic order. Louise constantly has to educate Thelma about the way this order operates. Thelma naively believes that simply telling the "truth" will exonerate them. Louise has to teach her that the symbolic order is a masculine imaginary in which their truths have no credibility.

Louise's journey has obvious affinities with that of Oedipus, most clearly in her attempt to circumvent the trauma rather than traversing it. Had she been willing to go through Texas, that direct route might have allowed the women to make it to Mexico. Thus, like Oedipus's, her journey is inscribed as a circle that repeats the wound in the effort to elude it. As the refrain from the film's theme song, "Part of Me, Part of You," repeats, Louise and Thelma are standing at the crossroads, evoking the mythical topos where the hero makes his fated, fatal move. For Oedipus, however, the lyrics that follow would have to say "from this day on you'll *always* walk alone." For Thelma and Louise, the crossroads motif signals each juncture in their deepening commitment to each other—"from this day on you'll *never* walk alone."

But *Thelma and Louise* is an Oedipal narrative by virtue of its structure alone. Teresa de Lauretis has brilliantly demonstrated that all narrative is governed by an Oedipal logic in which each reader—"male or female—is constrained and defined within the two positions of a sexual difference thus conceived: male-hero-human, on the side of the subject; and female-obstacle-boundary-space, on the other."[25] Perhaps there is no narrative more transparently Oedipal than the conventional buddy film in which the female obstacles have *already been eliminated* before the action begins. As, until recently, an exclusively masculine domain, what the buddy films might show us is the already-achieved homosocial order that underpins a purportedly heterosexual economy. By skipping the step of hiding the bonds between men behind the male subject's pursuit of a female object, male road movies might radically subvert dominant ideologies *or* powerfully substantiate them. Whether they are hetero-subversive, homoerotic, or disruptive of the distinction, the form has been presumed to be inherently masculine.

Developing Roland Barthes's hunch that pleasure and narrative move along the triple track of language, narrative, and the Oedipus, de Lauretis shows how this movement is one of masculine desire. Barthes writes, "The pleasure of the text is . . . an Oedipal pleasure (to denude, to know, to learn the origin and the end)."[26] But the fulfillment of that desire is not guaranteed, for as de Lauretis points out, unlike reproduction—the " 'aim of biology' "—which "may be accomplished independently of women's consent, the aim of desire (heterosexual male desire, that is) may not. In other words, women *must either* consent or be seduced into consenting to femininity,"[27] so that they come to represent the end point of the male journey.

Not only does Louise resist that Oedipal pleasure by refusing to disclose her "mystery," but also both women's journey is figured as precisely a *flight* from femininity. As they move through the phallic landscapes of the film's scenography, we watch them discarding the external trappings of their proscribed gender and appropriating the cultural markings of masculinity: Louise exchanges her engagement ring for a man's hat; Thelma dons the cap of the driver whose truck they blow up; Louise trades sunglasses with the state trooper whom they lock in the trunk of his car; their long flowing hair gets tucked up under the hats; they stop carrying purses and strap on guns and ammunition. In one particularly pointed scene, Louise exchanges looks with two elderly women who are watching her quizzically as she waits for Thelma to finish robbing a store. When she sees the women watching her, she throws her lipstick out of the car. The most striking instance of this appropriation is Thelma's imitation of J.D.'s style of committing armed robbery. Her husband and the detectives are later shown watching this incident on videotape; and this is the moment when they recognize the women as unrecuperable. As Louise jokes to Thelma, "There's no such thing as *justifiable* armed robbery." So there is no turning back. Thelma and Louise have, from this moment on, crossed the boundary that represents women's space in the symbolic order. They are no longer simply women in trouble but full-fledged outlaws.

We can then understand this film's "incoherent geography" to be enacting the oxymoronic logic of a narrative that sets out to show the "impossible"—two women together outside the confines of the patriarchal symbolic. Theoretically, as women, Thelma and Louise are excessive to the representation. And indeed reviewers' responses indicate that women cannot be seen as women within the buddy-film conventions. So, for example, one reviewer says that Thelma and Louise are "free to be-have like—well, men."[28] Or at best, the "good ol' boys are gals" who become "parodies of men."[29] The semantic awkwardness that refers to *Thelma and Louise* as a "female buddy film" points to the conceptual inability to think of the film in terms other than that of substitution. The dilemma is posed by David Denby: "In some ways, I suppose, we've seen all of this before. . . . But in crucial ways, we've never seen it before."[30] Of course, we have seen the plot structure of two heroes on the lam many times before; what we have not seen is simply two women occupying the same topography. The issue is whether this substitution constitutes differ-ence, sameness, or the same difference. *Thelma and Louise* thus engages us directly in the problems and paradoxes of the sameness/difference debates.

Thelma and Louise are hemmed in by spaces they cannot enter or will not pass through; Texas and the "Grand Canyon" become structural me-tonymies for these female "buddies." For in the phallocratic libidinal economy, it is precisely the absent space that signifies "woman," the lack that is necessary to uphold the symbolic order. Theoretically, this is the space where they always already were and to which they will ineluctably return. And yet, in the diegesis, Thelma and Louise stake out their terri-tory in the middle ground, the place of the masculine hero. Ostensibly, it is their inhabitation of this landscape that has produced so much anxiety in response to the film, indicating that the reverse discourse holds some promise for destabilizing the masculine/feminine dichotomy. However, the mechanism of reversal alone does not fully account for the cultural hysteria that this film has elicited. When we examine the "logic" of the reception of *Thelma and Louise*, another possibility begins to emerge that is more subversive than appropriation of the "other's" territory.

First, spectators' responses to the film manifest the familiar denuncia-tion, couched in aesthetic terms, of its lack of verisimilitude, and *at the same time*, the fear that its content is all too imitable. The *Time* cover story sought out feminist scholars to reassure readers that the film was "not . . . a cultural representation but . . . a fairy tale," or "a dramatic piece, not a [literal] description of what's going on in our society."[31] The point here was to restore cultural confidence in *real* women's passivity. Then there is the need for reassurance that the women involved in the making of the film as well as the fictional characters do not hold any malice toward men. Thus we are told that the screenwriter, Callie Khouri, does not hate men.[32] Nor do Thelma and Louise *really* hate men, as one reviewer offers: they "basically like men, as most women do."[33] Another tells us that Louise is really a "man's woman," who is forced, "by circum-stances, into a much tougher attitude towards men than she started out with."[34] The last piece of this developing narrative is the representation of the real lives of the women in and behind the film. Thus we are taken behind the scenes to learn that Khouri is about to celebrate the first anniversary of her wedding, that Sarandon's boyfriend frequently visits her on the set, that Davis is recently divorced but has a long history of heterosexual romance.[35] If within the film we are reminded periodically that Thelma and Louise are attracted to men, so reporters seem to be concerned to emphasize that the women offscreen are heterosexual—as *most women are?*

In summary then, real women would not act like Thelma and Louise. In case there is any doubt, we have feminist authorities to tell us that they are fairy-tale characters, so real women could not act like them anyway. By the rule of substitution, only men can act like Thelma and Louise. This representation is not really about women; it is about men. Now you see women, now you don't. What is it that we *are* seeing when we see women who are *not really* women but are perhaps "really men"? One answer would be the projection of male fantasies in which the woman's body is simply the screen, *pace* the psychoanalytic reading of the fetishized spectacle of woman. While I do not quarrel with this account, it is nonetheless important to recall a specific history to this woman's body-as-screen. For the woman who is really a man—the woman, shall we say, "trapped" in a man's body—has a very specific historical materialization, not just a fantasized space in the masculine imaginary. When we speak of women who are somehow "really men," we conjure the specter of the invert. If Thelma and Louise are circling around the absent spaces where woman is located in the discourse of men's desire, response to this film is hovering anxiously around the threat of the lesbian as the unspeakable sign.

Keeping in mind the constitutive dubiety of sighting a lesbian "subtext" in *Thelma and Louise*, I want nonetheless to propose that what sets this film apart from the numerous other recent productions indiscriminately marked as "killer women" films is *not* the content of Thelma and Louise's actions, but the fact that they are *together*.

The violence in *Thelma and Louise* is patently understated compared to the gruesome conventions borrowed from the "slasher" tradition that characterizes other films in this purportedly newly emerging genre. While critics are squabbling over which of these representations are the most violent, they are overlooking what distinguishes this film from other recent "killer women" films. None of these other portrayals of outlaw women has generated as much controversy in the name of *feminism* as *Thelma and Louise*. And none of them has generated so much reassuring rhetoric about the women's "normality." Critical responses to *Thelma and Louise* have evoked lesbianism as a haunting presence through denial and negation as well as through the rhetorical circumlocutions that supposedly merely cleverly describe the film. For example, *New York* magazine prints a photograph of Thelma and Louise sitting in their Thunderbird. The caption reads, "Girl Crazy."[36] The conceptual dyslexia produced by this idiomatic expression is apparent if we imagine the caption "Boy Crazy" used to advertise *Butch Cassidy and the Sundance Kid*. "Girl Crazy" is not meant to translate outside the terms of heterosexuality. The caption simultaneously connotes the women's desire for each other and reinstates the historical equation between homosexuality and pathology. The connotation of desire circulating between Louise and Thelma has been hinted at only through such "slips"—or through negation, as in the case of the *Vogue* reviewer who thought the film was riddled with cliché and found almost nothing positive about it *except* for the *absence* of any overt lesbianism: "One of [the film's] admirable mercies is that . . . the women do not come on to each other," an omission "that makes the final scene all the more poignant and exhilarating."[37]

In the film itself, we are reminded rather too insistently that the women are heterosexual, even though and perhaps especially since their heterosexuality is established from the beginning. As they go on the road, the film seems pressured to reinforce their sexual identities. A number of reviewers have pointed to Thelma's one-night stand with the hitchhiker J.D. as ideologically problematic.[38] That the film chooses to engage Thelma in a casual sexual encounter with a stranger just a day after she has been sexually assaulted by a man she met in a bar is improbable at best. When Louise's boyfriend, Jimmy, shows up in the Western Union office to deliver her money to her personally, we are as surprised as she. Given the way the film has characterized Jimmy up to this point, we would expect him to steal her life savings rather than fly across three states to hand it to her. When this man who cannot make a commitment to her is, in addition, bearing an engagement ring, the film further strains a spectator's credibility. I think, however, that we can read the improbability of these episodes as more than issues of verisimilitude. For these romantic/sexual encounters allay any potential anxiety about the women's desire for men.

Summoned through negation in both the film's action and the critical responses is a history of identification between the female criminal and the lesbian. Given this history, the expectation for lesbianism between women who violate the law is so strong that the film works overtime to disavow it. If the lesbian has been constructed as the manifest figure of women's "latent" criminality, we can expect that representations of violent women will be haunted by her absent presence. This historical association/conflation is particularly problematic in the context of a film that focuses on women bonding together outside the law since lesbianism has been used to maintain rivalry *between* women. Caroline Sheldon was one of the first film critics to show how homosexuality operates within the heterosexual family unit as "the criminal element—both as a warning to those stepping out of line and a method of containment of anti-social (anti-heterosexual) tendencies." Sheldon's analysis shows that when lesbians do appear in cinematic representations, it is almost always as "castrating bitches and sadists."[39] Given this history, it is likely that when women are represented as violent, predatory, dangerous, the reverse would also be operative—the "castrating bitch" would carry the presumption of lesbianism.

Nevertheless, even though lesbianism is produced *within* this system as a necessary boundary to rein in and provide closure to the heterosexual imperative, this does not necessarily contain a potential disruption to the system that produces it. It is not a matter of looking for the lesbian *behind* the content of the criminal woman. Rather, we need to understand how the lesbian functions as a structural dialectic of appearance/disappearance in the process of making women's aggression visible. These representations carry with them the weight of a culture that has made the lesbian and the female criminal synonymous by *displacing* women's aggression onto the sexually "deviant" woman.

Whereas there exists a well-documented history of representing lesbians *as* criminals in avant-garde, pornographic, and grade B films, recent films that depict and eroticize violence by and between women take excessive measures to heterosexualize the women.[40] By reading these later representations in a historical context, one can see in them a voyeurism in which the spectacle of a woman assaulting or killing a man makes an unconscious appeal to lesbianism and thus perpetuates the ways in which the presence of lesbians has been used to facilitate the heterosexual pleasure of male spectators. When the two women in the representation work with rather than against each other, their aggression almost unavoidably connotes lesbianism. The anxiety these films generate will be in proportion to the incoherencies in the narrative that permit some glimmer of this recognition.

If on the one hand the narrative of *Thelma and Louise* imitates a heterosexual chase, it also plots Louise's gradual winning of Thelma. As the older, wiser woman who seduces the flighty and inexperienced younger woman, Louise is not unlike the dominant butch, usually working-class, who preys on innocent, virginal femmes, a relationship that is commonplace outside the classic cinema and has served to reiterate the conflation of the lesbian and the criminal. From the opening of the film, Louise's dominance is established. When one of her co-workers takes the phone from her and flirts with Thelma, Louise wrests it away and says to him, "Not this weekend, honey, she's running away with me." It is also common for the predatory older woman to seduce through narcissistic identifications. This "bad influence" theme is exemplified in *Thelma and Louise* by Thelma's husband, Daryl, who assumes that Louise has led his wife astray. This is reinforced as we watch Thelma taking on Louise's bad habits. As they drive away together in Louise's Thunderbird, Thelma, a nonsmoker, lights one of Louise's cigarettes. Louise laughs at her and asks what she is doing. "Smoking," Thelma answers: "I'm Louise."

Implications of erotic desire between them begin in the roadside bar where they stop for a drink. Thelma initiates by suggesting that Louise "tell Jimmy to get lost." Instead of responding to the question of her desire for Jimmy, Louise suggests an exchange: "Why don't you get rid of that no-good husband of yours?" This dialogue could be read as that of two women commiserating about the inadequacies of their heterosexual love lives; but it also unmistakably flirts with the potential for their freeing themselves up for each other. This latter possibility is reinforced when Thelma then says, "Let's dance." Louise clearly takes this to mean that Thelma wants to dance with her. She follows Thelma to the dance floor, then realizes that Thelma is going to dance with Harlan. Louise makes a gesture indicating frustration and embarrassment and returns to her seat. Both women end up dancing with men, but this moment is superfluous to the narrative movement. It serves no formal function but connotes that Louise is in some sense already "woman-identified" while Thelma must be persuaded. When a few scenes later Harlan tries to rape Thelma in the parking lot, spectators might recall that Thelma chose the wrong dance partner.

The film titillates spectators with the possibility of desire between the women, then recuperates that desire by introducing male lovers in heightened moments. Structurally, this matches the convention used in pornographic films in which two women are presented together amorously only as prelude to a man's entering the scene as "the real thing." This procedure is particularly clear when the hitchhiker J.D. is introduced in the film. Thelma has just told her husband to "go fuck [himself]," a moment that marks her unwavering commitment to Louise. Thelma joins Louise in the car and says, "So how long before we're in goddam Mexico?" Until this moment, Thelma has hesitated, responding to Louise's questions about whether she is "up for this" evasively: "I don't know, I don't know what you're asking." When Thelma indicates that she is prepared to go to the end of the line with Louise, the women exchange a glance of complicity with an erotic valence. But Thelma's gaze is quickly refocused on J.D., who appears in the side and rearview mirrors of the car. This overly cautious presentation of him at exactly the moment when Thelma has relinquished her allegiance to Daryl reinforces my reading of the film's excessive repudiation of the very desire that it evokes through negation.

"Lesbian" is the aporia in this narrative. Functioning as a placeholder for the reproduction of masculine desire, it is both necessary and disruptive. Subtle suggestions of its possibility lend the film an erotic charge, but if it were overtly represented the mainstream audiences targeted by this film would almost surely lose all sympathy for the characters. In fact, it is important to recognize that this display of women's aggression could be produced only in the context of a certain guaranteed innocuousness; this is achieved through manipulation of both the sexual and the racial politics of the film. It is striking that the men in the film are so *un*threatened by the clear menace of a woman aiming a gun at them that they respond to her warnings with additional provocations. Harlan says, "Suck my cock" when Louise is holding the gun on him. When Louise demands that the truck driver apologize, he answers, "Fuck that." We could understand these curious responses as confirmation of Hélène Cixous's point that "[men] need femininity to be associated with death; it's the jitters that give them a hard-on!"[41] But we need not theorize what turns men on to see what is operating in this film: the historical alignment of women with passivity that has been ideologically enforced so powerfully that even when the women are presenting a clear danger, they are not perceived as capable of carrying out aggressive action. This alignment, however, is grounded on the usually unspoken assumption that the "women" in question are white, generally middle-class, and conventionally attractive. Women who deviate from these prescriptions would certainly not appear as sympathetic *or* as nonthreatening. Could we imagine black women in these roles, or women whose physical appearances signified lesbian? Louise's working-class toughness alone does not overcome the images that Davis and Sarandon command as glamorous white actresses.[42]

These subversions are constantly at risk for recuperation by the narrative form. For the referent of these transgressions cannot but be the dominant racist and heterosexist ideologies against which they strain. Thus the film holds the most promise in what it fails to show and tell. To borrow Valerie Traub's expression, it is what *Thelma and Louise* "(dis)articulates"[43] that holds the most potential for undoing the hegemony of white heterosexist patriarchy.

If Thelma and Louise's origin is the traumatic space signified by Texas, their end point is another locus of absence—the "Grand Canyon."[44] Hovering over this death-space, the hood of their Thunderbird points downward as if to signify a forever-deferred penetration. They linger above it out of time, suspended, waiting. On its edge, they can marvel at the splendor, the sublimity of its enormous absence. "Isn't it beautiful?" Thelma says as they catch their breath. Moments later, surrounded by artillery, Thelma suggests that they drive into it. Louise at first has difficulty understanding Thelma's desire to "go," to "hit it," but when her recognition comes, she kisses Thelma on the lips. The camera is positioned behind Sarandon's head, so that we do not actually see the women's lips meet, but the kiss is too prolonged for friendship, and the camera's angle reminds us of Louise's earlier parting kiss with Jimmy. Louise hits the gas pedal, the car hurtles forward, the camera zooms in on the women's hands interlocking; then they are stopped in midair. Desiring from a distance, even one so close as the very edge of the precipice, is permissible. Disappearing into it is not.

It is tempting to read the canyon as a feminine space, a uterovaginal anomaly in the midst of the excessive phallic images that surround the women at this moment. But the canyon is much more interestingly ambiguous than that. What makes the canyon a sublime object is its vast emptiness. One can contemplate its "nothingness" only by looking at the contours of the frame that surrounds it. The canyon is thus a perfect "anamorphotic object," a nothing to be seen that is nonetheless visible by virtue of the boundaries that encircle it. Only the background is visible, but it is the black hole of the center that constitutes the canyon as such. Its presence is a blank. In this sense, the canyon is the very image of the relationship between Lacan's "Real" and "reality." If the Real is that which resists symbolization, the unseen impossible that is necessary to maintain the consistency of the Symbolic, "reality" is the ideological order that depends on the relegation of the Real to the status of a central lack.[45]

It is scarcely necessary to rehearse once again how this relationship is gendered so that "woman" is constructed as this lack. The Real is thus the zone that must be excluded, represented only as nonrepresentable in order to constitute the fiction of the phallocratic symbolic as truth. It may be impossible for Thelma and Louise to break through this boundary, just as it is impossible for the film to represent their desire as lesbian. For in the phallocratic economy of desire, on the other side of that boundary there is only madness. *Thelma and Louise* cannot tell a truly different story, but it points to this narrative as just one story among many. And in this sense it historicizes it, setting it in motion and indicating that it is susceptible to transformation.

Thelma and Louise are not criminals because they shoot a rapist, rob a store, or blow up a truck. They are criminals because they are *together*, seeking escape from the masculine circuit of desire. At the beginning of their journey, Louise holds a camera at arm's length and takes a photo-graph of them together. As they drive out over the canyon, the camera zooms in to show us this photograph flying out of the car's backseat. The picture they have taken of themselves disappears into the offscreen space, and we are left with the static image of them hurtling to their deaths. If the canyon is the absent space that signifies woman in the semiotics of the narrative, Thelma and Louise cannot enter it because it is where they always already were. There is no place for them to go except the place designated for them in the masculine symbolic. But the photograph's dis-appearance allows us to imagine an elsewhere that resists representation. If we look at the map of the film from Louise's perspective, we might fix our gaze on the unseen real of her desire, exit from the endless circuit of masculine desire, and enter her imaginary landscape.

Shameless Liaisons: *Mortal Thoughts*

Advertised as a suspense-thriller, *Mortal Thoughts* is, on one level, more accurately a classic "whodunit." The film also enacts the crucial dynamic of the buddy film. *Mortal Thoughts* is above all a film *about* Cynthia's and Joyce's relationship. It makes their bond into an enigma that the narrative sets out to detect but fails to disclose fully. In classic detective fiction, Tzvetan Todorov argues, there are always "two murders." The first—the story of what really happened—is little more than a pretense for the second: the detective's narrative. Likening these two murders to the Russian formalists' distinction between "fable" and "plot," Todorov points out that the fable of the murder is always subordinated to the plot of the investigation. The second story, serving as "a mediator between the reader and the story of the crime," is an excess generated by the murder, having "no importance in itself." Thus the classic "whodunit" is struc-tured as a duality of narratives: the first "absent but real," the second "present but insignificant."[46]

These distinctions resonate with the Freudian interpretation of dreams, where it is not the hidden content of the dream (the "first murder") but the dream-work itself (the "second murder") that commands our atten-tion. Dreams, like detective fiction, are subjected to the hermeneutical code, their units functioning "to articulate in various ways a question, its response, and the variety of chance events which can either formulate the question or delay its answer; or even, constitute an enigma and lead to its solution."[47] Todorov's "intermediary," the figure who leads us out of the absence of the first story and into the "insignificant present" of the investigation, correlates with the Freudian analyst (or the Lacanian subject-supposed-to-know), who accomplishes the "crucial step toward a *hermeneutical* approach and conceive[s] the dream as a meaningful phenomenon" (author's emphasis).[48] As Barthes reminds us, the hermeneutical code is the offstage "Voice of Truth."[49] The hermeneutics that drives the detective narrative is a demand for Meaning.

In "Psycho-analysis and the Establishment of the Facts in Legal Proceedings" (1906), Freud spoke of the similarities and differences between criminal investigative strategies and psychoanalysis. Drawing an analogy between the criminal and the hysteric, Freud makes the point that both are "concerned with a secret, with something hidden." The fundamental difference between them is, of course, that the criminal knows his own secret and willfully conceals it, whereas the hysteric's secret is "hidden even from himself."[50] Both the magistrate and the therapist are charged with the task of disclosing the secret, but the former's aim is to *un*cover its contents, whereas the latter's is to *dis*cover the form of the secret itself. The Law, in other words, is on the side of consciousness and the relative banality of the "fable"—what "really" happened. But psychoanalysis's territory is the unconscious and the structure of the "plot": the story of the detective's coming to knowledge, the relationship between the observer and what is being observed.

These juridical and psychoanalytic discourses intersect in *Mortal Thoughts*, which foregrounds the relationship between classic detective stories and the subject in analysis. As the opening and closing credits are running, we watch images of the protagonists passing from infancy to adolescence engaged in ordinary activities such as skipping rope, dancing to a record player, playing on the beach—images that evoke the women's lost innocence. As in the secondary revision of the dream, these images attain their full import only retrospectively. After we watch the girls become murderers in the narrative of the film, these opening shots are no longer isolated, nostalgic moments, but narrative commentaries on their "normal" progress through the formative years. Retrospectively the audience is invited to consider the question "What went wrong?"

After the credits roll, the film then opens with a slow-motion tracking of Cynthia Kellogg as she is brought into police headquarters for questioning, and this setting will serve as a framing device for a series of flashbacks that promise to constitute a linear, coherent narrative answering the question "Whodunit?" As in classic detective fiction, it is Cynthia's interrogation by detective John Woods and his assistant Linda Nealon that commands our attention even as it appears to serve only as a pretense for the revelation of "what really happened." Cynthia is what the law might call a cooperative witness, but what Freud might consider a paradoxical criminal, or a hysteric, for she immediately abjures her right to remain silent and expresses her desire to cooperate fully with the investigation. The criminal, Freud reminds us, "does not work with you; if he did, he would be working against his whole ego."[51] The hysteric, on the other hand, because she hopes to gain recovery from the analysis, consciously combats her resistance. Alternatively, Cynthia might be simply employing the talent that, according to Lacan, distinguishes animals from humans—deceiving the Other by means of the truth itself. By deploying the "mask of truth" she may be attempting to lead the detective astray.[52] It is this dialectic between truth and deception that constitutes the interrogation as the film's framing device.

Through the interrogation of Cynthia Kellogg, which constitutes the plot of Mortal Thoughts, the spectator is aligned, on one plane, with detective John Woods, who is carrying out the investigation into the death of James Urbanski. That is, to the extent that the question we ask of this film is what happened, it is Woods's point of view with which we are complicit and it is the past that concerns us. As spectators, however, we are invited to watch what is happening between them, and thus we are positioned as objective observers of the interactions among Woods, his assistant Nealon, and Kellogg in the present tense. And yet for the vast majority of this film what we are actually watching are Kellogg's flashbacks. We are thus inside her memories, suffering through her reminiscences with her. And the film thereby sets up a contest between the verbal exchange of the interrogation scene and the visual flow of events as Cynthia remembers them. The contest for the "truth" is not the truth of what really happened, but a truth that the visualized memories make manifest in excess of the events that Cynthia narrates. Which will finally be more believable? The words that Woods extorts from her, what we hear her tell him, or her memories—what she shows us that he cannot see? When the subject of interrogation/analysis in this contemporary film is a woman suspected of murder, the boundaries between hysteric and criminal blur and the professional detective finds himself positioned as amateur analyst.

Freud tells his audience of jurisprudence students and faculty that they need not take into account that the "psychoneurotic," unlike the criminal, "is invariably concerned with a repressed sexual complex."[53] But it is precisely this insignificant difference that (dis)appears in Mortal Thoughts, not as a "latency" in the consciousness of the accused, but rather as a trace in the form of Cynthia's secret itself. It is not just that "something is wrong here," in Cynthia's testimony about what happened, as the detective John Woods queruously repeats. Woods is convinced that she is prevaricating, and his incredulity is summoned by Cynthia's loyalty to Joyce. "Cops don't protect each other!" Cynthia fires back as Woods shakes his head and mumbles, "I don't know, some-thing's . . . I don't know." Amateur analyst that he is, Woods searches for the hidden meaning behind the manifest content of Cynthia's story. But we, as spectators, are intrigued by the *form* her secret takes.

If his suspicion is aroused by his inability to believe in her devotion to another woman, Cynthia, on the contrary, assumes the primacy of her bond with Joyce and hence attempts to use it as a deception. The discrep-ancy between her assumption and his vision can be read only as the differ-ence between his voice as the representative of a patriarchal unconscious that has foreclosed the primacy of a woman's bond with another woman and her "hallucinatory" evocation of that bond. In *his* consciousness, we are back in the musty archives of the British Museum with Virginia Woolf and the nearly unutterable sentence: "Chloe liked Olivia." But enough to risk her life? Enough to kill her abusive husband for her? Enough to sacri-fice her own husband and children? Because Woods cannot believe in such loyalty, he demands that Cynthia produce an explanation, a reason.

The film will finally give him that reason, through the classic "trick" ending of the detective narrative. But by the time this ending is revealed, the "unreason" of Cynthia and Joyce's fidelity has been too powerfully conjured to be undone by the trick. That is, if we read the story that Woods elicits as a secondary revision, it is one that does not fully succeed. For the investigation itself produces an excess, something that surpasses the coherency of the narrative, which can only be read as a void around which the questioning circles. This unrepresentable excess is Cynthia's desire. As detective, Woods wants to find out what she *did*; but as analyst, he needs to know what she *wanted*.

The story of *Mortal Thoughts* conforms rather neatly to the first mur-der of classic detective fiction. The mystery is not cleared up until the last moments of the film; the ending reveals the "trick" that has been the second story's aim to isolate; and the investigator is granted immunity. Once all the "facts" are in, the story appears to be linear and coherent. One reviewer sums it up in this mock headline: "Bayonne Wives Slay Hubs in Murder Swap."[54]

The women's story does finally, though circuitously, take shape: Jimmy (Joyce's husband) is stabbed by Cynthia as he attempts to rape her. Cynthia confesses to Joyce, and Joyce decides to assist Cynthia by dumping Jimmy's body on the side of the highway. Since he is not dead from the stab wounds, technically the two women kill him together. They then work together to cover up the crime. When their alibi begins to leak, Joyce is arrested and held for suspicion of murder. Released on bail, Joyce finds out that Cynthia has told her husband, Arthur, that Joyce had killed Jimmy. Joyce then kills Arthur. Cynthia is brought in for questioning, tells the detective that Joyce killed Jimmy, and admits to being an accomplice after the fact. At the end of the film, Cynthia returns to police headquarters, presumably to confess the "real" story. The film thus supplies a satisfactory resolution to the generic detective tale whose end point is the production of a linear story.

Yet the question this film leaves open, and what some reviewers interestingly perceived as an incoherence in the *what* of the narrative, is *how* such events could have occurred. There must, the film suggests, be something else that remains hidden in the psychic exchange between these two women that accounts for their actions. The trick in the ending—that Cynthia did not simply assist Joyce after the fact but initiated the murder—confirms the detective's suspicions that Cynthia has to have been motivated by more than loyalty to her girlfriend. And yet there is something between these women that the juridical inquiry cannot penetrate. What the film constantly evokes as an incomprehensible excess is the primariness of the bond between these women. For even when the "trick" is revealed and we might be satisfied that Cynthia was indeed acting in her own self-interest, the film adds one more twist: Cynthia returns to the police station to take her place beside Joyce.

If homosociality between men is the necessary but invisible ground of the patriarchal symbolic, homosociality between women would seem to be impossible in reality but always threatening to erupt from the Real. It falls outside of symbolization, drops out of discourse, but occasionally emerges as a destabilizing rupture in the margins of a dominant order that cannot quite banish it. It is not too surprising, then, that when women enter representation ineluctably together, they do so as criminals.

Mortal Thoughts finally frustrates the narrative desire for epistemological certainty. Woods appeals to Cynthia's maternal empathy with Joyce (the only fully legitimized bond between women in patriarchy) in order to extract a confession from her. But through Cynthia's flashbacks, which the spectators can see but the detective cannot, we know that it is much more than a shared concern for their children that brings Cynthia back into the station. Rather, it is her memories of the murder and Joyce's devotion to her that she replays as she gazes at her own image in the rearview mirror of her car. The film ends with the promise that Woods will extort the "real" story from Joyce and Cynthia. And in a final image we see Cynthia's face captured on the video monitor and Woods's disembodied voice: "Ready, let's get started."

Even so, the recuperative power of this ending is not strong enough to undo the incoherencies that Cynthia and Joyce's relationship has generated. Woods might be able to bring these women to "justice," but he is not likely to bring truth to them, or to make meaning *of* them. The hidden content of Joyce and Cynthia's secrets is uncovered, but the *form* of their secret remains partially occluded. For the film persists in naturalizing their priority for each other from the women's perspective. Joyce and Cynthia persistently presume that their loyalty to each other takes precedence over everything else, even as it violates their matrimonial and maternal contracts. From the perspective of the law's representative, this loyalty is constantly rendered as incomprehensible. When Woods solves the first murder, he does not resolve the second problem.

The immense popularity of a film like *Sleeping with the Enemy*, which has brought the subject of domestic violence to a mainstream audience, would indicate that battered women who kill their spouses can sell tickets at the box office, as long as the heroine is sufficiently pretty and the husband monstrous. Demi Moore (Cynthia) and Bruce Willis (Jimmy) ably fulfill these requisites. *Mortal Thoughts*, however, takes several steps away from that model. First, it is not the battered wife herself, but her best friend, who initiates killing the abusive spouse. The trick ending takes care of any anxiety that might erupt on that score, since we finally witness Jimmy sexually assaulting Cynthia herself. Nonetheless, this closure does not succeed in sealing over the threat of the women's bond as primary. Mainstream American audiences would seem to be prepared to justify a woman who kills in *self-defense*, but they are outraged when a woman rescues another woman from a sexual assault. I would submit that it is because Louise and Cynthia occupy the position of the traditional male hero that these representations have aroused so much cultural censure or outright bewilderment.

Less obviously, but finally more profoundly, *Mortal Thoughts* pushes even harder at the dominant culture's tolerance than does *Thelma and Louise*. We see Cynthia constantly intervening to rescue Joyce from Jimmy, coming between them on several occasions to lend Joyce comfort after his verbal and physical attacks, and also using her body to break up physical fights between them. She not only saves Joyce from Jimmy, but also saves Joyce from herself in the scene in which Joyce takes poisoned sugar to Jimmy and Cynthia interferes by knocking over his cup of tea before he drinks it. Finally, Cynthia actually takes Joyce's place, by killing Jimmy. We might overlook Joyce's cavalier attitude when she finds out that Cynthia has mortally wounded Jimmy; we might even understand how a battered wife would be relieved to have him out of the way. Since Joyce continuously fantasized killing Jimmy herself, it is not too incredible when she assists Cynthia who has realized her fantasy. Even though Cynthia believes that Joyce's threats were a bluff, she expresses no doubt that Joyce will be on her side, even as she tells her that she has cut her husband's throat.

The film, however, marks a significant turning point when Joyce pre-
meditatively waits until Cynthia is visiting her mother, then goes to her
home and shoots Arthur in cold blood. Shoots him, as Woods points out,
full of so many bullets that the coffin could not be opened at the funeral.
Arthur is a bit obnoxious, but he and Cynthia seem to have had a working marriage. Joyce kills Arthur when, having found out that Cynthia
told him about Jimmy's murder, she has come to perceive him as a
threat—not just to her, but to *them*. It is Cynthia's betrayal of the primacy
of her relationship with Joyce that motivates the second murder. The
common strategy of rendering the women insane is discarded. Joyce and
Cynthia are never presented as anything other than very ordinary
women, the kind you meet every day in the supermarket or on the street
pushing baby strollers.

Mortal Thoughts presumes the "we" of women and thus performs
gender in excess. As Woods interrogates Cynthia, he catches her saying
"we," referring to herself and Joyce. "We could have got rid of him,"
Cynthia says in response to Joyce's plan to put poison in James's sugar.
You said "we," Woods reminds her. She denies saying it; he threatens to
run back the videotape for proof. She claims it "doesn't mean anything";
he, good analyst, tells her that everything means something. It is this moment, when the detective catches the woman speaking the "we" of
women, that he believes he has isolated his first clue, a sign to confirm his
theory that these women planned this murder together.

Connoted here is Woods's suspicion of an "unnatural" relationship
between Joyce and Cynthia. To insert homosexual implications in the
ellipses of Woods's "I don't know"s and "something's missing"s may
seem dubious. However, as Woods's questioning proceeds, it becomes
clear that what he cannot fathom is Cynthia's betrayal of her husband. At
least implicitly, it is her breach of the heterosexual contract that makes
him doubt her testimony. I am not suggesting that Woods suspects that
Cynthia and Joyce are lovers; rather, I am pointing to an aporia in his
analysis of her response that he is himself incapable of articulating. The
referent for this inarticulation is persistently Cynthia's *choice* in favor of
Joyce. How she could choose Joyce over Arthur is his question. It is
Arthur himself who answers it: "If you've got to keep your nose so far up
her behind all the time, you should just pack your bags and go with her."
And later, as he is packing his own bags and threatening her with divorce,
he says, "All these years you've been married to her."

What is striking in this film is that these suggestions of lesbianism do
not accomplish their usually quite effective purpose of dividing the
women through fear of ostracization from society or the threat of defem-
inization. Cynthia dismisses her husband's accusations as *his* hysteria.

While the blanks in Woods's expressions connote an unnatural relationship between the women, this is the *false solution* that will be supplanted
by the trick of reality—that Cynthia killed James herself. But in the detective's epistemological quest, it is only *through* the false solution that he
can arrive at the truth. The truth, as Lacan persistently reminds us, always arises through a *misrecognition*.

When Woods implies that Cynthia and Joyce are more than just
friends, the film's unconscious renders the women's disarticulated lesbian
desire as the false solution, which inevitably gives way to the reality that
is made manifest. Lured by the diegetic content, the audience, reports one
reviewer, exploded with rage, "cheated by the last minute cop-out." The
final flashback, however, does not entirely "jettison what we have just
spent two hours watching,"[55] for Cynthia's story—the false solution—
retains a certain truth. She is able to construct this story coherently because, as signified by her own memories played back for the spectators,
she can imagine herself and Joyce as interchangeable. Cynthia simply
puts Joyce in *her* place as she reconstructs the scene of the crime.

This interchangeability is most forcefully conveyed in the two scenes at
the carnival where the murder takes place. In the first account, Cynthia is
playing roulette when Joyce frantically summons her to return to the van
where James is lying in a pool of blood. Cynthia remembers this first
scene with herself in the role of accomplice to the cover-up. The second
time she remembers the scene is the flashback where the "trick" of the
film is revealed. Now it is she who signals to Joyce at the roulette table,
and Joyce who assists her in disposing of Jimmy's body. This exchange
does not produce the paranoia of a masculine gaze in which "the other is
in my place"; rather, it facilitates the women's mutuality. Cynthia and
Joyce, in other words, are always "we" in Cynthia's memories. She
makes little or no distinction between herself and Joyce. Blurring of the
boundaries between self and other, a typically "feminine" problem for
psychoanalytic femininity defined as a lack of proper distance, abets both
their violence and their deception. If we cannot tell the difference between
them, how can we know which one of them did it?

It is surprising that *Mortal Thoughts* has not generated as much anxiety as *Thelma and Louise*. After all, in the latter the women kill a would-
be rapist who is a stranger; in the former, two women murder each
other's husbands. It would seem that *Mortal Thoughts* would much more
profoundly threaten the heterosexual contract that maintains the phallocratic symbolic. Perhaps it is the fact that Thelma and Louise escape the
law, whereas Joyce and Cynthia are apprehended by it, that soothes the
cultural anxiety. As dead women who get away, Thelma and Louise appear to be more dangerous than living ones who are locked up. Their

narratives do not seem to be as significant as the images the camera produces: that of Louise and Thelma flying freely over the canyon's vast ex-
panse, with the detectives left in the dust behind them, has more power
than Cynthia captured in the frame of the detective's video eyes. The lure
of the image, its hyperreality, means in excess of the stories themselves.

But how finally are these films operating in our contemporary cultural
consciousness? If women acting together to the exclusion of their bonds
with men is represented as murder, from whose perspective has this become a prominent pattern for women together to enter representation? Is
there a certain line that women in representation cannot cross over in
regard to their fidelity to each other *without* being criminalized? Perhaps
these films are testing the boundaries, capitulating to the history of asso-
ciating women who are too "loose" with criminality and yet subverting
that association by insisting on their representativeness. For despite the
formal recontainment of these killer women in the iconic final moments
of the films, the characters do not succumb to retribution, they do not
repent, and the freeze-frames are hardly the "tableaux of sympathy" that
returned the nineteenth-century villainess to the moral order.

Cynthia Kellogg's mistake is her attempt to deceive with a truth that
the symbolic order has foreclosed. If Cynthia's original story *were* true, it
could appear only as a psychotic discourse. And yet, for some spectators,
her story might seem plausible. The film gives us a way of continuing to
see it as true. For even as she tells Woods that she made her choice, that
her place was with her husband, she returns to be with Joyce even *after*
Joyce has murdered Arthur. Cynthia's actions are thus trapped in the
circuit of meaning that Woods has manufactured, but her desire eludes
symbolization and frustrates the hermeneutical resolution.

5

Reconsidering Homophobia: Karen Finley's Indiscretions

KAREN FINLEY wants to get even. She believes that "revenge can be art." As for forgiveness, she does not "necessarily believe in forgiving at all!" She "feels that forgiving is: *never letting go. . . . a myth* by which you in actuality think you can still maintain control over someone." [1] Not very "ladylike" of her, is it?

When Finley was embroiled in the National Endowment for the Arts (NEA) debates as the center target of the "NEA Four," C. Carr provocatively suggested in the *Village Voice* that it was a "short step from rude girl to rude queer" [2] in the censorious fantasies of the New Right. Among the four performance artists whose grants were rescinded after recommendation by the NEA peer panel, Finley received by far the most media attention as well as the greatest number of direct attacks on her art. The other three artists—Holly Hughes, John Fleck, and Tim Miller—all openly claim lesbian or gay identities, and their work is heavily marked with homoeroticism. Finley was the "token" heterosexual, yet her work seemed to elicit more opprobrium than the performances of a self-identified lesbian like Holly Hughes. The argument that homophobia was at the heart of the obscenity charges was thrown something of a curve by Finley's inclusion in the group.

The movement from rude to queer is, I think, a large leap rather than a "short step." But as I have been setting out in this book, a woman who is perceived as aggressive carries with her the shadow of the lesbian. My project in this chapter is to track the steps that led to Finley's singular positioning within the NEA controversy, and along the way to reconsider how insidiously homophobia operates in these cultural debates.

Identity politics haunted the NEA debates just as they continue to ghost the rhetoric of feminist politics and poststructuralist theory. Although the NEA has quietly dropped the antiobscenity pledge, [3] and the "NEA Four" have won their lawsuit, this history is worth returning to as it opened up a juridical space where identity politics collided with coalition building. David Leavitt argued that homophobia was the constitutive impulse behind NEA chair John Frohnmayer's July 1990 decision to deny funding to the four performance artists. In so doing, Leavitt emphasized Finley's singularity: "Ms. Finley was the only heterosexual among the four performance artists whose grants were retracted."[4]

However, homophobia is a more complex mechanism and produces more subtle reality effects than can be read simply in the targeting of self-identified *or* ideologically interpellated gays and lesbians. I want to argue that Finley's ostensible exceptionality exposes rather than impedes a reading of this decision as homophobic, and expands our understanding of homophobia as a broader and more pervasive discourse. Just as we have come to understand a pluralism of homosexualities, so we must contemplate a multiplicity of homophobias, some of them elicited by the performances of a heterosexual feminist.

The conclusion that sexual anxieties permeated these debates is inescapable. From the Mapplethorpe and Serrano censorings—the former explicitly in reaction to the artist's depiction of gay and sadomasochistic sexual practices, the latter in response to a representation of the body of Christ submerged in urine—to the defunding of the four performance artists, the NEA controversies were explicitly concerned to police displays of the body. As Simon Watney points out, sexual anxieties necessarily respond to "our attitudes to our own bodies and one another's."[5] The sexualized body is always a body in relationship to others, and this body is the site where "identities" get constructed. Because the signifiers of lesbian and gay "bodies," as opposed to racial, ethnic, or gendered bodies, are less secure, harder to read, presumably less fixed in a visible economy, the gay and lesbian affirmative slogan "we are everywhere" must indeed seem ominous to the paranoid gaze that seeks identifiable objects.

The dilemma about identity politics is ongoing, for when identity becomes radically indeterminate, as it may in the classic deconstructive mode, it risks replacing stable, immobilizing identities with idealized transcendent subjectivities.[6] Linda Alcoff poses the problem when she writes, "In their defense of a total construction of the subject, poststructuralists deny the subject's ability to reflect on the social discourse and challenge its determinations."[7] This crisis in the politics of representation has been met with proposals such as Gayatri Spivak's "strategic essentialism": "a strategic use of positivist essentialism in a scrupulously visible political interest." But such a strategy is risky, for, as Spivak recognizes, it shares the "constitutive paradox" of humanism "that the essentializing moment, the object of their criticism, is irreducible."[8] Even as a tactical maneuver, essentialism is difficult, if not impossible, to implement when the subjects are defined by their sexualities. We could argue that Fleck and Miller were defunded because they are gay, or that Finley and Hughes were denied funding because they are women. But then we would erase Hughes's lesbianism, which she insists upon emphatically. Even momentarily, it has been all but impossible to construct a coherent category for gays *and* lesbians, or even for gays *or* lesbians. The ontological instability of sexualities troubles political affirmations within existing legislative frameworks. But the strength of sexuality politics lies in their *already* mobilized status. More than ever we need ground to stand on together; but constructing that ground on the basis of identity risks reifying an ontology of race, gender, and sexuality that creates "objects" vulnerable to the conservative assaults.

While there is certainly some validity to Leavitt's emphasis on the overt targeting of gays and lesbians, the limits and dangers of isolating groups based on identity alone are apparent when Leavitt implies that situating the word "homoeroticism" next to "a taboo extreme of sexual behavior few would be willing to argue in favor of"[9] (sadomasochism) detracts from the defense of homoeroticism. Such rhetoric reinscribes the same system that has brought us to this historical moment. Leavitt writes, "Female in a world of men, Jewish in a world of gentiles, black in a world of whites: it's the same difference."[10] But certainly it is *not* the same difference. These comments demonstrate how homogenization always reduces by excluding.

One of the most important things that queer theory has to contribute to discussions of subjectivity formations is that not only are identities fluid across and between categories but they are also always unstable and shifting *within* the categories themselves. There are no targeted "objects" of hostility at different historical moments. On the contrary, creating the illusion that such objects exist is precisely the anxious effort of groups that depend on making these categories to shore up the fiction of their own impermeability. It is those performers who explode the seamless body of humanist discourse and slip out of such naturalized categories who pose the greatest threat. Lesbian and gay "content" does not have to enter the specular field according to the dominant culture's rules of recognition in order for us to read that culture's efforts to silence these representations as homophobic. Indeed when lesbians and gays enter into the "visible" from the dominant spectator's position, it is on terms that practically guarantee a homophobic reaction. Hence homophobia becomes virtually synonymous with homosexuality, a realization that has spurred efforts to discard the term "homophobia" in favor of "heterosexism." Joseph Neisen, for example, puts forward the argument that substituting "heterosexism" for "homophobia" shifts the emphasis from the latter's suggestion of something inherently abhorrent to the former's stress on the constitution of the oppressor. Neisen points out that homophobia is not a "true phobia" anyway, for a "phobic reaction is one in which the object that provokes anxiety is avoided."[11] Neisen's point is well-taken. How-

ever, I would caution against discarding "homophobia" for precisely the
reasons that Neisen makes clear. That is, I think we are always witnessing
a *displaced* response. For the "object" under attack by the homophobe is
the presumed stability of his/her *own* identity. Certainly homophobia targets self-identified gays and lesbians. But as evidenced by the defunding of
these four performance artists, all of whom challenge the containment of
the human body by dominant ideologies, policing the boundaries of the
body is forcefully instituted by the naturalization of heterosexuality. Homophobia might be more broadly understood as a diffuse and pervasive
psychic mechanism that reacts to the adulteration of all binary constructions which reinscribe sameness *by* positing oppositional differences.

   Jonathan Dollimore has addressed the political problematics of both
the psychoanalytic and materialist accounts of homophobia. From a psychoanalytic perspective, "homophobia might well signal the precarious-
ness and instability of identity, even of sexual difference itself," whereas
in the materialist version, homophobia "typically signals the reverse, that
sexual difference is being secured."[12] Dollimore finds fault with the psychoanalytic understanding of homophobia for leaning toward a poly-
morphousness that might abet the loss of sociohistorical specificity, hence
producing such radically deconstructed subjects that identity becomes entirely meaningless. This is the familiar complaint against psychoanalysis's
"ahistoricism." On the other hand, the materialist reading could produce
a functionalism reinstating the hierarchical oppositions that empower the
dominant order. Between the two accounts, Dollimore finds an uneasy
alliance in that they both propose that identities are formulated through
exclusion and negation. What I find most intriguing about Dollimore's
argument is his claim that homophobia most often works to secure a
dominant cultural definition of masculinity, and only incidentally to target gay men. Since his emphasis is on masculinity, Dollimore does not
mention that homophobia is also used to keep women within the confines
of a historical construction of femininity. And surely the opposition femi-
ninity/homosexuality has produced a discursive and material violence as
virulent as the opposition masculinity/homosexuality.

   These oppositions, however, have not produced parallel effects. When
men are excluded from the category "masculinity," they *fall* into the "degenerate" category of femininity, which is where lesbians, as women, always already were. Gay men become recognizable to the heterosexist
spectator as they are "seen" to enter the feminine. In contrast, lesbians are
invisible precisely as they are contained within representational appara-
tuses that depend on Woman as the ground while simultaneously constructing women as the elusive enigma. When lesbians enter the field of
visibility as it has been constructed within gender dimorphic parameters,

the threat that they pose to the dominant order is seen as a usurpation of masculine privilege. Peggy Phelan has pointed out that "gay men implicitly 'feminize' all men which is why they arouse so much hatred. Lesbians are not as overtly hated because they are so locked out of the visible, so far from the minds of the N.E.A. and the New Right, that they are not acknowledged as a threat."[13] In both cases, there is no simple switching back and forth between categories permitted by the dominant order of sexual difference. Both the male and the female homosexual are positioned by the naturalization of heterosexuality in a space that is abject— the nonhuman. But this is a space that is not "other" than masculinity or femininity. On the contrary, as exemplified by gay men who fall into this space and lesbians who are always already there, the abject is *consonant* with the very oppositional hierarchy masculine/feminine. However, I am not convinced that lesbian invisibility arouses less hatred or poses less of a threat to the homophobic spectator. As I have indicated earlier, historically the "indifference" toward lesbians masked a series of projections and displacements that reveal a threat perceived as virtually apocalyptic. That the "lesbian" could *not* be seen might mean that she is nowhere; but it could also indicate that she is *everywhere*; and her more pronounced unidentifiability therefore phobically renders her invisibility omnipresent.

Her very absence could thus make her implied presence even more terrifying. If in the materialist account the homophobe reacts with hostility to the "otherness" of the homosexual, and in the psychoanalytic account it is the "sameness" that produces the phobic reaction, this opposition indicates the impasse of the sameness/difference binary itself. We might turn to consider the operation of homophobia from the perspective of colonialist discourse. As Homi Bhabha argues, what is "English" in the discourse of colonial power "is determined by its belatedness," not by its fullness or "presence." Like the meaning of "English," the meaning of heterosexuality is acquired *after* the scene of difference is enacted. Bhabha brings together a materialist and a psychoanalytic way of understanding the enunciation of colonialist discourse that is productive for an analysis of heterosexism/homophobia as well. He proposes "two disproportionate sites of colonial discourse and power: the colonial scene as the invention of historicity, mastery, mimesis, or as the 'other scene' of *Entstellung*, displacement, fantasy, psychic defense, and an 'open' textuality." These two scenes are not exclusive. They operate together to produce an authority that Bhabha calls "agonistic" rather than antagonistic. And this authority achieves its domination through a disavowal that "denies the *différance* of colonialist power—the chaos of its intervention as *Entstellung*, its dislocatory presence—in order to preserve the authority of its identity."[14] If heterosexism and homophobia can be understood not as separate discourses but as effects of a double inscription that is mutually reinforcing, then the ambivalence can become ground for interventionist strategies launched from the very uncertainty that makes possible the conditions for domination.

While "lesbian" has been located as an eccentric position from which the paradox of "Woman" can be exposed in order to construct alternative fields of vision,[15] one need not claim a lesbian "identity" in order to locate the reification of gender in the heterosexual contract. In other words, one can perform "lesbian" *acts* without "being" a lesbian. Indeed, women do so with or without intention. If we understand homophobia as the fear that the homosexual/heterosexual dyad is *already* adulterated, a performance artist like Karen Finley is just as likely to produce a homophobic response, even though and perhaps even more so *because* she claims a heterosexual identity. In Karen Finley's work and in her position within the NEA debates, I think we can read the absent presence of the lesbian specter, which haunts the entrance of the aggressive woman into representation.

Long before the NEA denied her funding, Finley became notorious for a performance called "Yams up My Granny's Ass." C. Carr covered her work in a *Voice* article entitled "Unspeakable Practices, Unnatural Acts: The Taboo Art of Karen Finley" (1986).[16] In our heterosexist culture, the reference to "unnatural" acts invariably evokes homosexuality. In this case, the unnatural act performed by Finley was the smearing of canned yams on her buttocks. Carr's article was followed by a deluge of letters to the *Voice*, which constitute a gloss on the borderline that Finley crossed. Even the usually liberal *Voice* readers were outraged. Two themes dominate the letters—filth and madness. Some examples: one "greatly disgusted" reader threatened to send "a lump of shit in an envelope" to make *Voice* editors "feel more at home." The same writer referred to the editors as "a pack of crazies." Another reader equated Carr's "rationalization" of Finley's work with "those who justified receiving their entertainment at Bedlam and Charenton." One drew an analogy between Finley's art and a man on the street relieving himself under a billboard advertising tequila. This debate continued for several weeks in letters debating whether or not Finley inserted the yams into her anus, whether the yams were cooked or uncooked, and whether it was possible to insert uncooked yams.[17]

As ridiculous as these letters seem, I think they are a text worth contemplating seriously. For this was the moment when Finley's work became linked in the public imagination with bodily orifices and the boundary between what is inside and outside the body. And it is important to notice that it was not just any bodily orifice, but the anus, the opening to the body that historically has been most associated with "unnatural sexuality." It is particularly worth noting that respondents read this performance not only as dirty and disgusting, but also as *gender* transgressive. As Eve Sedgwick has pointed out, the only part of a woman's body that has been singularly *unmarked* by cultural inscriptions is the anus. Whereas anal eroticism has been virtually conflated with gay male sexuality, Sedgwick remarks that after classical times *"there has been no important and sustained Western discourse in which women's anal eroticism means.* Means anything" (author's emphasis).[18] By rendering public what is necessarily privatized in order to uphold the reign of the phallus, Finley's emphasis on anality created strong associations with (male) homosexuality and thereby also constituted an attack on heterosexual supremacy. As Guy Hocquenghem explains:

> The desires directed toward the anus are closely linked to homosexual desire and constitute what can be described as a group-mode of relations as opposed to the usual social mode. The anus undergoes a movement which renders it private; the opposite movement, which would make the anus public, through what might be called desirous group-formation, provokes a collapse of the sublimating phallic hierarchy, and at the same time, destroys the double bind relation between individual and society.[19]

Finley's indiscretion was thus not only a violation of the "purity" of womanhood, but also a willful crossing over into a domain that has been preserved for gay men in homophobic discourse. Hence in one performative gesture, Finley not only violated the boundaries of gender but also transgressed the hetero/homo binary. And in doing so she forced a response that revealed how the latter is necessary to shore up the fictive coherency of the former.

Whether her supporters are valorizing her or her detractors are vilifying her, Finley's "indiscretions" have been persistently described as prior to or outside of culture. Here we can see the double operation of any discourse that depends on inside/outside oppositions. On the one hand, Finley's performance was considered "obscene" because it was perceived as "dirty" on the level of gender (she was "outside" the category of womanhood). At the same time, the obscenity could be accounted for by her association with an act that connoted gay sexuality. Thus she was, at once, not properly "discreet" as a woman and "indiscrete"—not separate and distinct but mixed, adulterated. It is, of course, the former connotation that has dominated the discourse of womanhood. But it is the latter indiscretion that troubles the binary opposition of heterosexuality/homosexuality. It was this separation that was muddied when Finley performed "Yams up My Granny's Ass," and it was the beginning of her association with homophobic constructions of homosexuality.

In addition, Finley's performances have an unusually aggressive edge in the history of women's performance art. Her shows might be likened to the "complaint" tradition that Lauren Berlant describes as a paradigm of public female discourse. The complaint is a "discursive deployment of . . . rage, a litany of injuries," a discourse that Berlant perceives as holding little possibility for change since it is deterministically vulnerable to phallic discourse.[20] Berlant's use of the word "witnessing" to describe the complaint seems especially appropriate for Finley, who is often described as a performer with a calling and who describes herself as a "medium" for a collective message. Also, Finley often delivers her monologues with evangelical fervor: her voice—something like a cross between a televangelist's and a game-show host's—uncannily resonates with the twinning of theology and capitalism.

Certainly Finley complains. She rages incessantly about the unjust treatment of women, children, the homeless, the working class, and ethnic, racial, and sexual minorities. These "themes" are well within the tradition of American feminist performance art. And her demands are within the rhetorical parameters of liberalism. For decades partial nudity and strong sexual content have been used by feminist performers. And yet Finley has been perceived as particularly threatening in her transgression of the limits that other feminist performers have crossed without garnering much attention.

Rather than having been hysterized by phallic discourse, as Berlant's paradigm would suggest, Finley's complaints seem to have rendered her spectators hysterical. Catherine Schuler finds, for instance, that most of the male spectators she interviewed could not even *remember* having seen or heard Finley's "Cut Off Balls" monologue in *The Constant State of Desire*. Rather than concluding, as Schuler does, that Finley's performances depend too much on an understanding of feminist theory to reach mainstream audiences,[21] I would say that what Schuler has observed is a bit of male hysteria.

Like all feminist performers, Finley struggles against the presentation of herself as an already-eroticized object. While the persistence of the Oedipal configuration and its concomitant heterosexual mandate permit little movement outside of the ideology of gender, Finley's performances do accomplish radical critiques of patriarchy, bourgeois culture, and sexual difference. Gender, as a social construct, and psychoanalytic sexual difference are both relentless repetitions in her work. As a gendered subject, Finley consistently presents herself in the roles of housewife, mother, rape victim, or incest survivor: the daughter whose father rapes her with vegetables from the icebox bin; the woman tormented by her decision to abort a fetus conceived through incest; the girl whose gang rapists throw her under the wheels of a train when they discover that she was born without a vagina. But Finley deploys these positions with a violent humor that does not play to the spectators' sympathy for the victims, as radical feminist performers often do. Rather, her graphic enactments of sexual abuse and her scatological rage assault the sex/gender system that produces these damaged female bodies by historicizing it.

For example, Finley frequently locates herself within the Oedipal family structure where the female body functions as a closed system opened only by the penetration of a man or the birth of a child. But Finley manipulates her own body, calling attention repeatedly to her bodily orifices and what enters and leaves them. This autoerotic work threatens the heterosexual contract. For in a culture that has made so thoroughly available the public display of nude female bodies to be looked at, touched, and penetrated by men, what could be so disturbing about Finley's performances? I would suggest that it is their autoeroticism that makes them threatening; and, furthermore, that the historical conflation of autoeroticism and homosexuality is still operative in perceptions of these performances.

In addition, Finley's rituals and metaphors of filth and waste cross the borderline that secures sexual difference. As self-proclaimed "Queen of the Dung Dynasty," Finley calls attention to the abject female body. But she does not merely imitate the body in pain. Rather, she *mimics* the psychosocial structures that describe, theorize, and construct the patriarchal female body. Her performances enlist the possibilities for multiple, shifting identifications that psychoanalytic discourse permits without abandoning a materialist critique. In the gaps between her rhetoric and performance, she negotiates the psychic/social split that troubles the feminist project of enlisting psychoanalytic concepts in a materialist critique.

Unremittingly, the media have focused on Finley's excretory actions—defecating, spitting, urinating—as well as the application of various substances to her body: eggs, chocolate, glitter, sprouts. It is, in other words, the rendering of her body as indiscrete, a violation of the female body's naturalized seamlessness and a manipulation of her body as malleable, that has aroused so much controversy. In her performance, *We Keep Our Victims Ready*, the single gesture foregrounded by the conservatives who pushed to deny her funding was the smearing of chocolate on her nude body.[22] The materials that Finley applies to her body are always viscous—eggs, Jell-O, ketchup—products that are in themselves ambiguous, liminal, occupying an intermediate zone between solid and liquid.

As something of a signature, Finley's engagement with waste cannot but conjure abjection. In abjection, Julia Kristeva writes, "as in true theatre, without makeup or masks, refuse and corpses *show me* what I permanently thrust aside in order to live. These body fluids, this defilement, this shit are what life withstands. . . . Such wastes drop so that I might live" (author's emphasis).[23] Abjection is not about a lack of cleanliness or health; rather, it is an act that "disturbs identity, system, order . . . what does not respect borders, positions, rules."[24] If the "I" is produced through the expulsion of waste products, this process can be understood as a kind of elemental "othering," a construction of subjectivity based on excluding or expelling the "alien" within. The body makes waste in order to constitute itself as autonomous, sovereign, pure. The formation of subjectivity is thus a process that occurs not between discrete subjects but rather through the concealment of differences that exist within the subject.

Finley's performances might be read as inhabitations of the abject, but she does not challenge the master from this banished zone. Rather, her insistence that spectators reflect on waste launches violent assaults on a binary system that maintains its metaphysical closure by constructing the illusion of discrete terms. Finley strikes a nerve by touching the boundary that reveals what this culture's ordering system cannot tolerate. Her public display of waste products adulterates the boundary between interior and exterior. As Mary Douglas argues, maintaining a discreteness between what is properly inside and what is outside constructs a system, for "ideas about separating, purifying, demarcating and punishing transgressions have as their main function to impose system on an inherently untidy experience."[25] Hence to violate borders is to *reveal how a system is constructed*. Thus I would argue that Finley's excremental performances do not merely reproduce the female body's victimization but rather perform the cultural operations that render victims and perpetrators distinct. She puts pressure on the contradictions that make such dichotomies invisible.

One of Finley's most memorable defiling rituals occurs in *The Constant State of Desire* when she strips down to her underpants, puts unboiled colored Easter eggs in a plastic bag, and slams the bag on the floor until all the eggs are broken. She then takes a stuffed Easter bunny and uses it to sponge her body with the sticky mass. Over this she applies glitter and paper garlands. Layering her body with these substances produces a narrative of the construction of the female body as an impossible object. First we see the nude female body; then it is covered with sticky waste products that might have been reproductive; then the glitter and frills only partially cover the waste products beneath them. The final ef-

fect is a palimpsestic body that is both seductive and repellent. The destruction of the eggs is a crucial signifying gesture in this performance.
From a patriarchal perspective, Finley is Woman and thus always already
Mother. But here she enacts the destruction of the raw materials of reproduction, layers them on her body, and thinly disguises them with se-
ductiveness. By making the application of this process visible, she demonstrates the contradictory inscriptions of the female body in dominant
discourse.

Similarly, in *We Keep Our Victims Ready*, Finley smears melted valen-
tine chocolates on her body, covers them with sprouts (which she announces should be read as sperm), and then layers on brightly colored
paper icicles. This is a body that at once allures and disgusts—a courtship
ritual manqué. If the iconic body of the reproductive woman is always
there for the scopophilic gaze, Finley brilliantly alienates that body by
historicizing it. Like the Brechtian social gest, Finley plays this body "as
a piece of history." Elin Diamond has pointed out that "the gestic moment in a sense explains the play, but it also exceeds the play, opening it
to the social and discursive ideologies that inform its production."[26] The
hidden reproductive body of woman as the allure of the sexually seductive female is unveiled as a governing construction in these stunning gestic
moments.

This representation also counters the perpetual return of the maternal
body as a site for celebrating the essential female that relegates women to
the reproductive economy. In one sense, Finley re-creates herself in patriarchy's image—as both mother and whore—but in the contiguity of the
signifiers Finley performs the construction of this doubling, thus historicizing it, setting it in motion to imply its mutability, and instigating an
alternative: that women can destroy and reject reproductivity. Whereas
patriarchy persists in reducing women to mothers by controlling their
bodies through material interventions as well as perpetuating an ideology
of the sacredness of motherhood, Finley performs the female body as topography for enforced fertilization, then desecrates and defiles it so that
it cannot be recuperated. Her laminations recall the patriarchal construction of Woman/Motherhood, but in their "seaminess" they show the
rough, unfinished edges of this seemingly smooth surface. Her gestures
are thus situated within this history and excessive to it.

Less directly, Finley addresses the primary site where the woman/
mother is perpetually reinscribed—the heterosexual dyad. One highly
charged moment in *The Constant State of Desire* bears close attention. In
this performance a four-tiered wedding cake remains upstage for the entire show. Finley destroys all the other emblematic props but saves the
cake until the end of the performance. It is the one item that appears to

escape her rage. Following a monologue in which she lists a number of strategies for social change, each item followed by an emphatic "Nothing happened!" she wheels the cake to center stage, lights the candles, and in the dim light that frames her face as she peers over this emblem of heterosexual union she ominously intones: "But something's gotta give / Something's gotta give / Something's *gonna* happen."[27] The implacability of this prop is ambiguous. But accompanied by the rhetorical shift from "it has to" to "it is going to," Finley suggests at the very least that heterosexuality is the site where resistance is most necessary.

Finley continues her anti-Oedipal critique in *The Theory of Total Blame* in a performance that most overtly targets the maternal body as the site of abuse and co-optation. Whereas the pain of the victim remains foregrounded in *The Constant State of Desire*, it is the laughter of a mother grotesquely inscribed as such that dominates *The Theory of Total Blame*. Much more conventional than her earlier one-woman shows, *The Theory of Total Blame* has a full cast of characters (a nuclear family), and it is set in a fairly realistic lower-middle-class American living room that is grossly overcrowded with cheap material possessions, circa late 1950s and early 1960s. This shift in form necessitates a diffusion of the voices that Finley usually performs solo. The ritualistic quality of her earlier work, in which she takes on and performs the suffering of a collective, becomes "individualized" as she historicizes the nuclear family as an ideological social unit. In a sense, Finley rejects the internalized pain of her former performances by displacing it onto the family. This movement is duplicated by Irene, the mother played by Finley, who expels her entire family from her house, including her husband whom she must arouse from a coma in order to do so. Irene plays out her imposition as a Mother with a parodic vengeance.

Defilement remains an important strategy in this play, here represented as food loathing. Beginning with a benignly comical scene in which Irene digs Jell-O out of a mold with her hands, the play accumulates images of the nurturing mother that are increasingly sinister. Playing self-consciously on the American domestic drama, Finley presents a family that has returned home to partake of mother's meal. Irene dutifully treads back and forth between the refrigerator and the table carrying armloads of food, none of which is palatable. Irene's meatloaf is a disgusting mass of raw beef slathered with ketchup, which she manipulates with her hands and shoves in one son's face. Bits of raw beef dangle from Irene's nose and lips; ketchup runs down her arms and stains her face. Irene almost merges with the meatloaf; it becomes difficult to tell where she begins and it ends.

Instead of nurturing meals, Irene serves up fantasies of the devouring mother and voices the culture's matrophobia: "I made you and I can unmake you,"[28] she threatens, boldly proclaiming the issue of the mother's responsibility for castration anxiety. If, as Freud argued in "Femininity," the woman's remembrance of the father's incest is a fantasy of seduction whereas the mother's seduction has some basis in reality, Finley's Irene plays this game in hilarious mockery. Irene tells her children that she made them all sleep with her so they could not masturbate; she openly acknowledges lust for her children; she stands on a chair and shoves her genitals in one son's face. Irene is the phallic mother unleashed in diabolical fury. "I'm in living hell and I intend to keep my devil *out*," she warns them.

This exorbitant mimicry does not, of course, simply dismiss the power of the nuclear family and its Oedipalization. If it is "the father in all of us" that haunts the monologues of *The Constant State of Desire*, it is still the Father who menaces and maims the family in *The Theory of Total Blame*. Classically absent in the former performance—a dead father who killed himself because his daughter was insufficiently attractive—the father in the latter performance is a marginal presence, lying comatose on the living room sofa for most of the play. Persistently, Finley makes and unmakes the Father. If in earlier shows the Father was the irremediable return of the repressed, in the later work Finley moves toward the suggestion that intervention is possible. Irene shakes her comatose husband awake and forcibly ejects him from the house. If the Father/phallus is the original lost object that constructs desire as a ceaseless urge for that which can never be found, Irene "finds" the phallus, shakes him out of his death-like sleep, and pushes him offstage in a brilliant parodic capture of the Lacanian transcendental signifier. What remains are waste products, spit out, regurgitated, excreted. Irene will not permit any corpses to take up space in her living room.

Finley cannot, of course, simply step outside of the Symbolic Order and discard the Law of the Father. According to the psychoanalytic narrative "there can be nothing *human* that pre-exists or exists outside the law represented by the father; there is only either its denial (psychosis) or the fortunes and misfortunes ('normality' and neurosis) of its terms."[29] In order, then, to read Finley's performances at all, one may have to understand them as limited responses of a woman who strives to disrupt that order. That is, Finley would become the hysteric. But Finley's performances directly address the paradoxical positioning of Woman within that order. Certainly for her children, Irene's maternal body is the hysterical body, "a theater for forgotten scenes,"[30] onto which they project their anxieties. Irene, however, refuses the terms of that contract, and like the sorceress she claims the ironic status of her marginality.

Michelet's hysteric "resumes and assumes the memories of the others,"[31] much as Finley does in the collective voices of her monologues. But the sorceress-mother Irene holds tenaciously to her own memories in order to repossess them, cut them up, dismember them, and remember them. The hysteric keeps absorption and craving to herself; but the sorceress "cooks up her affects . . . mix[es] up in dirty things; . . . has no cleanliness phobia . . . handles filth, manipulates wastes." The sorceress-mother turns her banal family dinner into a sabbat where she "is completely exposed—all open skin, natural, animal, odorous, and deliciously dirty."[32] Irene is the Freudian mother unleashed from the unconscious in travesty—powerful, devouring, terrifying, seductive—and, most important, self-consciously performed rather than unwittingly inhabited. Produced from her children's nightmares, she refuses to stay there. Instead, she corporealizes, taking on a body that assaults the model from which she was constructed. Her wild presence permits her to speak another story, the story of her own making and unmaking, the production of her image through a theory that becomes unsettled when confronted with her unrepressed materiality.

Finley ends *The Theory of Total Blame* by stepping outside the realistic frame of this play into one of her more characteristic monologues: the "Black Sheep" monologue is an expressly antifamily tract in which she counts herself a member of a community that the family cannot contain. The black sheep transgress the limitations of the nuclear family. Refusing to be enclosed by it, they bond with other "outcasts" in alternative communities. This monologue is also the finale to her piece *We Keep Our Victims Ready*. Here it is juxtaposed resonantly against a scene in which Finley portrays herself as a friend keeping vigil by the bedside of a person with AIDS. Having already been well-established as a performer whose work involves the manipulation of bodily fluids as well as anal eroticism, Finley has undoubtedly elicited AIDS hysteria as well. Indeed it may well be within this context that she has been perceived as dangerously aggressive, even as a "fatal woman." As Leo Bersani has so astutely argued, there is a correspondence in the minds of conservative fundamentalists between the "promiscuity" of gay men and female prostitution. In this heterosexist imaginary, "those [who are] being killed," gay men and persons with AIDS, "are killers." Bersani elaborates:

> Promiscuity is the social correlative of a sexuality physiologically grounded in the menacing phenomenon of the nonclimactic climax. Prostitutes publicize (indeed, sell) the inherent aptitude of women for uninterrupted sex. Con-

versely, the similarities between representations of female prostitutes and male homosexuals should help us to specify the exact form of sexual behavior being targeted, in representations of AIDS, as the criminal, fatal, and irresistibly repeated act. This is of course anal sex.[33]

We Keep Our Victims Ready begins with a monologue about Jesse Helms's attacks on the NEA. "It's Only Art" projects a future in which America has no museums, television, newspapers, or performances of any kind. Sculpture has been banned because it is too much like handling waste products. Hot dogs at Coney Island are outlawed because they are phallic symbols. Museums display only announcements explaining why the artists' work has been removed: Mary Cassatt for painting nude children, Jasper Johns for desecrating the flag, Michaelangelo for being a homosexual, Georgia O'Keeffe for painting cow skulls.

By beginning this performance with an assault on the New Right's censorship efforts and ending it with a monologue addressed to a person with AIDS, Finley constructs a frame of reference that connects the desire to censor with the fear that the "black sheep" will unite in an understanding of shared oppressions, that the discreteness of constructions of subjects conceals constitutive indiscretions, that the sexual subjugation of women, gays, and lesbians depends on the prioritizing and naturalization of gender.

While Hughes, Fleck, and Miller were undoubtedly made immediately suspect and vulnerable to what Frohnmayer called the "political realities," it is important to recognize just how pernicious homophobia is in this culture. It is not a phenomenon that oppresses only those who have named themselves lesbian and gay. Without question gays and lesbians are targeted as quintessentially unstable, unseamless bodies. But Finley's performances and the responses to them are texts that expose homophobia as a much broader and more complex psychic mechanism. Homophobia is not fear of the same, nor is it fear of difference, just as homosexuality is not reducible to same-sex object choice or to difference from heterosexuality. More productively, we could think of homophobia as a reaction to the visibility of sexualities that expose the fallaciousness of the sameness/difference binary itself. Rendering those terms indiscrete produces an instability in sexual difference that points to the heterosexual/homosexual binary as always already undone.

6

Race and Reproduction: *Single* White *Female*

> The term "lesbian" without racial specificity,
> focuses on and refers to white lesbian culture.
> White lesbian culture, or the white lesbian, has
> become the quintessential representation of les-
> bian experience, of the very concept "lesbian."[1]
>   (Ekua Omosupe)

> White women are constructed as the apotheosis
> of desirability, all that a man could want, yet
> nothing that can be had, nor anything that a
> woman can be.[2]
>   (Richard Dyer)

> One loves ultimately one's desires, not the thing
> desired.[3]
>   (Friedrich Nietzsche)

IN Sheila McLaughlin's film *She Must Be Seeing Things*, Jo is a white woman and Agatha is a woman of color. In the postpresentation discussion following Teresa de Lauretis's analysis of the film, Nancy Graham asks her to comment on the film's treatment of racial difference. De Lauretis responds that she wanted to focus on fantasy, an issue the film seriously considers. For, she argues, while the film poses the question of racial difference, it then avoids it by collapsing it into questions of cultural or ethnic difference.[4] Many long questions later, Ada Griffin resurrects the question: "Maybe it's just because I'm black, but I am astonished that race does not have to be a priority for women, especially for lesbians, because it always is for me."[5] Griffin's remark must surely make all of us pause. Why does she say "especially for lesbians"? In this context, she must mean *white* lesbians; and she implies that white lesbians should have a particularly strong stake in attending to racial differences.

In her article, de Lauretis opens by commenting on the ambiguities in the film's title. *She Must Be Seeing Things* can mean that she is "imagining things that aren't 'real,'" or she *must* be seeing things—there are things that are mandatory for her to see.[6] The ambiguity pivots on the question of what constitutes a hallucination; and de Lauretis brilliantly reads the film's reversal of phallocratic reality, in which "lesbian" desire can appear only as what Freud would have said were "external returns,"[7] by showing us that the film positions Agatha and Jo to see together that heterosexuality is a mandatory hallucination. It is precisely this "seeing" together that makes Jo and Agatha inhabit what de Lauretis identifies as a lesbian subject position, and it takes two women to accomplish this fantasy.[8]

But the elision of Jo and Agatha's racial difference remains troubling. Jo, the white woman, is a filmmaker. Jo makes movies, "things" that people can see. Her vision is validated in the symbolic order. But Agatha makes "pictures [that are] more like hallucinations."[9] Agatha really does seem to be hallucinating. She imagines that she sees Jo with men, and the camera's eye shows us that what she saw was not really there. Within the diegesis of the film, Agatha appears to be classically paranoid. But as de Lauretis demonstrates in analyzing the film's engagement with the problem of representation, Agatha may actually occupy the more privileged position. For it is her "hallucinations" that foreground the double enforcement of heterosexuality: first, in the sense that "women can and must feel sexually in relation to men," and second in that "sexual desire belongs to the other, originates in him."[10] Yet Agatha's ability to make this double enforcement visible depends on Jo's affirming vision. Again, it takes both of them together to create an alternative way of seeing, a recognition that heterosexuality is the hallucination.

De Lauretis is right, I think, when she says that this film does not build in an overt critique of the racial dynamic between the two lesbians. And I would not want to say that de Lauretis *must* be seeing anything other than what she says she sees. But I think the film's failure to engage with racial differences comments on "what can be *seen* and eroticized and on what *scene*,"[11] and makes it possible to see something else about the historical erasure of sexual desire between women.

Psychoanalytically informed feminist theory has been taken to task for its inability to theorize racial differences between and among women. Jane Gaines was one of the first film critics to acknowledge and confront this difficulty, arguing that "the psychoanalytic model works to block out considerations which assume a different configuration, so that, for instance, the Freudian-Lacanian scenario can eclipse the scenario of race-gender relations in Afro-American history, since the two accounts of sexuality are fundamentally incongruous."[12] The problem of applying psychoanalytic formations to race is not simply a matter of insufficient attention or disregard; rather, it appears that inherent in psychoanalysis is a blind spot when it comes to racial differences. Mary Ann Doane explains:

> The allegation is not simply that psychoanalytic feminist theory has *neglected* the analysis of racial difference but that there is an active tension between them. If certain races (associated with the "primitive") are constituted as outside or beyond the territory of psychoanalytic endeavor—insofar as they lack repression or neurosis (perhaps even the unconscious)—the solution cannot be simply to take this system which posits their exclusion and apply it to them.[13]

Gaines advances the by-now-familiar refrain that lesbians and women of color have come forward to challenge the ways in which feminist theory, informed by psychoanalysis, too often reproduces an uninterrogated concept of "women" that is white, middle-class, and heterosexual. But Gaines also repeats the division of lesbians and women of color when she writes: "In the US, lesbian feminists raised the first objections to the way in which film theory explained the operation of the classic realist text in terms of tensions between masculinity and femininity." Then later: "Thus it is that women of colour, like lesbians, an afterthought in feminist analysis, remain unassimilated by this problematic."[14] Lesbian theorist Sue-Ellen Case refers to the "feminist genuflection of the 1980s—the catechism of 'working-class-women-of-color' [that] feminist theorists feel impelled to invoke at the outset of their research," and asks, "What's wrong with this picture?" Her answer: "It does not include the lesbian position."[15]

But what is really wrong with this picture is that the lesbian remains implicitly marked as *white* by these very divisions. The 1981 anthology *This Bridge Called My Back: Writings by Radical Women of Color* is frequently cited as the ground-breaking publication that brought voices of women of color to the forefront to challenge feminist theory's monolithic white, middle-class presumptions. And yet at least half of the contributors to that collection are lesbians who explicitly discuss their sexualities in their essays.

White feminists, both lesbian and heterosexual, have undoubtedly been complicit in reifying this segregation. But the making of the (modern) lesbian as white is also an inheritance from nineteenth-century sexology and criminology that became further encoded in the discourse of psychoanalysis. And it is a division that carries with it significant ideological consequences. For it seems impossible not to conclude that The Woman produced in the discourse of psychoanalysis and the lesbian who ghosts her entrance into representation—both of them "things" that are "(no)-

things"—are "white (no)things." And this would then mean, within the terms of racial difference as it has been constructed as a binary opposition, that the nonwhite things are (some)things—indeed perhaps the thing itself. That is, what is "nonwhite" becomes inscribed with a certain immobilizing positivity, a "presence" that stabilizes and hence creates the illusion that there is no possibility for historical change.

Although I have been tracking the construction of an object that does not exist, this does not mean that the "object" has not been inscribed with a certain positivity. On the contrary, The Woman, overdetermined as both heterosexual and white, is a representational absence that is necessarily constituted by a displaced "presence." Let us consider the gap between representations of violent white women and the data on female offenders in the recent past and the historical present.

Of the 398 females executed (primarily for homicide) in the United States since 1632, most of them, not surprisingly, were poor, uneducated, and lower-class. Sixty percent of them were women of color; 189 of them were slaves, all but one black, the other a Native American. All of the women executed for crimes other than homicide—arson, assault, petty treason—were female slaves or freed black women just after the Civil War. Of the ten female offenders under the age of eighteen who have been executed in North America, only one was white, but all of their victims were white. Providing the statistics cited above, Victor Streib conducts his research in the interest of ascertaining why comparatively few females have received the death penalty. And, given evidence that supports a gender-bias *away* from imposing death sentences on female offenders, why these 398 women did not escape the penalty.

Streib offers some speculative answers: their victims were preponderantly white and/or of socially prominent classes; they tended to act alone, and hence could not have arguably been "under the domination of another"; and finally, "perhaps most fatally for them, they committed shockingly 'unladylike' behavior," indicating that "their crimes and behavior could be characterized as more like those of male killers than female killers, perhaps removing them from the normally protective constructs for female offenders."[16] Streib does not elaborate the particulars of this "shockingly unladylike behavior," but his research points quite blatantly to the fact that these women do not merely fall, but have *already fallen*, outside the bounds of prescriptive femininity. What is already out of bounds, and therefore already criminalized, are nonwhite women and women who act alone, i.e., without men. Women of color and white lesbians have committed "unladylike" behavior by virtue of their race and sexual preferences alone. That much should by now be evident.

What is curious, then, and cannot go unremarked because it attains its power precisely because of its invisibility, is that these *representations* are so overwhelmingly of *white* women in the particular formulation I have been interrogating: the ghosting of the deadly woman with a spectral homoeroticism as she appears in a coupling that repeats a masculine imaginary's equation of sex and death. These lesbian "ghosts," it would seem, have a certain privilege. As the specters in the machine of white, heterosexual patriarchy, their invisibility affords them a certain power that makes them particularly threatening. For it is through the logic of the white heterosexual male imaginary's own identity formations that they come to occupy, sometimes subversively, these subject positions. If they are, in a sense, wish-fulfilling ghosts, or, in some cases, the white heterosexual male's worse nightmares realized, they are nonetheless produced by a desire that wants them to be almost, but not quite, "like" their dreamers. Gender preserves this distance within sameness. Racial difference, however, perhaps does not appear because it would constitute an alterity that could eliminate the pleasure which undoubtedly attends the terror.

In chapter 1, I argued that the construction of lesbianism *as* a "secret" was an ideological maneuver designed to serve the interests of white European patriarchy. For the most part, what I have been tracking in these readings is a constitutive absence in a heterosexual masculine imaginary, a void which is necessary in order that the desire of those who occupy the subject positions in this imaginary may be reproduced. This is a form of desire that forever seeks, but never finds, presence but at the same time projects that presence as a lost "positivity" which can be located on an other radically outside the system. Homi Bhabha points out that there is a "paradox central to . . . anti-epistemological theories."[17] This paradox, which makes the deconstructionist reading possible, "requires that there is a constitutive discourse of lack imbricated in a philosophy of presence."[18] Citing Mark Cousins, Bhabha argues that the *desire* for presence "carries with it as the condition of its movement and of the regulation of its economy, a destiny of non-satisfaction."[19]

The movement of this desire, as Luce Irigaray has so brilliantly demonstrated, persistently reinscribes sameness where difference is ostensibly elaborated.[20] Pursuing the limits of critiques of logocentrism, Bhabha argues that for these repetitions of sameness to be avoided, it is required that the "'non-satisfaction' should be specified *positively* which is done by identifying an anti-west. Paradoxically, then, cultural otherness functions as the moment of *presence* in a theory of *différance*."[21] Cultural otherness then becomes a stabilized site of subversion that continues to serve the interests of Western metaphysics by being "appropriated by the west as its limit-text, anti-west."[22]

I would suggest that a similar relationship exists between the historical construction of the (white) lesbian *as* a secret and the displacement of the "real" lesbian onto lower-class women and women of color, a relationship that renders white lesbians and lesbians of color differently marked. As Bhabha develops a four-part strategy for analyzing the stereotype in order to "provide a structure and a process for the 'subject' of colonial discourse," he makes the crucial point that "the fetish of colonial discourse—what Fanon calls the epidermal schema—is not, like the sexual fetish, a secret":

> Skin, as the key signifier of cultural and racial difference in the stereotype, is the most visible of fetishes, recognized as common knowledge in a range of cultural, political, historical discourses, and plays a public part in the racial drama that is enacted every day in colonial societies. Second, it may be said that the sexual fetish is closely linked to the "good object"; it is a prop that makes the whole object desirable and lovable, facilitates sexual relations and can even promote a form of happiness.[23]

Following Bhabha's argument, it is possible to speculate that the absence of women of color in the representations I have been examining is explicable in terms of a differing relationship to the structures of sexual and racial "secrets." For, if the fantasy that motivates these representations resides largely in uncovering, or dis-covering, the sexual rapaciousness and hence violence hidden "within" these women's appearance, the fantasy can be sustained only if anything that would already mark the women as "deadly" is not disclosed as "visible." Whereas the fetishization of skin color renders the lesbian of color already marked as a "terrifying presence" and thus not se-creted, the sexual fetish necessarily appears as a secret and is associated with the "good object." The white woman is then likely to appear as an ambivalent figure who is both pleasing and terrifying.

In chapter 4, I pointed out that it is difficult to imagine these violent female "buddies" played by anyone other than glamorous white actresses. The fact that they are white is not incidental; on the contrary, it would seem to be obligatory. In his article "White," Richard Dyer proposes several strategies for bringing into focus "whiteness," which is elusive precisely because it attains the property of being "everything and nothing," and thereby gains its representational power.[24] The ways in which women of color *are* represented as violent will not be the subject of this chapter. While that project bears considerable further theorization, this book is about popular representations that have been produced by the dominant culture. The fact that the "subjects" of these representations have been overwhelmingly heterosexual, white women should not, then, be surprising. But if, as I have been arguing, the "ghost" of the lesbian pursues the entrance of these women into representation, the question that must be raised is how these "lesbians" function ideologically, not just as sexual "deviants," but specifically as *white* sexual deviants.

Dyer argues that for white people to begin "see[ing] whiteness" it seems possible only "where its difference from blackness is inescapable and at issue."[25] Hence he looks at mainstream cinematic representations in which ethnic differences are manifest, and suggests other approaches that might prove productive, such as studying how whites are represented in Third World or diaspora cinema or in "avowedly racist and fascist cinema."[26] These approaches, however, still depend on looking at representations in which, in one way or the other, racial differences are already marked *within* the representation. Dyer's final suggested strategy, "the imaginary substitution of black for white performers" and the question he raises—"If these are unimaginable played by black actors, what does this tell us about the characteristics of whiteness?"[27]—indicate the deep entrenchment of oppositional thinking in considerations of racial differences. Rather than falling into the trap of "positivity" or "presence," a pitfall that all too often occurs when white feminists turn their lens to focus on women of color, I want to persist in my negative critique, pursuing the absences that ground the figures which do appear. And, once again, it is not my project to make visible the figures that constitute this ground, but rather to show how white, heterosexual masculinity reproduces itself through this repetition of absent-ground/present-figure.

Weaving a complex critique of Hillary Clinton–bashing as the "anxiety of impending Gender Trouble," Patricia J. Williams links a number of seemingly unrelated social/political events and popular representations. From the commercial for Gitano jeans aired at the height of the 1992 Republican convention featuring Marie Osmond as a "writhing, nubile, young woman . . . who professed that living with 'more than several men before marriage' . . . is perfectly consistent with traditional 'family values,' "[28] to Vice President Dan Quayle's attack on T.V. character Murphy Brown, to the enormous popularity of films like *Basic Instinct*, *The Hand That Rocks the Cradle*, and *Single White Female*, Williams finds consistency in their collective backlash against feminism.

The film *Single White Female* classically repeats the thematics that have been this book's concern: the deadliness of the inseparability of women, the return of a "repressed" homoeroticism in their relationship, the uncanny meeting of two women who function as a dual construct that reproduces a masculine imaginary. Playing on readers' familiarity with the cult film *The Attack of the 50-Ft. Woman*, Williams alludes to it in her article's title: "Attack of the 50-Ft. First Lady: The Demonization of Hillary Clinton." The immense popularity of *The Attack of the 50-Ft. Woman* is undoubtedly due to its rendering so apparent the fears and fantasies that motivate a great many mainstream Hollywood productions.

Originally billed as a "sci-fi drama," this film now circulates widely as a "classic camp thriller."[29] Not a thriller in the technical sense that I will discuss in chapter 7 in regard to *Basic Instinct*, *Attack of the 50-Ft. Woman* is, however, a film that features a hysterical woman whose truth-telling status is at issue. Nancy Archer encounters an alien satellite in the desert one night from which emerges a giant white man who kidnaps her, takes her invaluable "star of India" diamond, and deposits her unconscious on the roof of her home. Her unfaithful husband, who is hoping to have her committed so that he can take her money and run away with his girlfriend, takes advantage of her incredible tale and calls in a doctor who he hopes will declare Nancy insane. Nancy persuades her husband to drive into the desert with her, promising that if they do not find evidence to corroborate her story she will admit to being insane. While the entire town, including the law enforcement officials and the local newscaster, are mockingly broadcasting Nancy's story, Mr. Archer does see both the satellite and the giant and abandons Nancy in the desert to the mercy of the alien. She returns, however, and begins to grow to gargantuan proportions. Despite the pulleys, chains, and morphine administered with an elephant's syringe, Nancy's body spills out of the frame of their middle-class home. When she awakens from the narcotic administered to subdue her, she ransacks the town, pulling off the roofs of dwellings in search of her unfaithful man. Nancy Archer is finally killed by electrocution, but she takes Mr. Archer with her and no one doubts the truth of her tale. Her enormous body in its entirety becomes the symptom that unequivocally testifies to the real of the trauma. The terror of unrestrained, unconfinable femininity is raised to ridiculous proportions in this cult classic. Excessively rendering the fear of femininity as a *body* that is grotesquely out of control, *Attack of the 50-Ft. Woman* also makes a salient point. It is the touch of the alien white man that sends Nancy Archer off onto her rampage of revenge. The violently hysterical female is a giant white man's fantasy.

But what I find most provocative in Williams's critique is the implication that this backlash attains a certain unity around the issue of reproduction. Although she repeatedly refers to the noxious insistence on "family values" that was the hallmark of the Republican platform, she does not directly mention how markedly abortion rights were pushed into the background in this campaign. At the same time, however, she does emphasize that it is the issue of sexual and reproductive freedom which animates each of her examples, and that the demonization of Hillary Clinton depends largely on her deviance from conventional ideas of motherhood.

Connecting this deviance to Quayle's attack on Murphy Brown, Williams points out that Quayle's criticism of single motherhood was a thinly veiled assault on African-American women. Citing Anna Lowenhaupt Tsing's argument that the "monsterization of the liberated middle-class female" is a representational strategy that masks what is in fact a rage "unleashed upon the bodies of poor women and women of color,"[30] Williams illustrates her point in reference to Quayle's linkage of Murphy's "illegitimate" reproduction with the riots in south-central Los Angeles following the acquittal of the police officers who beat up Rodney King: "The not-very-subtle implication of this [being] that all those rioters were the unfathered wild children born of loose wombs, not 'legitimate' mothers."[31]

While one need not look hard to see that Republican "family values" are not only patriarchal and heterosexist but also white supremacist, the latter hand is not often shown so blatantly as in David Wattenberg's article "Boy Clinton's Big Mama," which, as Williams reminds us, invokes a connection between Hillary's threatening self-assertion and the stereotype of the dominating African-American matriarch. It is only a small step from there to the "presumptively degenerative man-hating insouciance" of the single woman.[32]

"The *single* woman" is a phrase so overdetermined with connotations of both African-American motherhood and lesbianism that it is often difficult to discern whether either or both of them are conjured by the phrase. They share the opprobrious charge of "mocking the importance of fathers,"[33] and where one is implicated, the other is not likely to be far away. The threat of their proximity constitutes a sufficient danger in patriarchal fantasies; the fact that they can and often do inhabit the same space appears to be a possibility so terrifying that it is constantly erased. The resulting historical product has been an entrenched separation of the two. And the most effective means of perpetuating that division has been to construct the "lesbian" as *white*.

Williams argues that what made the vice president's remarks on Murphy Brown so "controversial was his mixture, not mere juxtaposition, of images of white and black women's *unmarried* bodies: corrupt by virtue of their autonomy, their uncontrollability" (my emphasis).[34] I would suggest, moreover, that the fear/fantasy of this mingling of white and black women's bodies—"single" bodies—scarcely veils the threat of these bodies' coming together. That is, there is the danger not only that white women would "imitate" the unruliness of single black mother-hood, but also that these bodies might perform together. If the single mother is "sweepingly portrayed as 'mocking the importance of fathers,'" and the single woman who chooses not to reproduce is condemned for her presumptive "degenerative man-hating insouciance,"[35] the latter characterization has powerfully informed heterosexism's construction of the lesbian while the former has been located most emphatically on the bodies of single women of color.[36] As the dominant culture continues to reproduce this division, its effects have been to enforce a racial segregationism of sexual preference.

In the film *Single White Female*, a single white woman breaks up with her fiancé and seeks a roommate to share her rent-controlled Manhattan apartment. The title immediately refers to the advertisement she places in the paper. As Williams points out, the film is terrifyingly unselfconscious about its segregationism.[37] There is, however, something quite interesting in the way this segregationist desire operates in the film. When Allison Jones runs the ad, it reads, "SWF Seeks Female to Share Apartment in the West '70s." Although she marks herself as both "single" and "white," it is only the sameness of gender that she specifically requests in the identity of her prospective roommate. Furthermore, the ad unmistakably echoes the rhetoric of the "personals," advertisements that solicit sexual partners, not merely roommates, and thus the tension between sexual and racial differences is evoked. By announcing herself in terms of both marital status and race, and leaving her desired roommate unspecified in these two respects, Allison (Bridget Fonda) effects a curious reversal of the dominant culture's designation of "minority cultures."

Whereas white is usually the invisible race, here it becomes the category that is made visible. That the impulse is segregationist is unquestionable; by identifying herself as white, Allison indicates that she is seeking "the same." In fact, the rhetoric of advertising for roommates is more likely to read "seeks same," and the novel by John Lutz upon which the film was based was originally entitled *SWF Seeks Same*. Allison's intention is borne out in the scene that follows when she interviews four candidates. The first woman who answers her ad is a heavyset, large-boned, white woman dressed in working-class clothing who aggressively begins talking about the physical work she can do around the apartment. The second applicant is a black woman who is stylishly and provocatively dressed in a miniskirt and high heels. The third visitor is a white woman who announces that she is an incest survivor who has not yet remembered the actual incident but who is convinced, along with all of her therapists, that she has "survived something." Each of these women appears for only a few seconds; and with each of them the camera shows us Allie's face registering her obvious disapproval.

These three women are immediately recognizable as dominant-cultural stereotypes of the working-class butch, the hypersensual black woman, and the militant feminist. Significantly, the dyke and the feminist are both white, thus reinscribing the separation of the woman of color, who, on the basis of her race alone, is sufficiently identified as a type and distinguished from either of the other two categories.

The fourth candidate is a white woman—soft-spoken, demure, modestly dressed in department store–bought slacks and a blouse. Allie is just about to call this last woman when she breaks down and phones her unfaithful fiancé, Sam. Gathering her strength at the last moment, she hangs up after hearing his voice and sinks to the floor in tears. At this moment, Hedy (Jennifer Jason Leigh), the shy, awkward girl who becomes the film's fatal woman, enters. Catching Allie in this moment of extreme vulnerability, Hedy wins her affection and half of the apartment.

What is interesting in this parade of choices is that, as her ad implied, Allie was seeking the "same," someone just enough like herself but not quite. The first three women were clearly unacceptable. As the butch, the woman of color, and the feminist, they were too alien to Allie's own identity. The fourth candidate was perfect—just enough like her, the "all-American girl" lacked Allie's affluent airs and sensual sophistication but probably shared her "values." She did not, in other words, threaten Allie with too much difference. But the film is going to show us Allie learning a terrible lesson, one that will nearly cost her her life, and one that will take the life of her fiancé. For, on the one hand, Allie is shown to make the right choice by seeking the same, as long as that same was same gender, same race, and same values. Although she would certainly have been better off choosing any one of the three unacceptable candidates, the film makes each of them so unappealing, by stereotyping them so blatantly, that there is not much room for spectators to identify with any one of them. Instead, we are meant to identify with Allie and her rejection of them and their differences. And yet Allie pays an exorbitant price for failing to recognize the terrors of "sameness," for what she gets by seeking the same is a pathological "lesbian," who only appears to be drastically different from Allie.

At first, Allie and Hedy are marked as radically different. As one movie critic writes: "Immediately, the contrast between the roommates is blinding. Hedy is as painfully self-conscious as Allison is outgoing; as plain as Allison is ravishing; and as sullen as Allison is bright. But where Allison is romantic and naive, Hedy is a realist with a keen sense of horse hockey."[38] But Hedy's deep, dark secret is the loss (possibly the murder) of her identical twin sister, a part of her that she has always felt was missing. And thus Hedy, we discover, is also seeking the same; indeed she is seeking the self-identical. And to refind this missing other she will slowly transform herself into Allie's double, first borrowing her clothing and makeup, then purchasing exact duplicates of them, assuming Allie's gestures and mannerisms, and finally cutting and dyeing her own long dark hair into an exact replica of Allie's flaming red hairstyle. Thus Allie's segregationist impulse is, in a sense, punished. By seeking the same she risks forfeiting her own identity. In this respect, the film challenges the equation of the field of vision with knowledge: "seeing" is not to be mistaken for truth/knowledge. For what Allie sees is not what she gets.

One of the advertisements for this film cautioned, "Living with a roommate can be murder."[39] That *Single White Female* is a warning for women who think they might achieve a certain escape from dependency on men by turning to each other in financial arrangements, as well as for comfort, companionship, advice, and protection, is comically obvious as Hedy exacts a horrible penalty from Allie in exchange for these gifts. Hedy kills Allie's boyfriend (with whom she has reconciled), ties her up in a locked apartment, threatens to cut her throat (Allie saves her own life in this moment by kissing Hedy on the lips, which makes her put away the knife immediately), and finally, after failing to force Allie to swallow a lethal dose of tranquilizers, attempts to kill her with a grappling hook. Allie's smug confidence that she can do without Sam simply by getting a roommate backfires rather spectacularly. Sam's little sexual indiscretion (sleeping with his ex-wife) can scarcely be compared to the horrors of Hedy's pathologized desire for the "same."

While gender and sexual difference/sameness remain at the film's forefront, the "White" of the title appears to have dropped out of the picture entirely. It seems to be only an incidental remark, perhaps just a slip of the filmmaker's pen. But let us return to speculate on the significance of this evocation of whiteness and its rapid erasure. Williams asks "what a movie entitled *Single Black Female* might look like," and observes that "in some ways the movie industry has not been as straightforwardly libertine with images of black women as it has with those of white women, except in pornography and of course maid-motifs."[40] While Williams's point, that with a few exceptions "black heroines—or antiheroines—simply don't exist in films,"[41] is well-taken, it does not explain their absence.

Given the history of white culture's association of women of color with licentiousness and dangerous hypersexuality, one would think that representations of the sexually lascivious/violently aggressive woman would include at least a fair share of women of color. And yet not only are the overwhelming majority of classic "femmes fatales" white; the "fatal woman" who acts with conscious deliberation appears to be almost a wholly white construct in popular, dominant cultural representations. Indeed we might speculate that the formulation sex = death is a "white thing."

I think that the whiteness of this construct can be explained on two fronts. First, as I have been suggesting throughout this book, sex = death is a fantasy formation of a *heterosexual* masculine imaginary; when it makes an appearance, the trace of the "lesbian" is often recuperable. As I pointed out in chapter 1, the lesbian enters representation via the construct of the invert, a construct that was made, in part, in response to the demands of white supremacy. This lesbian has thus entered representational histories *as* white; for the sexologists she was the "enemy *within*," and therefore racially marked to mirror the white supremacists' *own* imaginations of the other within *themselves*. Second, as I discussed previously the fantasy of sex = death is built on a biological metaphor in which "sex" is consonant with reproduction. As we know, the lesbian bears the onus of the nonreproductive woman and her threat to the future of the species. The "unnaturalness" of the lesbian has always had much to do with a sexuality that is nonreproductive. In that the nonreproductive woman is located in a category constructed as sexually abnormal, women who aspire to normality are simultaneously enjoined to reproduce and to be heterosexual. Indeed sex and reproduction are thereby made entirely consonant, and any woman who fails to prove herself in either category is vulnerable to the suspicion of lesbianism. It is not insignificant to note that most of the women in the representations I have discussed are childless.

Still, is it enough to point out that the lesbian was constructed as white in order to create a category that coerced white women to reproduce? If, finally, the masculine fantasy that equates sex with death is about the risk of being "subtracted" that must be "heroically" undertaken in order to reproduce the species, the species that is at risk of being annihilated is the white race. This fear of annihilation is traceable in the rhetoric of "race suicide" that attended the declining white birthrate in the United States toward the end of the nineteenth century. Although urbanization largely accounted for this decline, irrational fears produced an anti-abortion campaign that was targeted mostly at white, middle-class women. Carroll Smith-Rosenberg argues that in response to the declining birthrate and the needs of a patriarchal medical profession, anti-abortion rhetoric and imagery were produced that constituted a "new male metaphoric language" portraying the white bourgeois matron as an "unnatural and monstrous woman, lethal to *men* and babies alike . . . who threatened social order and the future well-being of the [white] race."[42]

To return to Williams's hypothetical *Single Black Female*, here we surely are confronted with a figure that is not likely to make too many appearances since she is *already* constituted as a formidable threat to white supremacy. Small wonder that so many of Dan Quayle's political cohorts rushed in to silence his egregious slips of the tongue, slips that clearly disclosed the collective unconscious of his allies. For despite historical efforts to isolate the single woman of color from the white lesbian, they are intimately associated with one another in the white masculine imaginary as figures who constitute serious threats to the reproduction of white men—both fail to reproduce *him*, even when they do reproduce.

These representations of the single (heterosexual) white female are produced as *exceptions*; but they are figures that can be represented only on the unarticulated ground of white lesbians and women of color. Let me return for a moment to the opening dialogue of *Single White Female*. The very first words we hear are a conversation between Sam and Allie that is seemingly as incidental as the "White" of the title:

> SAM: So how many kids do you want?
> ALLIE: I don't know. What's the statistical norm?
> SAM: Ah, you and your statistics. 1.2
> ALLIE: Okay, then I want 2.2, and I want them to look like you.[43]

Allie and Sam thus locate themselves as white and upper-middle-class aspirants to this statistical norm, with one to spare. Furthermore, Allie makes it quite clear that she understands and is willing to accede to the conditions of motherhood as it is constructed under the reigning ideology—"I want them to look like you." Allie's destiny is to reproduce Sam. Hedy, the pathological lesbian, interrupts this reproduction. But her violent intrusion into this arrangement not only effects a disruption of Allie's heterosexuality but also cancels out what is clearly a reproduction of a "normative" white procreativity.

What is too often forgotten, not only in gender theory but also by white lesbian theorists, is that heterosexuality is not just about sexual difference. Heterosexuality, as an institution, is also an economy that maintains white supremacy. One can see this quite clearly in the history of reproductive legislation, and especially the more recent "right-to-life" movement, which coerces white women to reproduce and, paradoxically, restricts access to abortions for women of color and working-class women—the *majority* of American women—the same group for whom it otherwise encourages sterilization. Rosalind Petchesky explains that these contradictory policies are "inherent in a society geared historically to the need to control both its 'relative surplus population' and the sexual and reproductive maneuverability of women."[44]

Although *Roe v. Wade* has been effectively overturned for more than a decade for the majority of American women who seek reproductive freedom, that is not a sufficient victory for the right-to-lifers. The women who count for them can still get abortions: primarily middle- and upper-class white women who have connections with the few private physicians who still perform abortions, women who can travel across states, women who have greater access to scarce commodities.

Anti-abortion protesters who scream the word "dykes" at the escorts as well as the women seeking the services of abortion clinics point to another strand in the ideological web. It is often asserted, most recently in a *Newsweek* cover story, that lesbians' highly visible activity in the pro-choice movement is not self-interested since reproductive rights is an issue that is "unlikely to affect them directly."[45] This view overlooks what should be the most obvious agenda of the right-to-life movement. On one level, the historical association of lesbians with nonreproductivity is evoked as an opprobrious charge that signifies a falling from "woman-hood." Peggy Phelan points out that in addition to "dyke" the protesters scream "whore" at both the clinic workers and the counterdemonstra-tors, appellations that reveal the "breathtakingly crude" logic of Opera-tion Rescuers: "all feminists are lesbians; all pregnant women contem-plating abortion are sexually promiscuous."[46] While I agree with Phelan's reading of the underlying logic of these charges, I think that her larger argument supports a less obvious and hence more insidious connection between the "dyke" and right-to-life ideology. Citing Frances Wilkinson, Phelan reminds us that 56 percent of Operation Rescue's members are men; but, perhaps even more significantly, "almost all of its members are white."[47] Phelan also points out that the members of this organization see themselves as performing "missionary work," and hence "catalyze the conversion narrative so crucial to Christian culture."[48] Both the rhetoric and the performances of Operation Rescue thus unmistakably are en-gaged in a colonialist project.

At a recent anti-abortion rally in New York, demonstrators made their racist agenda abundantly clear when they shouted: "Abortion is the new holocaust. Only Blacks and Jews should be going in there."[49] As Phelan's article so powerfully demonstrates, the right-to-life movement is grounded in an identification between the fetus, which is "always already gendered—and not surprisingly, gendered male," and the would-be white male rescuers, who in the guise of protecting women and children are in fact attempting to rescue themselves from the loss of control of reproduc-tivity.[50] The "murdering mother" who appears in their imaginary is a figure that they attempt to displace onto "dykes," "whores," and women of color; for these are the historically "proper" places where the women are not expected to reproduce and/or are discouraged from doing so. Phelan writes that "Operation Rescue has attempted to hide the fact that the baby it wants so desperately to rescue is that mythically innocent white man, still caught in the silent womb of the maternal body."[51] That white man is indeed the quintessential "unborn."

Lesbians' stake in the fight for reproductive freedom is not at all *not* self-interested. For, in a sense, even the white lesbian is disaffiliated from the "white race" even as she has been, paradoxically, constructed *as* white. Because the "real" of female homosexuality was historically displaced onto women of color and working-class women, the white middle-class lesbian was considered an impossibility. And yet the lesbian, like the whore, is perceived as "not-woman" and therefore also not "really" white. For The Woman, who is always already both heterosexual and white, has the primary function of reproduction. Here I do mean reproduction in the biological sense—and I emphasize that what she is enjoined to reproduce is white men—but my sense is also, as I have been arguing all along, that her function as a placeholder serves to reproduce the white masculine imaginary's desire for desire—*their* desire, for *themselves*.

Historically, the woman of color, the prostitute, and the lesbian have been intimately connected with each other, sometimes nearly conflated in the imagination of white hetero-patriarchy. Sander L. Gilman illustrates that by the late nineteenth century the "perception of the prostitute" had "merged with the perception of the black,"[52] both of whom were distinguished from the white woman on the basis of physical attributes, most notably in the overdeveloped, "primitive," or degenerate sexual organs of the black woman and the prostitute. Furthermore, both the prostitute and the black woman were associated with the lesbian. As Gilman demonstrates, Theodor Billroth's standard gynecological treatise links the Hottentot's sexual anomalies with irregularities of the labia and overdevelopment of the clitoris, "which [Billroth] sees as leading to those 'excesses' which 'are called lesbian love'"; the "concupiscence of the black is thus also associated with the sexuality of the lesbian."[53] While this passage would imply that the lesbian as a type precedes the construction of the black woman as a hypersexualized and thus degenerative image of female sexuality, it is also possible to conclude that "lesbianism" was here being constructed as a *product* of the black woman's "primitive" sexual anatomy. Gilman argues that the black woman and the prostitute merged by the late nineteenth century; he does not go so far as to say that the lesbian was also subsumed within this merger. But in his analysis of atavistic theories of the prostitute's physiognomy, the emphasis on the "stigmata of criminal degeneration" accords with contemporary accounts of the invert's physical attributes. Especially prominent is the focus on the prostitute's "masculine" characteristics. Particularly as they age, prostitutes were seen as beginning "to appear more and more mannish." And in this context Gilman makes the point that Billroth's gynecological handbook links "the physical anomalies of the Hottentot and those of the lesbian."[54] Furthermore, in his discussion of Zola's *Nana*, he points out that her "atavistic sexuality, the sexuality of the Amazon, is destructive."[55] As Nana dies, she is described as reverting "to the blackness of the earth, to assume the horrible grotesque countenance perceived as belonging to the world of the black, the world of the 'primitive,' the world of disease."[56] Significantly, it is Nana's seduction by a lesbian that propels her into this decomposition.

If not quite made entirely synonymous, the prostitute, the black woman, and the lesbian were nonetheless drawn together to form a triad onto which the white male patriarch's terror of sexuality was projected. If the black woman and the prostitute were seen as "corrupted and corrupt[ing] through sexuality," and miscegenation was made "parallel to the barrenness of the prostitute," and both were feared for leading to "the decline of the population,"[57] it was not only an aversion to *difference* that was embodied in these historical constructions and conflations. Rather, it was also a fear of *sameness* that propelled this ideology. What links the lesbian, the prostitute, and the woman of color in this ideological web is that all three, separately and therefore together, did not facilitate the reproduction of the white man.

If the black woman and the prostitute bore the stigma of sexual difference, the lesbian bore the stigma of sexual sameness. Despite their differences, the three became linked in the white heterosexual male imaginary as figures that carried the apocalyptic threat of the demise of "the species." This connection continues into the twentieth century in the antiabortion movement. Played out in earlier decades by the now rather suppressed rhetoric of "race suicide," it continues in the more recent fetal imagery deployed by organizations such as Operation Rescue, whose "missionaries" offer to take us on a "discovery" of the heretofore "dark continent" of the maternal womb.

In his reading of the film *Night of the Living Dead*, Dyer provocatively argues that this film takes the hints of other representations to a logical conclusion, that "whiteness represents ... death."[58] Having argued through his readings of *Simba* and *Jezebel* that blacks are represented as having "more 'life' than whites," he pursues the obvious antithesis, that "whites have more 'death' than blacks."[59] Not only are all the "living dead" in *Night* white, the film also shows that living whites can be mistaken for the dead. Dyer argues that the "body horror" in these films is not merely a conventional use of the symbolism associated with the horror genre, but that "body horror is the horror of whiteness" and that the fear of "one's own body, of how one controls it and relates to it" is linked to the "fear of not being able to control other bodies, those bodies whose exploitation is so fundamental to capitalist economy." Thus in these films of the "dead," the fear of loss of control over one's own body and the projection of that fear onto others are "at the heart of whiteness."[60] Dyer's argument ties in neatly with Gilman's: "The 'white *man's* burden' thus becomes his sexuality and its control, and it is this which is transferred into the need to control the sexuality of the Other, the Other as sexualized female."[61]

Having thus made the connection between whiteness as the white man's fear of losing control over his own body and the projection of that fear onto the bodies of others, Dyer makes an interesting segue into a brief conclusion about the ideological function of the white woman's body in Hollywood cinema. Not attempting to make a "rounded conclusion," Dyer states that he is pursuing another tack in describing the way in which Marilyn Monroe, who was referred to as "The Body," is represented in *The Seven Year Itch* (1955) as "a classic instance of woman as spectacle."[62] In the scene Dyer analyzes, Monroe is framed within a doorway, and the lighting and architecture combine to create a strong perspective that emphasizes the male protagonist's gaze. Monroe herself is just a silhouette, and she "looks translucent." In a later scene, a similar effect is created when Monroe is shot standing, apparently nude, in front of a dark wall that makes her "face and shoulders stand out as white. Such moments conflate unreal angel-glow with sexual aura."[63] Monroe, Dyer argues, becomes an "impossible dream, offering another specifically white ideal as if it embodies all heterosexual male yearning, offering another white image that dissolves in the light of its denial of its own specificity."[64] His essay then ends with the words that serve as this chapter's second epigraph.

Although Dyer asserts that his conclusion diverges from the thesis he has so meticulously worked out in his readings of *Jezebel*, *Simba*, and *Night*, I would like to tease out the implications of this return to the white *woman* as the "apotheosis of desirability" within the context of "white representation *in general* [as obtaining] this everything-and-nothing quality."[65] Dyer's persuasive linking of whiteness with death accords with his discussion of whiteness as repression. If the white woman is represented as an exception that permits the equation of sex (reproduction) and death, this representational exceptionality, I would suggest, is linked through a series of displacements to the "others" who are ideologically interpellated as the "rule."

If the invert was constructed as the "secret" of white Eurocentric patriarchy, she was assimilated *within* that discourse, and hence the white lesbian becomes the enigma that is constitutively inside the white male imaginary. By contrast, the "real" homosexual women—working-class women/women of color—were located outside and hence did not partake of the structure of the secret. Doane argues that "repression becomes the prerequisite for the construction of white culture," and psychoanalysis can be understood as "a writing of the ethnicity of the white Western psyche."[66] The form of desire that this psyche represents can be expected to manifest itself according to a model that reproduces the white woman as the "apotheosis of desirability" in a writing of sexual difference that is inherently violent. But another kind of violence, a violence that exceeds this discursive formation, will be exacted on the bodies of those women who do not partake of the enigma but are a priori excluded from its terms.

As I have discussed in earlier chapters, the apotheosis of this white male imaginary's desire *for* desire is encapsulated in the rhetoric of courtly love. And when we return to its terms and conditions, we find that indeed The Woman of the courtly love tradition is by no means "universal woman," but an aristocratic "lady" who occupies the position of the forever unattainable ideal, the obstacle that is constructed, according to Lacan, to mask the fact that the (hetero)sexual relation is impossible. But while this lady—posited as the placeholder of a lack that facilitates the reproduction of the hom(m)o-sexual economy—represents the "nonsatisfaction" that guarantees this economy's reproduction, her absence did not preclude acknowledgment of the courtier's need to find satisfaction prior to his ascent to the heavenly bridegroom. For that satisfaction, he was enjoined to divert his desire to the peasant woman, who could, if necessary, be taken by force.

Andreas Capellanus, author of *The Art of Courtly Love*, thus advises his friend Walter on the "love" of peasant women: "Be careful to puff them up with lots of praise and then, when you find a convenient place, do not hesitate to take what you seek and to embrace them by force. For you can hardly soften their outward inflexibility so far that they will grant you their embraces quietly or permit you to have the solaces you desire unless first you use a little compulsion as a convenient cure for their shyness."[67] Louis Mackey explains that courtly love was "motivated by aristocratic disdain and a regard for the feudal order: If (*contra naturam*) farmers cultivate the art of love rather than the art of agriculture, the upper classes will get nothing to eat."[68] The courtly lady became something of a monster of disdain, but this "monsterization," like modern representations of fatal women, was in fact unleashed upon the bodies of peasant women. James Hillman argues that "we feel cleansed of shadow in the supremacy of white," and that while some alchemists believe that the work stops there, the

> "moral aspect of whitening" may in fact be that self-deception in which the ghosts are driven out by blending in, formulated in philosophy as the "identity of indiscernibles." Although the differences between white and its shadow are not perceptible (e.g. we can't see the shadow in our bright ideas, good deeds, true beliefs, honest motives, beautiful feelings or any of the other Christian virtues which ennobled the conquests, glories, triumphs and spoils of the Christian mission), they are there nonetheless.[69]

What appears in what was once one's blind spot is not always the return of the repressed. To borrow a phrase from Bhabha, what we are not seeing when whiteness blinds us with its all-encompassing nothingness may be the "return of the oppressed."[70]

7

Why The Woman Did It: *Basic Instinct* and Its Vicissitudes

> . . . it has to be said that morality stops short at the level of the *id*. In other words, what it is all about is the fact that love is impossible, and that the sexual relation founders in non-sense, not that this should in any way diminish the interest we feel for the Other.[1]
>
> (Jacques Lacan)

IN THE INTERVIEW that follows the uncut version of *Basic Instinct*, director Paul Verhoeven insists that Catherine Trammell (Sharon Stone) is definitively the murderer despite the complex compilation of evidence that points, all but decisively, to Dr. Beth Gardner (Jeanne Tripplehorn).[2] Until the film's final image—the ice pick under Catherine's side of the bed, her hand dangling toward it as she makes love to the detective Nick Curran (Michael Douglas)—we are led to believe, along with all the duped detectives, that Beth did it.

Avoiding the controversy about the film's homophobia, which instigated a massive protest based on the contention that the film portrayed lesbians and bisexuals as predatory murderers, Verhoeven sticks to a discussion of the film's formal conventions. At the same time, however, one cannot help but notice Verhoeven's verification of what became the gay and lesbian activists' strategy for ruining the film's box-office appeal: "Catherine did it!"—the ubiquitous signs that marked the demonstrators' protests were intended to ruin the element of suspense that is the hallmark of the detective narrative.[3]

If the gay activists' plan was ultimately unsuccessful (*Basic Instinct* made $15 million in its first weekend), it failed not only because it was grounded in an assumption that moviegoers would attend the film only to find out "who did it." For the film itself much more interestingly fails to deliver the certainty upon which the queer protesters banked. And despite Verhoeven's confirmation, the film exceeds his intention to wrap up the mystery of the murderer's identity as neatly as we have come to expect from a classic whodunit.

In his review of *Basic Instinct*, Richard Schickel makes an interesting double move. On the one hand, he claims that the film cannot be fairly termed antigay: "Catherine is certainly bisexual but it is just another aspect of her cultivated air of differentness, her love of high risk games and shock effects."[4] Catherine's sexuality is thus irrelevant for Schickel, who, like Verhoeven, wants to focus on the film's formal aspects, which for him are where the *real* problems lie. Thus Schickel criticizes the film for the "chilly, self-conscious sleekness of its production design" and Verhoeven for the "heartless and relentless thrill seeking" of his direction. Mainly though, the film is a failure because its plot is flawed. It fails to be persuasive because it breaks "faith with the most inviolate convention of the whodunit—refusing to state firmly which of the two women [Catherine or Beth] dunit."[5] Schickel is perturbed by the film's smart, smug attitude, its arrogant belief that it is fast and sleek enough to "wow the yokels." Not wishing to identify with the "yokels" himself, Schickel separates himself from them, parenthetically marking them as the "gay activists" who erred in their "confident naming of [Catherine] in a publicity campaign aimed at undermining the movie."[6] Schickel is certainly not a gay activist, naive or not; nor is he a homophobe, he wants us to believe. He is simply a neutrally positioned film critic who can name a generic violation when he sees one.

I want to propose that what is most intriguing about *Basic Instinct* is precisely this failure to confirm the conventions of the detective genre. Furthermore, I want to suggest that this failure is bound up with, perhaps even inextricable from, the film's homophobia. This film is not homophobic because of its negative portrayals of lesbian and bisexual women; rather, the film quite markedly displays the systemic, structural homophobia of the masculine imaginary. *Basic Instinct* is a film worth the notice of feminist and lesbian theorists not because of its excessive rendering of the equation lesbian/man-hater—which is not much more than a banal repetition of male anxieties, fears, and fantasies—but because the film inadvertently makes evident the condensations and displacements that reproduce this link as a *structural* mechanism necessary to the power and pleasure of heteropatriarchy.

Let us return to the question of the genre as such. *Basic Instinct* does not qualify as a classic "whodunit" in the first instance. Although Verhoeven uses the terms "whodunit" and "thriller" interchangeably,[7] they are not merely substitutive terms. As a subcategory within detective fiction, the thriller, according to Tzvetan Todorov, reverses the situation of the classic whodunit. In the latter, the detective enjoys a certain immunity. Never a victim himself, the detective can be thought of as a "pure and unpunishable murderer," who "kills" (literally or figuratively) the first murderer.[8] Thus following the "two-murder" structure of the classic whodunit, the story (what the Russian formalists called the *fable*) is what "really" happened (the first murder), and the plot (*subject*) is the retelling, or re-presentation of the story (the second murder).

The hermeneutical structure of the classic whodunit is defined as the duality of these two elements, and the classic detective is always presented *as* a representational figure whose task is to expose the "truth"—the first (real) murderer's story—while remaining himself immune from danger. The thriller not only reverses this paradigm by exposing the detective to risks from which he was formerly safeguarded by convention; it also creates a different dynamic of suspense. Whereas the whodunit's formal conventions depend on a reconstruction of the past, the thriller's form is in the mode of anticipation and uncertainty: "Prospection takes the place of retrospection."[9]

There is, then, no formal guarantee in the thriller that a careful reconstruction of the past can recover the truth. Rather than providing the satisfaction, characteristic of the whodunit, attained by a neat compilation of evidence that solves the mystery, the thriller leaves the reader suspended along with the detective, who may well remain in peril and doubt: "No thriller is presented in the form of memoirs: there is no point reached where the narrator comprehends all past events, we do not even know if he will reach the end of the story alive."[10]

The thriller represents a transgression of the classic whodunit, and its formal alterations signify a significant shift in the reader/spectator's experience. For the classic whodunit gives us, in the figure of the detective, a subject whom we can comfortably assume to know—the one who will ultimately reveal to us the truth. But the thriller, in its derivation from and thus evocation of the whodunit, gives us a "subject-supposed-to-know" who turns out *not* to know. If, in the thriller, "everything is possible,"[11] it is because we can no longer suppose the subject-supposed-to-know. The thriller exposes the detective/analyst as a fraud. The transference is broken.

In "God and the *Jouissance* of The Woman," Lacan sets out to elucidate "*There is something of One,*" which in Freud is set forth in the concept of Eros, "defined as a fusion making one out of two, that is, of Eros seen as the gradual tendency to make one out of a vast multitude."[12] For Freud, this "making one" is metaphorized by the fusion of the ovum and sperm—reproduction makes one from two, but not without "a quite manifest subtraction for at least one of the two just before the conjunction is effected."[13] Beginning with this biological metaphor, we have the familiar formula, elaborated by Bataille among others, that sex (reproduction) = death.[14] Lacan, however, interrogates this "One" on the level of language—that is to say, in the unconscious, which is structured like a language. Within the discourse of psychoanalysis, Lacan argues, we are always dealing with this "one alone," and it is only there that we can grasp this thing that for centuries has been called love, which is indistinguishable from transference. Lacan's formula for grasping this phenomenon is "the-subject-supposed-to-know." Love/transference can be understood only in relation to this formula: "He whom I suppose to know, I love." And love's opposite—hate—is also dependent on this formula: "When I say that they hate me, what I mean is that they de-suppose me of knowledge."[15]

If the formal movement from the whodunit to the thriller can be understood as a transformation of the detective from a subject-supposed-to-know to a subject-desupposed-of-knowledge, we might simply hypothesize that these conventions invite a spectatorial response that shifts from love to hate. However, the thriller always carries within it the trace of the whodunit, and to some degree the expectations of the whodunit are carried forward into the thriller. For if the classic whodunit (which, like all "classics," is a deduction from an abstract schema, an ideal to which no actual representation conforms but always aspires) promises the spectator the truth, the thriller also makes this promise but breaks it. The thriller is not by any means the whodunit's opposite; rather, it is a transgressive form that, like all transgressions, necessarily conjures the model from which it departs. The thriller would, then, not be about love, or about hate, but rather about their proximity. In evoking the always vacillating movement between these two opposites, the thriller's form might be understood as inhabiting the space in between, where love and hate are not each other's opposites, but each other's doubles.

The formal conventions of the thriller could be said to embody the "content" of a film like *Basic Instinct*. Or rather, its form *is* its content, and the pulsating rhythm of the love/hate relationships is not thematic, but rather constitutive of the form. And so the dominance of "doubling" within the film's diegesis can be read as a compliance with the formal conventions of the thriller. The thriller, then, would seem to command a particular shape to the representation of the "deadly woman." And the shape in which this ubiquitous figure appears in the thriller will be intimately bound to the status of the detective, as the subject-desupposed-of-knowledge.

Three of the four primary female characters in *Basic Instinct* are killers. Roxy, Catherine's live-in lesbian lover, attempts to kill Nick Curran, and after her death graphic police photos reveal that she slashed her two younger brothers to death with her father's razor. Hazel Dobkin, an older woman who is Catherine's friend, was convicted of killing her husband and her three children, slashing them to death with a knife she had received as a wedding present. Neither Roxy nor Hazel ever explained why she did it; Hazel said it was just a sudden impulse, and Roxy said that the razor was just there, so she used it. Their characters, together, establish that "women" can be suddenly and inexplicably violent. That point established, the film's primary interest lies in distinguishing between the good girl and the bad girl, that is, securing the identity behind the appearance of the third woman.

Like nineteenth-century criminology, *Basic Instinct*'s real interest lies in the fear of ambiguity, the inability to detect which woman might be the real offender. The contest is between Catherine Trammell and Beth Gardner. Catherine is implicated in the murders of her parents; one of her lovers, the ex–rock and roll singer, Johnny Boz; her college professor Noel Goldstein; and the detective Neilson. Dr. Beth Gardner's husband was shot to death under mysterious circumstances; and all of the hard evidence in the film points to Beth as the murderer of Johnny Boz (whose murder sets the whole plot into motion and makes Catherine a prime suspect) and of Gus, Nick's closest friend and right-hand man, who is ice-picked to death on the elevator in a building where he was summoned to meet with Catherine's college roommate. Retrospectively, Beth is also the primary suspect in the murders of Goldstein and Neilson.

Basic Instinct is thus an almost comical rendition of the deadliness of women. This thematic overkill, however, is not achieved simply by addition. For it is the complicated relationship between these women that produces the film's horror. It is not, in other words, so much what they *do* individually that makes for the film's gripping suspense as it is the mystery of their relationships with each other. Roxy and Hazel, for example, are seemingly minor characters. Neither of them is necessary for the plot to move forward. Rather, they are decorative additions to a story that does not require their presence to tell its tale strictly on the level of the plot. While Roxy is used in the early part of the film as a possible suspect, the suggestion that she might have killed Johnny Boz in a jealous fury is not presented convincingly. Her primary significance is to fill out Catherine's character; specifically, Roxy serves simply to signify Catherine's bisexuality. Once that function has been fulfilled, Roxy is eliminated.

Hazel's function is more enigmatic. There is never any suggestion that she is implicated in the murders in any way. The only explanation the film offers for her presence is that Catherine, who is herself a writer of thrillers, struck up a friendship with her because Hazel could teach her about the workings of a homicidal mind. Hazel presumably is a research interest for Catherine. Her appearances are minimal, but we do see her at one very charged moment in the film when Catherine's allegiance to Nick is broken. And Catherine chooses in Hazel's favor. Both Roxy and Hazel function as signs that Catherine is capable of forming lasting, affectionate, loving bonds. We see Catherine lose her cool, detached air of indifference when she hears about Roxy's death, an emotional outburst that contrasts markedly with her insouciance in the face of Boz's murder. With Hazel, Catherine is soft-spoken, affectionate, submissive. Catherine reserves her *real* love for women—and it is necessary for there to be more than one woman to make the point that this "real" love is for women only.[16]

Thus Hazel's and Roxy's roles make it understandable that protesters could read in the film that Catherine is a lesbian—despite her more obvious "bisexuality," her real love is clearly reserved for women. Furthermore, the film accedes to the historical myth of the lesbian as narcissistic: both Roxy and Hazel resemble Catherine physically. Roxy, in fact, is so like Catherine that it is not easy to distinguish between them, especially in the bar scene when we see them dancing seductively together. And Hazel could easily be an older version of Catherine. All three women are of similar build, have long blond hair, and manifest the stereotypical physical attributes of upper-class white women. The threesome resonates with the doubling effect that is characteristic of the lesbian as autoerotic/narcissistic. In these three, this history is repeated in its relatively benign incarnation.

But the diabolical doubling is between Beth and Catherine. And the whodunit plot turns not only on the inability of spectators to deduce from the evidence which one of them in fact did do it, but also on an identification between them that is revealed in their histories with each other. For as the plot unravels its clues, we discover that Beth and Catherine were students together at Berkeley. And that, moreover, they were lovers, for at least one night. Each of them, after having sex with Nick, tells him the same story: that the two women slept together once and that the other became obsessed. The obsession took the form of stealing the other's identity. Beth, of course, claims that Catherine was the compulsive-obsessive who began to imitate her hairstyle and clothing and to stalk her on the college campus. Catherine tells Nick exactly the same story, only claiming that Beth stalked and imitated her.

Once we have attained this information, the scene in which a group of psychiatrists, Beth included, is called in for consultation about the Boz murder resonates retrospectively with new meaning. Either Catherine's novel about a rock-and-roll star who is tied up and ice-pick murdered in his bedroom is Catherine's "perfect alibi," or the murderer is someone who is so obsessed with Catherine that she is willing to kill an innocent man to ruin Catherine. Is Catherine the victim of a crazed stalker, or is she a diabolical killer who has banked on her book as the perfect alibi? Is Beth the rejected lover who is bent on revenge? From this point on, the film never lets us stop guessing. Nor does it ever satisfactorily *resolve* these questions. For, despite the final shot of the ice pick under Catherine's bed, it is possible that now Catherine is the (potential) "copycat" killer. The ice pick that Catherine reaches for in the final scene is the expensive, steel one we have seen her use in her home several times in the film, not the cheap, wooden K-Mart brand that the film reminds us often enough is the favorite tool of the killer. In the interview with Verhoeven, he makes this distinction explicit, but he is puzzled himself by the point of this very important detail.

Furthermore, the evidence all overwhelmingly points to Beth. After "proving" to us that Beth did it by compiling a list of evidence that is seemingly incontrovertible, the film asks us in the end to overrule the altogether "reasonable" conclusion that Beth is the guilty one, and to turn once more to Catherine as the culprit. Catherine's capacity for diabolical machinations strains credibility if we are to believe that in at most a couple of days she has entered Beth's apartment and planted ice picks (K-Mart brand, of course), copies of her novels, a .38 caliber revolver (the type used to kill Neilson), enlarged photographs of the two of them together at graduation, and assorted news clippings of publicity shots of herself with various male escorts. In addition, she has lured Beth to meet Gus in the hotel, erased the phone message on Beth's answering machine, stolen a slicker marked "San Francisco Police Department" from the precinct where Nick and Beth work, killed Gus and left the bloody slicker, ice pick, and a blond wig on the staircase, gone home to shower, and driven out to Nick's apartment where she is waiting for him, fresh, repentant, and ready to make love.

Now, we could simply chalk this all up to bad plotting and agree with Schickel that *Basic Instinct* is a poorly written film. But I think that the ambiguity of this ending tells us something important about the masculine imaginary, something that is usually less blatantly exposed. The film's failures produce an excess that reveals the comedy of heterosexuality—the "non-sense" of the sexual relationship. For it is precisely in this film's inability to make sense that the (non)sense of heterosexuality is rendered patent. When we ask the film to tell us who *did* do it, the only answer it can give us is that the *women* did it, which is to say, The Woman did it.

When the subject-supposed-to-know is desupposed of knowledge, "he" is effectively annihilated. The link between breaking the transference and annihilating (murdering?) the subject-supposed-to-know is made quite explicitly in the film when Catherine finishes her novel (about a detective who falls for a woman who kills him) and tells Nick (her model) that their love relationship is over:

> NICK: I finished my research.
> CATHERINE: I finished my book.
> NICK: Yeh, so how does it end?
> CATHERINE: I told you, she kills him. Goodbye Nick.
> NICK: Goodbye?
> CATHERINE: Yeh. I finished my book. Didn't you hear me? Your character's dead. Goodbye.[17]

At this point one remembers that Catherine warned Nick early on, during the scene in which he first takes her in for questioning about the Boz murder, that this novel was in progress. Murder and transference (love) are here rendered equivalent. For if "falling for" someone and killing her are the same, Nick has fallen for the "wrong woman" (as Catherine had warned him her novel's hero would), and he has also killed the wrong woman (Beth). In other words, Catherine "kills" Nick in this scene (breaks the transference, thus rendering him the subject-desupposed-of-knowledge) because he has killed the wrong woman. In a sense, then, Catherine here avenges Beth's murder.

One might assume that love's opposite is hate and that, correspondingly, the subject-supposed-to-know is loved, whereas the subject-desupposed-of-knowledge is hated, but this is too simple an antithesis for the thriller. In "Instincts and Their Vicissitudes"—in which Freud endeavors to "confine [instincts] in definitions," always aware that such definitions are "strictly speaking . . . in the nature of conventions"[18]—he makes it clear that creating meaning is performative, an achievement that is effected by "making repeated references to the material of observation" in order that they may become "serviceable and consistent."[19] Freud suffers from no illusions that the meanings he will make of the instincts have any "true" content; rather, their serviceability is produced through repetition, and they are "constantly being altered in their content."[20]

Nonetheless, as Lacan reminds us, Freud was the ultimate subject-supposed-to-know: "He was not only the subject who was supposed to know. He did know, and he gave us this knowledge in terms that may be said to be indestructible, in as much as, since they were the first communicated, they support an interrogation which, up to the present day, has never been exhausted."[21] So, for the sake of argument, let us proceed as if the transference (the belief in Freud and Lacan as subjects-supposed-to-know) were not broken, and suppose that what Freud had to say about the instincts has attained certainty.

Freud points out that the transformation of *love into hate* is the only instance of a change in the *content* of an instinct (his emphasis), and that it is of special interest since this transformation "refuses to be fitted into our scheme of the instincts."[22] Freud thus has difficulty discerning what meaning to ascribe to the love/hate antithesis. It seems that this opposition does not properly belong to the instincts as such at all. What is clearer is that love has two other opposites, which Freud finds more explicable. There is also the antithesis "loving—being loved," and then there is "unconcern or indifference," which is not the opposite of love alone, but the antithesis of "loving and hating taken together."[23]

It is in the second set of oppositions—loving/being loved—that there is an exact correspondence to the "transformation from activity to passivity," and it is in the state of "being loved" that Freud locates the characteristic feature of narcissism.[24] As we know from Freud's essay "On Narcissism," this is the feminine condition par excellence, a state from which the "purest and truest" of women never emerge.[25] In tracing the genesis of love and hate, Freud posits that hate is preliminary to love. Love is an achievement that must pass through the narcissistic phase into object-love through an ambivalent phase in which the sexual aim is directed toward incorporating the object. In this ambivalent stage, love is "hardly to be distinguished from hate in its attitude towards the object."[26]

It is this ambivalence that we see Catherine Trammell performing particularly graphically in the last scene of *Basic Instinct* as she struggles with herself between making love to Nick and murdering him. The film foregrounds this ambivalence by showing us her split-second decision not to grasp the ice pick but rather to grab hold of Nick in a passionate embrace. Ostensibly, then, she makes the decision to love rather than to hate the object; she passes through this ambivalent stage and achieves "true" object-love. That is, she accedes to the order of heterosexuality: "Not until the genital organization is established does love become the opposite of hate."[27] *Basic Instinct*, in other words, consummates Catherine's heterosexuality. It is an allegory for the "becoming of woman" according to the teleology of the instincts that begins with autoeroticism and ends with "genital organization," that is, heterosexuality.

And yet this is a trajectory that only assumes the appearance of a linear progression. For the earlier "phases"—autoeroticism/narcissism and the suggestion of homoeroticism with which they are always overwritten— are not merely left behind. Catherine's ambivalence toward Nick leaves open a space where we can see that her heterosexuality always remains in doubt. And the ambiguity of the ending, the fact that we never know, with certainty, whether Catherine or Beth did it, makes of these two women a kind of eternal couple. Not a lesbian couple, but the coupling of women, the doubling, that underwrites a masculine imaginary. For in a sense, the film inescapably concludes that Catherine and Beth *both* did it; and that, furthermore, they did it together. Although this reading of the question "Who did it?" is based primarily on what I am arguing is the unconscious scene of a masculine fantasy, the possibility that Catherine and Beth are working together finds some patent justification in the film. For example, just after Beth provides Nick with an alibi when he is accused of killing the detective Neilson, Beth asks Nick why he believed that Neilson had sold Nick's private psychiatric file to Catherine. Beth is Nick's therapist, and when he answers, "She knows things that I only told you," the possibility is left open that Beth is Catherine's informant. More speculatively, while it is difficult to believe that either Catherine or Beth could have carried out such complex machinations individually, the theory that they were working together increases the plot's plausibility. Nevertheless, though the film lures spectators into engaging in such speculations, it is all the more interesting for failing to "make sense."

What is most pronounced in *Basic Instinct* is its insistence on erotic triads. Between the man and the woman, Lacan placed "a certain Other who seemed remarkably like the good old God of all times."[28] As a third party in this affair of human love, "this Other, while it may be one alone, must have some relation to what appears of the other sex."[29] That relation is Woman as man's symptom, the nonexistent obstacle that functions as the cause of man's desire. Men, in other words, make love to the Symbolic Order.

In Verhoeven's earlier film *The Fourth Man*, this ménage à trois is neatly encapsulated in the mysterious utterance of the hero as he ejaculates inside the deadly woman: "Through Mary to Jesus," he cries out.[30] Such is there "something of the One." But in *Basic Instinct*, the invisible fourth partner in this mystical ménage à trois makes appearances: once as Roxy, twice as Hazel, and as the third woman, the deadliest of them all, Beth, the "other woman," who is not just "other" as Nick's rival for Catherine, but Catherine's other/double. The one who "does it" *with her* must be eliminated: "Still like girls, Beth?" Nick screams hysterically just before he shoots Beth. If men need femininity to be associated with death, they also need representations in which masculinity survives the thrill of getting close to those flames.

One woman will not do the trick. Men need one who does it and one who doesn't do it. It is not "Woman" who doesn't exist; it is *The* Woman. Striking out the article that signifies her singularity, we can see how her relation to the "something of the One" suggests that perhaps she is always already *two*: one to have the phallus (the one who threatens to take his place and is subsequently erased) and one to be the phallus, the one who reproduces him. Thus *Basic Instinct* blatantly exposes what I have been arguing is usually unmarked in representations of violent women. For I suggest that we can read in this film what is less manifest, but no less informative, in other representations I have discussed: The Woman, who does not exist, makes possible the reproduction of the ménage à trois ("there is something of the One") as an empty space that is nonetheless phantasmatically inhabited by a double feminine figure—one whose desire is "like" his (the "lesbian" in a masculine imaginary that can only think homosexuality *as* heterosexuality) and one who is different (the straight woman).

From a lesbian spectator's position, I do not think there are *any* lesbians in *Basic Instinct*, which invalidates the claim that the film is homophobic due to its negative portrayals of lesbian/bisexual women. Nevertheless, *Basic Instinct* is surely a homophobic film in the sense that it renders visible the systemic homophobia of masculine heterosexual desire. Making these often unarticulated mechanisms readable, *Basic Instinct* perversely inscribes a challenge to the patriarchal symbolic to own up to what it conceals in order to maintain itself.

8

Surpassing the Word: Aileen Wuornos

. . . so we go into the woods. He's huggin' and
kissin' on me. He starts pushin' me down. And
I said, wait a minute, you know, get cool. You
don't have to get rough, you know. Let's have
fun. . . . I said I would not [have sex with him].
He said, yes, you are, bitch. You're going to do
everything I tell you. If you don't I'm going to
kill you [and have sex with you] after you're
dead, just like the other sluts. It doesn't matter,
your body will still be warm. He tied my wrists
to the steering wheel, and screwed me in the ass.
Afterwards, he got a Visine bottle filled with
rubbing alcohol out of the trunk. He said the
Visine bottle was one of my surprises. He emptied it into my rectum. It really hurt bad because
he tore me up a lot. He got dressed, got a radio,
sat on the hood for what seemed like an hour. I
was really pissed. I was yelling at him, and
struggling to get my hands free. Eventually he
untied me, put a stereo wire around my neck
and tried to rape me again. . . . Then I thought,
well this dirty bastard deserves to die because of
what he was trying to do to me. We struggled.
I reached for my gun. I shot him. I scrambled to
cover the shooting because I didn't think the
police would believe I killed him in self-defense. . . . I have to say it. I killed them all because they got violent with me and I decided to
defend myself. . . . I'm sure if after the fightin'
they found I had a weapon, they would've shot
me. So I just shot them. . . .[1]
    (Aileen Carol Wuornos, testimony)

AILEEN (LEE) WUORNOS figured correctly; no one believed that she killed
in self-defense. As of this writing she waits on death row in a Florida
prison. She has confessed to killing seven white middle-aged men, all of

whom picked her up on Florida's Interstate 75. The first man she killed, Richard Mallory, had a history of violent sexual assaults and was incarcerated for ten years in a Maryland institution after posing as a repairman and sexually assaulting a housewife. This evidence was not presented in the Mallory trial; it was not even uncovered by Wuornos's public defenders and was "overlooked" by the prosecution.[2]

I repeat her words at length here, hoping that somehow they will fill the gaping black hole from which they emerge and ineluctably return. I sink with her in and out of this incredible space. I want her words to stand in for the thing itself—to signify the event transparently—even as I know that testimony can never produce an effect of truth alone. "For the testimonial process to take place," writes Dori Laub, "there needs to be a bonding, the intimate and total presence of an *other*—in the position of one who hears. Testimonies are not monologues; they cannot take place in solitude. The witnesses are talking to *somebody*: to somebody they have been waiting for for a long time."[3]

Aileen Wuornos is waiting—on death row—and I am wondering if it is possible that a listener will arrive in time to save her. I will try repeating her story differently, in a way that perhaps can be heard. I do not, however, believe that I can save her. As her one girlhood friend has said, "She has been living with a death penalty since she was 12."[4] I can only tell one story of how and why she will be sacrificed, and try to document her resistance.

The media and the FBI have called her the first female serial killer. The serial killer has a particular legal and psychological profile. Writing in 1984, Steven Egger explained:

> All known cases of serial killers are males. . . . Serial killers commit subsequent murder(s) and they are relationship-less (victim and attacker are strangers) . . . killings are frequently committed in different or widespread geographic locations and not for any material gain, but a compulsive act for gratification based on fantasies . . . victims share common characteristics of what are perceived to be prestigeless, powerless, or lower socio-economic status, such as vagrants, prostitutes, homosexuals, children, single and often elderly women . . . and most of these murders have a basis of underlying sexual conflicts of sadistic lust. Many of these aberrants vent their hostile impulses through cruelty to animals, but their real hatred is against their fellow man.[5]

Wuornos embodies two incontrovertible reversals in the profile: she is a woman; and her victims were heterosexual, white, middle-class males, not members of powerless groups. The only point left in Egger's description that doubtless pertains to Wuornos is that the murders were subsequent and ranged over a geographical area. But by naming Wuornos a "serial killer," the prosecution built its case around the other characteristics—the "psychological" part of the profile—which are all obviously merely inferences in any case. Thus Wuornos has been depicted as a killer who stalked her victims, lured them with promises of sexual favors, and was compelled to repeat the crime because of a lust for domination.

Wuornos's own story is quite different. In her testimony, she claimed that she was a hitchhiking prostitute, who killed these men because they were raping her and/or threatening to kill her. Given her evident deviation from the serial killer's profile, even and indeed especially within the realm of what the law and its ministers consider concrete, observable facts, we might ask what purpose it has served to label Wuornos a serial killer, and indeed why she was so named even before the details of the murders were depicted.

Jane Caputi has argued that the hierarchy established between serial killers and their victims indicates that "these are crimes of sexually political import, crimes rooted in a system of male supremacy in the same way that lynching is based in white supremacy."[6] This obvious point is occluded by the way in which these murders are naturalized *as* deviant; despite the frequency and structural repetitiveness of these acts, each one is invariably represented, paradoxically, as *yet another* enigma—a pathological aberration—an act that is *outside* of culture and hence a violent intrusion into it. Caputi cites Kate Millett to support her view that "long-standing tradition" (naturalization) impedes the recognition of the serial killer's place *within* a patriarchal symbolic order. Millett writes:

> So perfect is [patriarchy's] system of socialization, so complete the general assent to its values, so long and so universally has it prevailed in human society, that it scarcely seems to require violent implementation. Customarily, we view its brutalities in the past as exotic or "primitive" custom. Those of the present are regarded as the product of individual deviance, confined to pathological or exceptional behavior, and without general import.[7]

More than twenty years after *Sexual Politics* first made such startling claims, the tedium of having to repeat them is almost unbearable. But perhaps Wuornos's acts have made a generative wedge in the sociosymbolic. For on a first consideration she would seem to have merely reproduced that order, only reversing it in two of its principal structural elements. But Wuornos has not acceded to her nomination as a "female" serial killer, and, furthermore, her actions on closer examination constitute much more than a reversal.

Elaborating the question "Why is *Woman* the Symptom of Man?" Slavoj Žižek identifies the "serial killer" as "the figure which comes closest to [the] role of a scapegoat embodying sacred violence . . . the madman

who, with no 'rational ground,' compulsively repeats murderous acts."[8]
Pointing to the doubleness of the Symbolic Order, which is *both* a "subject-supposed-to-know" and a "subject-supposed-*not*-to-know," Žižek
elaborates that in the first instance, the Other appears as a "hidden
agency," like divine Providence or the "invisible hand of the Market"—a
surplus or a "meta subject," which is within itself radically ambivalent as
it can serve either to reassure or to terrify. In the first case, it instills confidence and relieves us of responsibility; in the second, it is a "terrifying
paranoiac agency" that threatens to rob us of our pleasures. These two
mutually opposing qualities of the big Other are "united in the figure of
the psychoanalyst *qua* 'subject supposed to know' (Lacan)." At the same
time, however, the big Other functions as precisely the opposite of this
"hidden agency"—as an agency of "pure semblance, of an appearance
which is nevertheless *essential*, i.e., which should be preserved at any
price."[9]

It is in the latter understanding of the Other (which Lacan designates
the Name-of-the-Father) that we can recognize the Symbolic Order as a
"dead scheme," which derives its power precisely because it is "dead"
and thereby "dominates and regulates our actual lives. . . ."

> This is the way "tarrying with the negative" takes place, this is the way negativ-
> ity as such acquires positive, determinate being: when the very actual life of a
> community is structured by reference to symbolic fictions. In our everyday
> lives, we accept this as something so self-evident that we don't even notice the
> oddness of what is going on—to become fully aware of it, a philosophical
> experience of "wondering" is necessary.[10] (Author's emphasis)

Surely feminists from Millett on have been engaged in this "wondering."
There is not much difference between Žižek's description of the Symbolic
Order and Millett's patriarchy. But the question remains how one goes
beyond wondering and intervenes in this sociosymbolic in ways that can
alter it.

Although there is not any way "out" of the discourse of the symptom,
there are differing interpretations of what the symptom is saying when it
"speaks." Following Lacan, Žižek extols the virtues of "symbolic suicide" as an act of freedom that is beyond the scope of the performative,
and hence an eruption of the "Real" into the Symbolic Order. This eruption, however, in itself does not constitute a break with the Symbolic
Order; on the contrary, it depends on the Symbolic Order's function as a
barrier between the Real and the Imaginary. Symbolic suicide, as an act
of pure freedom, is an act, furthermore, that Žižek curiously allots to the
"feminine," personified most forcefully and paradigmatically in An-

tigone's "No!"—an exclusion from and dissolution of the community
that does not proffer anything new, any "positive" program to be erected
in the void left by her declaration. This "feminine" act is thus constative,
unlike the "masculine" performative. Žižek argues that this distinction
does not repeat the activity/passivity binarism (and its assumptive gendering), but rather indicates that masculine "activity" is always already "an
escape from the abysmal dimension of the feminine *act*" and hence nothing more than a "desperate attempt to repair the traumatic incision of this
rupture."[11] Nonetheless, it would seem that the masculine trauma is an
empty space that is "filled" with the feminine "act." That is, Žižek wants
to say that the trauma is without origin, without "real" status, and without any positive content. *But* there remains a need to narrativize the
trauma, for something is recovered in the act of testifying. When this act
is designated as feminine, The Woman is reinscribed as the symptom of
man. Woman remains the "not-all" that forever exceeds man's representations of himself; and it is precisely this excess that figures as the necessary condition for man to reproduce his desire. It says nothing of
women's desire; it merely repeats the desire for desire that is produced by
a masculine imaginary.

This "feminine" is a not altogether unappealing fantasy scene with
which women might identify, for the power of what cannot be symbol-
ized (murdered) should not be underappreciated. Nonetheless, the question remains: on what phantasmatic scene *can* women's desire take a
place? If the symbolic suicide is a pure act of freedom, performed as "feminine" but in order to reproduce the desire of a masculine imaginary,
what is the other/alternative to this suicide? Would suicide's complement,
double, or other—murder—also constitute such a pure act of freedom?

Still Unrepentant

The priest must look out for false tears . . . and
putting his hand on the woman's head, he will
say the following formula: "I beseech you by
the very bitter tears, shed by our Lord and Sav-
ior Jesus Christ upon the cross for the salvation
of the world, by the burning tears shed upon
the wounds of her son by the most glorious Vir-
gin Mary his mother, on the evening of his
death, and by all the tears shed in this world by
the saints and God's elect whose eyes he wiped:

if you are innocent, weep, and if you are guilty,
weep not." It is a perfect trap . . . everything is
the mark, everything is the sign of the devil.[12]

The media have dubbed Wuornos "the damsel of death," and have
rushed in to stake claims to her story. Movie deals, book contracts, made-
for-television specials were all in the works within days of her arrest. This
rush to repetitively narrate her story resonates ironically with the nomen-
clature of the "serial murderer." Robert Ressler, the FBI agent who
coined the term, explains that it derives in part from his memories of
Saturday afternoons at the movies during his boyhood, when "serial ad-
ventures" lured him back again and again with their cliff-hanger endings.
Likening these suspense fantasies, remembered from darkened movie the-
aters, to the repeat offender's desire to make the reality of the murder
accord with his fantasy, Ressler explains: "Serial killers . . . are obsessed
with a fantasy, and they have what we must call nonfulfilled experiences
that become part of a fantasy and push them on toward the next killing.
That's the real meaning behind the term *serial killer*."[13]

This is a structure of desire that is presented as if it were pathological,
anomalous at best. Nonetheless, it is easy enough to recognize in this
description an entirely *normative* relationship between the phantasmatic
and the real from a psychoanalytic perspective, in which the "real" is an
ever-receding, elusive kernel, an "object" that is retrospectively constructed in the scene of fantasy as perpetually lost. It is constitutive of
desire to repetitively construct this lost object in order to renew itself.
In a masculine imaginary, as we understand desire in a patriarchal symbolic, desire *is* precisely this perpetual losing and refinding of an object
that is not only always already lost but, more fundamentally, *necessarily*
lost. "Woman," in this economy of desire, is the *site* that makes this *scene*
renewable. Hence the enormous popularity of the "femme fatale" can
be understood as the symptom produced by this masculine imaginary.
As one reporter writes, "[Wuornos's] story [has] set off a frenzy . . . to
cash in on what is perhaps an unprecedented saga of a highway femme
fatale."[14]

But Aileen Wuornos is no femme fatale. A persistent figure of fascination in the texts of modernity, the femme fatale, as Mary Ann Doane
describes her, is "a function of fears linked to the notions of uncon-
trollable drives, the fading of subjectivity, and the loss of conscious
agency," and her "textual eradication involves a desperate reassertion
of control on the part of the threatened male subject." Although the
femme fatale may often exceed the representations that produce her in
order to eradicate her, she is not to be mistaken, Doane cautions, as a

"heroine of modernity." Rather, she is "a symptom of male fears about feminism."[15]

Aileen Wuornos has been and no doubt will continue to be represented as a femme fatale, the handiest construct available for reintegrating her into the Symbolic Order. But if the femme fatale is a functional construct of the masculine imaginary, a representation that, at once, expresses (while producing) a patriarchal sociosymbolic order's fear of femininity and disarms that fear by disabling her, Aileen Wuornos has exceeded this representational formula. In one sense, she is this masculine imaginary's dream come true—their metaphor realized. Fulfilling that fantasy, her actions confirm the "truth" of their theory, on the one hand; but on the other, she disrupts the theory by prying open its seamless dualism and exposing its deceptive monism. Aileen Wuornos will no doubt be swiftly sacrificed to maintain the illusion of phallocratic sexual difference, but in the interim she may well serve as a kind of subject of feminism, who, unlike the femme fatale, does not succumb to upholding the patriarchal sociosymbolic.

On the hand that quite expectedly is not the one the media or the courts are playing, Aileen Wuornos's story is banal, an all-too-ordinary repetition in a culture of paranoid male fantasies that eroticize their worst nightmares. This time, however, one might say that the fantasy has crossed a certain boundary. The hallucination has been realized. Aileen Wuornos has, quite horribly, acted it out. If the fantasies worked to preclude their actualization, something has gone awry; Aileen Wuornos has violated that barrier.

Elizabeth McMahon, the psychologist who examined Wuornos for a year and a half, makes a plea to save Wuornos from the death penalty on the basis that she has the emotional development of a three- or four-year-old child. "Lee is one of the most primitive individuals I've ever met," McMahon argues: "there's a whole set of rules out there that everybody else knows about and Lee doesn't."[16] Michele Gillen, interviewing Wuornos on "Dateline," asks her if she knows that most people could not understand how a prostitute could be raped. Wuornos responds that she cannot understand how they could *not* understand, then offers some horrifyingly graphic descriptions of just how she was tortured and raped by the seven johns whom she killed.[17]

"Still unrepentant," the "Dateline" voice-over introduces another segment of the interview. Gillen, again, pressing, incredulous: "Did you say to yourself, 'I'm out of control, I'm killing people?'" "No," Wuornos answers emphatically, "I thought to myself, 'Those men are out of control. I'm sick and tired of those men out there thinking they can control us and do whatever they damn well please with our bodies and think they can get

away with it.' Because this is a male-dominant society and 'we're goin'
to—we're going to treat you the way we want to. Abuse you, treat you,
destroy you—it don't matter to us, because we can get away with doing
that.'"[18] And earlier, Wuornos opens the interview: "I'm supposed to die
because I'm a prostitute. No, I don't think so."[19] Still unrepentant.

McMahon is partially right: there *is* a whole set of rules out there that
Lee Wuornos simply cannot seem to grasp. She does not understand, for
example, that it will not bolster her defense to point out repeatedly that
she slept with hundreds, thousands, perhaps as many as a quarter of a
million men, and only killed seven of them. From Wuornos's point of
view, these statistics are proof that she is not a predatory serial killer;
according to her logic, it is not unreasonable to believe that seven out of
thousands of men would become violent during a sexual encounter. "I'm
a *prostitute*," she reiterates, as if to bring home to her audience that she
is a member of a profession in which the likelihood of encountering sexual violence is somewhat higher than what the general population of
women experience. One of the "rules" that Wuornos does not understand is that prostitutes in a patriarchy are both necessary and utterly
dispensable. Usually they are the prey, not the predators. Mostly they are
the victims, and quite often, since Jack the Ripper, they are the most likely
victims of a serial killer. As "Dateline"'s Jane Pauley points out, without
seeming to recognize an irony deeper than mere reversal: "This is a story
of *unnatural violence*. The roles are reversed. Most serial killers kill prostitutes" (my emphasis).[20]

In an interview with Geraldo Rivera, Evelina Giobbe, president of a
support group for ex-prostitutes, confirms the credibility of Wuornos's
account: "Women in prostitution are commonly sexually assaulted,
raped, battered, and robbed by customers. . . . So what we're looking at
in Lee's case . . . is that she adequately . . . used deadly force to defend
herself against a real or perceived threat. . . . So Aileen's fears are not
unfounded. Close to 2,000 men a year . . . used her in prostitution. So to
say three to six a day, that seven of them may have sexually assaulted her
fits with the stats that are in there."[21] Rivera has to take a break. He does
not return to this subject after the commercials.

From the dominant cultural perspective, Wuornos's acts have produced something like a double negative. Whereas male serial killers are
"naturally unnatural," as a woman Wuornos has committed *unnatural
unnatural acts*. The "unnaturalness" of her crimes has, of course, everything to do with the fact that she is a woman. Women do not kill, lesbian
philosopher Jeffner Allen reminds us; their passivity is a heterosexist/pa-
triarchal imperative: "The heterosexual virtue that dictates what is a
woman also prescribes *what is violence*. Violence is defended as the right
to limit life and take life that is exercised by men, for men and against

women. A woman, by definition, is not violent, and if violent, a female is not a woman."[22] The heritage of nineteenth-century criminology demands a certain repentance. In order to reinstate themselves within the category "woman," they must experience remorse. This is a symbolic mandate that Wuornos has refused. She is not only, as she insists, "not guilty" because she was acting in self-defense; she is more profoundly not guilty—she will not allow herself to be sacrificed. Wuornos's persistent refusal to repent is the theme that runs throughout interviews:

> WUORNOS: I am not—I do not regret it. I do not regret it. They were going to kill me. I killed them. That is a normal thing to do.
> GILLEN [voice-over]: Why does she have no remorse? Who is Aileen Wuornos?
> GILLEN: Do you realize that what you did was wrong?
> WUORNOS: No. . . . Here's a message for the families: You owe me. Your husband raped me violently, Mallory and Carskadden. And the other five tried, and I went through a heck of a fight to win. You owe me, not me owe you.[23]

Appealing to her newly born Christianity, Rivera almost succeeds in persuading her to repent:

> RIVERA: Why don't you say, "I'm sorry. I'm sorry I killed those men"?
> WUORNOS: I am sorry I killed those men now, now that I'm into religion. I mean, I'm sorry it happened. I wish it never would have happened.
> RIVERA: But do you understand why they say that you don't show any remorse?
> WUORNOS: Because why should I? The cops made me so mad about all the lying and everything, I can't show any re—remorse.

Rivera tries to assume the role of father confessor, which only makes Wuornos dig in deeper:

> RIVERA: But deep down—here, I'm not a cop—I want you to say you're sorry to the fam—the innocent families.
> WUORNOS: The innocent families? Those families aren't innocent.
> RIVERA: Why not?
> WUORNOS: Those men aren't innocent. I'm not giving in. Those men are not innocent.[24]

We not only escape *from* guilt, Žižek reminds us; we escape *into* it. For the assumption of guilt, the readiness to become the sacrificial victim, is what saves the Symbolic Order from "the devastating knowledge of its inconsistency, impotence, inexistence."[25] Žižek explains that the Other is an agency that functions, in its mode of "pure semblance," the mode that is the exact opposite of the Other as a "hidden agency," as a subject "supposed *not* to know."[26]

If, for Lacan, the willingness to be sacrificed guarantees the desire (and hence existence) of the Other, it is this role that Wuornos has refused. Her acts are so incomprehensible because she has resisted the temptation of the sacrifice. Like Žižek's paradigmatic example, Job, who consistently asks what the Other wants of him, rather than simply following its mandates blindly, Wuornos has precipitated that "uncanny scene in which it is not simply a subject but the thing itself which starts to talk."[27] When they ask her about *her* desire, *her* motivation, *her* intentions, she turns the questions back around on them. What she has recognized, simply, is that the Symbolic Order is not a neutral agency with an ontological consistency; the big Other has a desire of its own. And Wuornos wants to know what it wants of her.

The "scapegoat embodying sacred violence" is a substitute, a double. Žižek's theorization of the serial killer's function alludes to René Girard's theory of the sacrificial crisis, which demands a scapegoat in order to interrupt what would otherwise be an interminable cycle of reciprocal violence precipitated by mimetic rivalry. The violence of the sacrificial crisis is propelled, according to Girard, *not* by differences but by their *loss*, which "forces men into a perpetual confrontation, one that strips them of all their distinctive characteristics—in short, of their 'identities.' Language itself is put in jeopardy."[28] In order to subvert this crisis, a scapegoat is selected to intervene as a third party, whose death then terminates the mimetic rivalry. This sacrificial victim must be a carefully chosen "ambivalent" object, one that is not quite *not* like the mimetic antagonists. In other words, the scapegoat must bear a certain resemblance to the antagonists, while also remaining distinguishable in some way. For if the scapegoat is too much like the antagonist, the cycle of vengeance would be perpetuated. Nonetheless, if the scapegoat is too different, then the sacrifice would not be efficacious. Using the Old Testament example of Jacob's substitution of himself via his imposture of the favored brother Esau, Girard explains that

> sacrificial substitution implies a degree of misunderstanding. Its vitality as an institution depends on its ability to conceal the displacement upon which the rite is based. It must never lose sight entirely, however, of the original object, or cease to be aware of the act of transference from that object to the surrogate victim; without that awareness no substitution can take place and the sacrifice loses all efficacy.[29]

Thus the sacrificial substitution might be understood as a *misrecognition* that takes the form of (appears as) a recognition. And the intervening "third party," the sacrificial victim, is never the *object* of the sacrificial rite; on the contrary, this "object" is nothing more than/other than the subject(s)—the antagonist(s)—himself/themselves, who are themselves nothing more than each other's doubles. In the mimetic economy of "sacred violence," then, two who are the "same" maintain their fictive distinctiveness (and thus autonomy) by erecting a third party to absorb the violence that would otherwise be directed at themselves. In short, the scapegoat serves the function of a symptom. Without "woman" as man's symptom, men are left without this object to exchange and are confronted with the commerce between themselves. How altogether fittingly ironic that a hitchhiking lesbian prostitute, Aileen Wuornos, has not only made this traffic in women apparent, but has also turned the brutality of this exchange back onto the primary players.

According to Girard, there is no violence that is not implicated in this "sacred" economy, and, furthermore, it is readily apparent that sexuality partakes of this violence. Not only, however, do sexuality and violence share certain common characteristics, such as the tendency to "fasten upon surrogate objects" if the original object is inaccessible, or the accumulation of "energy that sooner or later bursts forth,"[30] but they also share the same structure. Girard does not quite come to this latter conclusion explicitly, but it is everywhere implicit in his analysis.

What is left unarticulated in *Violence and the Sacred* is the gendering of violence itself, and the heterosexual imperative that compels it. One thus finds Girard attending to women in such special categories as in his discussion of culturally ambivalent responses to menstruation. Here he raises the question of whether there is not "some half-suppressed desire to place the blame for all forms of violence on women," even going so far as to suggest that a "monopoly [has been] established that is clearly detrimental to the female sex."[31] He nonetheless fails to recognize that this supposition is not confined to various symbolizations of female biological processes, but that indeed, the sacrificial crisis with its resolution through substitution is a virtual paradigm for the structure of "desire itself," a Desire that holds a monopoly in a phallocentric sociosymbolic.

The correspondence between Girard's theory of violence and Lacan's mirror stage reveals some interesting convergences on this question of the production of The Woman as symptom. In his early essay "Motifs du Crime Paranoïaque," Lacan wrote about Christine and Lea Papin, the infamous "murderers of Le Mans":

> For [Christine and Lea Papin] a common metaphor of hate, "I'll tear his eyes out," became reality. Public reaction to the crime is evident in the application of the maximum penalty. It is clear that the adage used by those who

fear psychology, "to understand is to forgive," is only applicable within certain societal limits and that outside these limits to understand is to condemn.[32]

On the basis of this "secret shared in common by . . . female crimes" Catherine Clément argues that "Lacan makes the discovery that becomes the source of *all* his subsequent thought."[33] This discovery is the mirror stage, the foundational moment in Lacanian thought, which is based on his lifelong fascination with female criminals—specifically female "paranoiacs" whose violent acting out manifested a repressed homosexuality. What was the "secret" shared by these women that led Lacan to theorize the mirror stage? Clément offers some intriguing suggestions: "the danger of too much closeness," the possibly disastrous consequences of "one person's identification with another," the notion of a "perfect love" that will inevitably explode in aggressivity when forced to "confront the Other."[34] From these cases, Clément concludes, Lacan must have observed that the "correct distance is the *opposite* of the feminine" (my emphasis).[35]

The negotiation of the "correct distance" is, let us not forget, what the mirror stage both is meant to accomplish *and* forever fails to achieve. If this is the moment when the child assumes a (fictive) identity, which will forever serve him as the shield that permits access into the Symbolic Order, it is an identity that is predicated on a misrecognition of himself as whole, autonomous, complete, and separate. It is this "jubilant assumption" of an identity that serves as a barrier between the Symbolic and the Imaginary. This identity is "orthopedic" because it enables the child to function within the illusion that "reality" is the real. It is an "achievement" that is necessarily always already *not* achieved. In the mirror stage, the child distances "himself" from the other by misrecognizing himself as a separate "self." The Other (the Symbolic Order) comes into existence for the child along with the mirror stage because this is the moment when the child disavows that he is lacking (incomplete).[36] Thus, paradoxically, the child's identity becomes an object of belief that is predicated on an *identification* with the other, who is aggressively incorporated into the illusion of one's separateness. But because the other is an absence, separation can never be more than a precarious distance that threatens to close up and engulf the subject, rendering the boundaries between "self" and "other" inchoate. In the mirror stage, as Clément points out, the child "in obtaining its identity . . . in fact only manages to achieve identification."[37]

Although Lacan posits the mirror stage as a universal psychic phenomenon, we might pause to wonder why this most critical moment in the child's psychic formation came to him by way of observing the "secrets" of female paranoiacs. As Clément points out, it was the "inseparability" of these women that led to their violent actions. The mirror stage is structured around a fundamental tautology; for the dangerous proximity that inevitably erupts into a violence that will characterize all subsequent desire was *already* gendered as feminine. The violence of identification that the mirror stage presumably produces is a reconstruction based on the observation of female criminals whose actions would become the paradigm for a generalized theory of femininity per se. Whereas male criminals would always be classified as anomalies, departures from the norm, female criminals would become the rule derived from these exceptions.

I return to the young Jacques Lacan, working on his thesis for accreditation in psychiatry, by chance observing a remarkable crime that would fascinate him throughout his career. In the small provincial town of Le Mans, France, in the year 1933, the year that Hitler became absolute dictator of Germany and Freud published "On Femininity," Christine and Lea Papin were quietly performing their domestic duties when they suddenly erupted into an outburst of violence unparalleled in the annals of French criminology. Madame Lancelin and her daughter came home to find their house in darkness and reprimanded their maids for blowing a fuse while ironing. Christine and Lea were later found huddled together in their garret bedroom; their employers' bodies were found

> lying stretched out on the floor . . . frightfully mutilated. Mademoiselle Lancelin's corpse was lying face downward, head bare, coat pulled up and with her knickers down, revealing deep wounds in the buttocks and multiple cuts in the calves. Madame Lancelin's body was lying on its back. The eyes had disappeared, she seemed no longer to have a mouth, and all the teeth had been knocked out. The walls and door were covered with splashes of blood to a height of more than seven feet. On the floor [were] found fragments of bone and teeth, one eye, hairpins, a handbag, a key ring, an untied parcel, numerous bits of white, decorated porcelain, and a coat button.[38]

The leftist newspaper *L'Humanitie* championed the maids' revolt against the oppressive bourgeoisie. Anarchists baptized the sisters as "angels of the revolution." It was two years before the formation of the Leftist Popular party. And it was a time in which the "nature" of female sexuality was at the center of debates within intellectual circles. The young Lacan joined the endless stream of commentators on the crime to diagnose Christine and Lea as a "délire à deux," a paranoid disorder that is "among the most ancient recognized types of psychosis." Lacan dubbed the murders in Le Mans a "social masterpiece."[39]

In his article on the maids published in *Minotaure*, Lacan compared the Papin sisters' crime to that of Aimée, the subject of his 1932 thesis, "De la psychose paranoïaque." Aimée also had a sister with whom she constituted a "délire à deux." Her crime was much less noteworthy than that of the Papin sisters: Aimée had attacked a famous Parisian actress as she entered the theater. Madame Z had blocked the blow from Aimée's knife, suffering only two cut tendons in her fingers, and declined to press charges. Aimée was sent to Sainte-Anne, and her official diagnosis was "persecutory insanity based on interpretation and with megalomaniac tendencies and an erotomaniac substrate."[40] It would be through his observations and study of the "female paranoiac" Aimée that Lacan would discover a "novel form of syntax, which enlists its own peculiar means of comprehension for the purpose of affirming the community of mankind."[41]

An aspiring writer herself, Aimée had written poetry and prose. Her attack on the actress was apparently motivated by the belief that Madame Z was in conspiracy with a novelist who threatened to expose Aimée's private literary life. Lacan wanted to compose a thesis that would expound the unconscious meaning of Aimée's paranoia. He theorized that "the figures of persecutory females were surrogates for a feminine imago."[42] Aimée's elder sister, as well as her mother, were the "original" imagoes, delusions that were later displaced onto other women, culminating in the attack on the actress. The "erotomaniac" component of her paranoid disorder, Lacan demonstrated, "went hand in hand with a homosexual dimension. Aimée became attached to famous women because they represented her *ego ideal*."[43]

In the case of the Papin sisters, there too a certain "repressed homosexuality" was the final explanation for their violent behavior. When Lacan learned of the "murders in Le Mans," he understood at once, argues Clément, that the separation in prison of the French maids, Christine and Lea Papin, caused the delirium of Christine, the older sister, "just as the close relationship between the two sisters was the cause of the crime."[44] The sisters' incestuous desire, as I have discussed at length elsewhere, was the obsessive focus of the trial proceedings during the height of the "woman question" in psychoanalysis.[45] If "repressed homosexuality" was the French law's final explanation for the unprecedented violence of the Papin sisters, it was not, for Lacan, the first explanation for the mystery of a distinctly feminine paranoia. As Clément points out:

> The first explanation involved language: this trail is already familiar to us. It begins with words and leads to action. In order for a paranoid crime to be committed, a metaphor must enter reality. "I'll tear her eyes out"—this is ha-

tred speaking, hatred at its most harmless. But when the metaphor is realized and the barrier between fantasy, imagination, and reality is eliminated, most people, Lacan tells us, react to the magnitude of the deed: their reaction is "ambivalent, double-edged, a product of the emotional contagion of the crime and the demand for punishment raised by public opinion."[46]

The trail from words to actions, from metaphor to deed, is one that is traveled by "madmen," "mystics," and "criminals." It is the path followed by one for whom the "talking cure" no longer suffices. The psychotic is one who takes things literally. Lacan bases his distinction between neurosis and psychosis on the subject's relationship to metaphor: the psychotic believes the voices, whereas the neurotic only believes *in* the voices.[47]

Psychoanalysis takes place within the scope of the performative. Its very kernel, as Žižek reminds us, is in "the dimension of language as speech *act*," for is it not "confined to this dimension by the very fact that it is a *talking cure*, an attempt to reach and transform the real of the symptom solely by means of words, i.e., without having recourse to an immediate operation on the body . . . ?"[48]

And yet there is some small particle of difference to which we cling, some distinction that we hold on to between words and acts, between representations and "the things themselves." Furthermore, it is precisely these "impossible" acts that constitute the "real"; hence Lacan's formulation that the "real is impossible." For Lacan, suicide is the only act that is more than a recollection, more than an *effect* of truth. It is the one "pure act" that is a deed, not a word. As Žižek demonstrates through the work of the Italian film director Rossellini, suicide is the " 'impossible' act of freedom beyond the scope of a performative."[49]

"I'll tear her eyes out": metaphor enters reality when the Papin sisters gouge out the eyes of their mistresses. For Freud, the edifice of psychoanalysis was built on his case studies of female hysterics, whose acting out was performed on their own bodies. For Lacan, female paranoiacs, whose language constituted a different syntax, and who acted out their family romances through violent assaults on the bodies of other women, was the cornerstone of his theory.

If Aimée was "inseparable" from a series of feminine "imagoes" that originated with her mother, her displacements onto other figures of threatening females, Clément argues, were what "probably . . . allowed her to stop short of murder," whereas Christine and Lea were two sisters who, "because they were brought up together, never had to face up to the existence of the Other, man."[50] In both of these cases of "délire à deux," there would be found the "clue" that the psychoanalyst would have been looking for—"the masculine dimension always present in the paranoiac."[51]

Both the French legal prosecutors and the analysts called in to deliver their opinions on the sisters' sanity made much of Christine Papin's statement that in another life she believed she had been, or would be, her sister's husband. Aimée imagined herself being "received as a bridegroom," who "shall go to see [his] fiancée."[52] Lacan's conception of the mirror stage would seem to be built on the observations of the dangerous proximity of women to *other* women; and furthermore, of a proximity, closeness, or inseparability *between* certain women—women who repressed their desire for women. Thus the mirror stage, the cornerstone of Lacan's conception of the formation of (split) subjectivity, is grounded in the heterosexual presumption. If the "proper distance" is the "opposite" of the feminine, "difference," it would seem, cannot be obtained by two who are alike. In the specular economy of the mirror stage, "same-sex" desire can only be thought of as resemblance—two who are "alike" are terrifying doubles, twinned copies of an ideal (ego). And it was precisely this doubling—the women's *proximity*—that was theorized as the cause of their aggression.

The theory of slight variation among women—the notion that all women are basically alike, which was so prevalent in the discourses of nineteenth- and early twentieth-century art, sexology, and criminology—would seem to have in some sense been verified by Lacan's observations of Aimée and Christine and Lea. This particular masculine imaginary not only leaves its trace in Lacan's mirror stage; it is also reproduced there and perpetuates a heterosexual imperative.

Délire à Deux?

> People are going to try to make [our love] into
> a "sexual perversion," but it's not like that at
> all. It's a soul binding. We're like Jonathan and
> David in the Bible.[53]
> (Arlene Pralle, Wuornos's adoptive mother)

Not surprisingly, the "inseparable" bond that Aileen Wuornos had with her lover, Tyria Moore, the woman for whose sake she confessed to the murders, has been implicated as the "cause" of her criminality.[54] Prompted perhaps by her legal advisers, Wuornos has eschewed the label "lesbian" and has insisted that her relationship with Moore was a spiritual bond. But Wuornos has not abandoned her devotion to women.

During her incarceration, she has formed another "inseparable" relationship, one that has been represented within the relatively safe confines of a mother-daughter bond.

A born-again Christian who has legally adopted convicted murderer Lee Wuornos, Arlene Pralle fervently believes that in Wuornos she has found her soul sister; the bond between them surpasses any love she has known before. Pralle's dream—that Wuornos's appeal will be successful and she will be released to live with Pralle forever on her horse farm northwest of Ocala, Florida—is not likely to be realized. From her intensive-care hospital bed, recovering from a riding injury, Pralle emphasizes that her will to live has everything to do with Lee: "I'm the one person Lee's bonded with in her whole life, and without me she'd have nothing."[55]

Too much closeness? The perfect scene for a "délire à deux"? But Wuornos has not played by the rules. Her "feminine imagoes" are not the targets of her violence. She does not understand how the Symbolic Order works. No condensation, no displacement. Perhaps Aileen Wuornos does not "have" an unconscious, or at least not a paranoid one. "They were going to kill me, I killed them," she says. She will not relinquish her Old Testament judgment, even though she has ostensibly found Jesus. McMahon, her psychologist, says that Wuornos cannot be held accountable for her decision (which she later reversed) to ask for the death sentence. McMahon claims that Wuornos does not understand death, does not grasp that if she were put to death she would not be here anymore. Why, then, did she change her mind and decide that she wanted to live after all? Why is she asking for appeals, fighting for her life, claiming that had anyone been through what she went through "in those woods . . . with these scum," she would have to conclude that "this woman deserves *nothing* [no punishment]."[56] Perhaps Wuornos knows more about death than most of us do. Maybe she has made a passage *beyond* death and has arrived, ironically, only at the point of death, at a place where she can assume her life.

Initiating the feminist defense of Wuornos, Phyllis Chesler stops short of proclaiming Wuornos the leader of a "feminist liberation army," but she admits to identifying with her deeply, understanding what motivated her actions. The feminist case for Wuornos's appeal, however, will not proceed on these terms, will not pursue the question "What would it mean if women started to defend themselves?"[57] Rather, the case is being made for her as a deeply disturbed victim of sexual abuse. The appeal will rest on the very pathology that reproduces the social conditions in which Aileen Wuornos performed her desperate actions.

Women may kill their children in the throes of postpartum depression;

they may kill their lovers or husbands in fits of jealous passion. Sometimes, recent evidence has begun to allow, women kill their batterers,
even occasionally when they are soundly sleeping. In a few rare cases,
these women have even been acquitted, when "battered women's syndrome" can be effectively diagnosed. Passion and/or pathology have been
the key historical constructs for explaining, and containing, women's aggression. Women like Aileen Wuornos are not supposed to exist.

Wuornos is undoubtedly a victim of years of sexual abuse. Leo
Pittman, Wuornos's father, was a habitual sex offender who hanged himself in prison where he was serving time for raping a seven-year-old girl.
In 1969, the year of her father's suicide, Wuornos was sent by her grand-
parents to a home for unwed mothers, where she was forced to give up
the child that she claimed was conceived in a rape. At the age of fourteen,
Wuornos began prostituting. Up to this point, Wuornos's story is tragi-
cally ordinary.

Despite the evidence that "Dateline"'s interviewers have uncovered,
which all but confirms Wuornos's story that Richard Mallory, her first
victim, was a habitual and violent sex offender, this "truth" is not going
to set Wuornos free. No amount of "evidence" has the power to counter
the systematic violence of white racist patriarchy. As Victoria
Brownworth reminds us:

> Over 84 percent of the men and women on Death Row were convicted of
> killing white victims—regardless of the race of the perpetrator. The majority
> were also convicted of killing men. In case after case before the US Supreme
> Court, it has been determined that the "value" society places on the victim is
> the factor that determines sentencing.[58]

Sexualized trauma, in particular, is an ineffective defense. Traumas, we
believe, are in the past; when these histories are acted out in the present,
"time" itself undergoes a radical disruption. The subject who repeats
them might win some sympathy, but the actions themselves are condemned, and she pays the penalty for upsetting the fiction of a chro-
nological procession.

Aileen Wuornos is "guilty" under the law; but she refuses to enact the
"guilt" that secures the fiction of law's justice. She confesses to the acts
but is still unrepentant. And although we might find her incredible when
she insists that her "past" has nothing to do with the crimes she has committed,[59] there is something fascinating, and unnerving, in her implacable
self-defense, her disregard for a linear narrative of a life's trajectory that
begins with victimization and ends in retaliation.

By refusing to accede to the narrative of her "traumatic past," Aileen

Wuornos repudiates not just a personal history but also the story of "vengeance," with its ever-threatening promise of repetition, that instigates the sacrificial crisis. She will not, in short, identify herself as man's symptom. Wuornos is caught between the logic of the law, which, as Peggy Phelan points out, "seeks to draw a line between the truth of the real and the fiction of the lie," and the psychoanalytic discourse of the symptom, "whose logic operates within the always unbalanced economies of displacement, disavowal, and the unconcious yes."[60] The only chance she seems to have is to appeal to her traumatic past. If the appellate courts can be convinced that Wuornos's actions are attributable to "post–traumatic shock syndrome," she may stand a chance of being delivered from death. This appeal, however, will not effect a decision that the phantasmatic repetition of her sexual abuse justifies her claim to self-defense. On the contrary, it will even more powerfully assert that Wuornos's perception of a "clear and present danger" was not *real*.

Finally, it is the question of what is being *repeated* that is at stake here. Wuornos killed not once, not twice, but *seven* times. She killed serially; serial killers repeat: she is a serial killer. The law will undoubtedly prefer witnessing her wounds opening, closing, reopening, reclosing—the beat, beat, beating of her personal, tragic trauma—to recognizing a cultural, collective trauma, a systematic, normative violence in which straight, white, middle-aged "everymen" repetitively assume their right of access to women's bodies. Wuornos knows this: "I say it's the principle," she says, "they say it's the number. Self-defense is self-defense, I don't care how many times it is."[61]

We all know how it is supposed to work: "the exchange of women derives from guilt; and their guilt—women's guilt—comes from the transgression of this exchange. . . . *The woman must circulate, not put into circulation*" (author's emphasis).[62] As an "unrepentant" prostitute, Wuornos circulated herself; and as a lesbian, she simultaneously insisted on controlling the terms of that exchange. The historical conflation of the prostitute and the lesbian, both of whom have been signified in patriarchy under the sign of transgressive sexuality,[63] returns to haunt a masculine commerce in the figure of Aileen Wuornos. By occupying *both* positions simultaneously, Wuornos has forced a recognition of this paradoxical commerce, in which the "woman" is phantasmatically constructed as an object that must submit to its status as a "real" object of exchange while failing to disclose the object's function as a cipher that holds open a space for the renewal of male subjectivity.

What happens when a woman refuses to be the symptom of man? It is an impossible position to occupy within this sociosymbolic order.

And yet Wuornos has exceeded the representational. She bears witness to that unseen other/scene—the mimetic rivalry between men acted out on the bodies of women. And it is for making this homosocial order visible, for calling its terms to account, that Aileen Wuornos waits on death row.

9

Afterword: Zero Degree Deviancy—
Lesbians Who Kill

> Murder is where history and crime inter-
> sect. . . . Murder establishes the ambiguity of
> the lawful and the unlawful.[1]
>   (Michel Foucault)

In *Lesbians Who Kill*, Deb Margolin's wry philosophical bent creates a dissident space of mimicry for Split Britches' butch/femme performers, Peggy Shaw and Lois Weaver, to play out their seductions. May (Weaver) and June (Shaw) abandon their house because it attracts lightning. While they wait out a thunderstorm in their car, they divine ways to kill time. When they "make time" with men, their eyes are as "open as bulletholes looking right at" each other as they kiss the men they dream of killing. Wanting to be remembered, they "kiss for memory . . . before fall[ing] into history."[2] Their kiss marks the hope of being together in the impossible present tense.

History is being made all around them while their desire grows in the garden where May plants seeds in the middle of the night when she cannot sleep. By the railroad tracks they pick wild raspberries in the dark. Crouched down in the "mouth of an animal" where the raspberries are hidden, May sucks June's fingers bruised by the brambles. All of this reads like a dream for June, but May insists that she never dreams, and June tries to believe her.

Lesbians Who Kill carves out a space in which the impossible-real of May and June's desire is an article of faith that can almost be believed for the few hours that we are drawn into their performance. Almost, but always not quite. Something is always obstructing their/our vision. Vision itself is a barrier reminding us that desire is always the desire of the Other. These lovers' desire is fueled by their rage against the repetitions of history into which they are inevitably falling. They kill time by playing a word game—"looks like/is like." It works like this:

> You pick a thing, and then you think of all the things that look like it or are like it, and if the other person doesn't understand why you think that, they can ask you for an explanation. And if you can make any sense out of it for them, they

lose! You have to tell them: does it *look* like the original thing, or is it like that thing in some *invisible* way? And if you're on to something that they couldn't see, they lose! The minute it makes sense to them. They lose everything! And then you start up all over again.

Losing the game is the promise of continuance. The failure to see, and thus to know, insures their relationship. May and June depend on accepting each other's explanations on faith. The game both perpetuates their desire and demonstrates how it is constituted. Each pushes the other in turn to acknowledge her insufficiencies; and with the acceptance of failure, the hope of reciprocity and recognition is continually renewed. The always-broken promise of the game is the promise of being, for the game always breaks down when the relationship between the word and the thing surpasses resemblance ("looks like"), which is intelligible to the senses, and depends on accepting the other's inexpressible interiority ("is like"). "Funny how one thing resembles another," May tells June. But resemblance is not really so funny; getting beyond it is the goal of the game.

Resemblance is the world of "reality" from which May and June outlaw themselves. Within it, they *are* outlaws. What is there in this world of simple division to separate them from the pathological discourse that displaces women's aggression onto the lesbian? How can they know that if they leave their fantasies they will not be apprehended by the law that has put out an all points bulletin for two lesbian killers, one blond, one brunette, who have left their traces on the Florida highways, "each signpost along the way, the body of a middle-aged white man riddled with bullets." May and June identify with Aileen Wuornos, the real killer in Florida who has been sentenced to death and labeled the "first female serial killer" by the FBI, and her lover, Tyria Moore, who was granted clemency for entrapping Wuornos to confess. May and June think they may be just as "guilty," for they have no alibi. They too are one blond and one brunette; they too are lesbians. What more evidence, in a "reality" ordered by resemblance, might be necessary to convict them? They are, they know, always already the guilty ones in this symbolic order.

They can dream, however, of differences that multiply and affirm. The darkness gives them a reprieve from the incarcerating light of mimesis. They fantasize about murder but choose instead to make poetry. "I'm not a poet, I'm a killer . . . don't get them mixed up," June says in one of her performances for May. But they do get mixed up. Metaphor can go either way. Resemblance can be deadly. "Resemblance," Foucault writes, "makes a unique assertion, always the same: This thing, that thing, yet another thing is something else." Resemblance negates, denies, and insists on the unity of the One. But similitude, the affirmation of the simulacrum, "multiplies different affirmations, which dance together, tilting and tumbling over one another."[3]

Lesbians Who Kill takes place in only one space—the front and back seats of the car that protects them from the storm. Like Hamlet, they depend on their fantasies to transport them outside this "nutshell," where they might command infinite space. May insists that she never dreams, and June doubts her. But they are not the mistresses of their own fantasies; they too are invaded by bad dreams, which are not phantasmatic but the stuff of their everyday waking reality. The voice of this reality enters their refuge by way of the car radio, which intermittently broadcasts reports:

> Willis, who has been serving her sentence at a state prison . . . outlining some of her reasons for ordering the killing. ". . . I'm asking that you place yourself in my shoes, knowing you had to lay awake each night knowing that your children have been molested by the man that is their father and your husband."

They have spent most of their time as escapees fantasizing about murder and playing word games to pass the time, as children do on a long car ride. The final game that they play is a fantasy about their own death, and how many times it can be repeated.

May is thinking about math, about "number[s] for everything, . . . a number of times . . . a number of times . . . that we'll do things and say things . . . let's say . . . how many times we'll kiss":

JUNE: How many times we'll fight . . .
MAY: How many times it'll rain . . .
JUNE: How many times we'll say How Many Times.
MAY: Before we . . .
JUNE: . . . die.

May contemplates the longest division, dividing a number by zero— "like putting a white sheet over the number." June asks, "Like it's dead?" May responds, "Yeah, like it died in the hospital." There is not enough time for June to count the hairs on May's head (they too have a number); but there is time for June to divide May by zero, cover her in white, and lay her to rest. June asks if there is "a number how many times [she] can do that." May answers, "Yes, . . . but I don't know . . ." June: "You don't know?" May: "No . . . I don't know." This failure to know keeps them from falling into history. It is the promise of infinity that they embrace in a passionate desire for the perpetual present.

This final game, the fantasy of the indeterminacy of their own deaths, is figured through the act of division. In a performance that constantly refers to, but never names, the "real" lesbian serial killer—Aileen Wuornos—who circulates throughout the performance as an absent model, this emphasis on division in the end might be thought of in terms of the Platonic theory of Ideas, which, as Gilles Deleuze describes it, is in the order of division:

> The Platonic project emerges only if we refer back to the method of division, for this method is not one dialectical procedure among others. . . . One could initially say that it consists of dividing a genus into opposing species in order to place the thing under investigation within the correct species. . . . But this is only the superficial aspect of the division, its ironic aspect.[4]

The real goal of division, Deleuze argues, is the erection of a hierarchy, "selection from among lines of succession, distinguishing between the [true and false] claimants, distinguishing the pure from the impure, the authentic from the inauthentic."[5] It is a secondary irony that characterizes Platonic division. Deleuze explains this other irony in the example of the *Phaedrus*: there the myth of the circulation of souls (a closed system) tells the foundational narrative of "true love," which belongs to "those souls who have seen much and thus have many dormant but revivable memories; while sensual souls, forgetful and narrow of vision, are denounced as false claimants."[6] It is these false claimants who occupy the simulacra, "built on a dissimilitude, implying a perversion, an essential turning away."[7] Unlike the true claimants, the icons, copies, or good images, who are authorized by resemblance, the "false claimants" are not just likenesses. On the contrary, the false claimant, or simulacrum, lays her claim "by means of an aggression, an insinuation, a subversion, 'against the father' and without passing through the Idea."[8]

The simulacrum is postlapsarian, constituting a break in time, a rupture in history, a difference not of degree but of kind. Deleuze summarizes this theological passage: "God made man in His own image and to resemble Him [the good copy], but through sin, man has lost the resemblance while retaining the image [the simulacrum]."[9] If we are to understand in this passage the curse that falls on the false claimant, who comes to embody an "evil power," it is also here that desire is born in this fall, this turning away that is perversion of the good and the true. And it is Woman who effects this passage, through her seduction, interrupting the resemblance between man and his model, insinuating herself everywhere and instigating a brotherhood of rivalry. Or so the story goes of how women brought evil into the world. Without this narrative, and its countless incarnations, one would have to create a different system of values, for life and for art, that did not raise reproduction to the pinnacle of these successive claims.

The simulacrum comes into being after the Fall, or through the mirror stage, where aggressivity becomes constitutive of desire and where secondary identifications will henceforth be based on the oscillation between insufficiency and mastery. The simulacrum's model is the Other, and desire has become the desire of the Other. The chaos of what Deleuze calls the "Eternal Return" reigns, and the "overthrow of the icons or the subversion of the world of representation is decided."[10]

By the end of the performance, May and June have assembled quite an impressive collection of guns. They are prepared to use them, if necessary, to protect their love. Although they never emerge from the car, never enter into the storm shooting, the possibility remains tangible. In this last scene, May appears to succumb to the fantasy of June's dividing her by zero and covering her over with a white sheet. Have they given up the fantasy of freedom? Not quite. Lacan writes:

> Everyone knows that if zero appears in the denominator, the value of the fraction no longer has meaning, but assumes by convention what mathematicians call an infinite value. In a way, this is one of the stages in the constitution of the subject. In so far as the primary signifier is pure non-sense, it becomes the bearer of the infinitization of the value of the subject, not open to all meanings, but abolishing them all, which is different.[11]

Peggy Phelan elaborates: "Different too is the distinction between the abolishment of meaning and the abolishment of value. For while metaphor can be understood as the erosion and loss of 'original' or 'singular' meaning it does not follow that this erosion negates value. On the contrary, metaphor makes value. And perhaps nowhere more meaningfully than in the metaphoric values of sexual difference."[12]

Lacan explains that this is why one cannot understand "the relation of alienation without introducing the word freedom," for what, "in effect, grounds, in the meaning and radical non-meaning of the subject, the function of freedom, is strictly speaking this signifier that kills all meanings."[13] This non-sensical signifier that kills all meanings and thus permits the foundational narrative of freedom is, of course, the phallus. The phallus, like the zero, is an integer—a whole number, complete in itself, entire, from the Latin *untouched*. The zero, as an integer, partakes of all these qualities but distinguishes itself from other "whole" numbers in that it signifies nothing. Its referent, if it could be said to have one at all, is a lack. If one is divided by any other integer, there is either diminishment or amplification, both of which produce differences. Dividing by zero, on the other hand, merely produces an infinity of reproductions of the Same.

Lacan reminds us that this signifier, which bears "the infinitization of the value of the subject," should not lead us to conclude that interpretation is therefore open to all meanings. This "non-sense" signifier "does not mean that interpretation is in itself nonsense."[14]

May and June understand these limitations. They know that there are only so many times that something can be repeated. This knowledge, however, does not preclude their desire for infinite returns. Nor does the reassurance that the phallus circulates without touching ground satisfy them. Perhaps the phallus reminds them too much of the ball of lightning that once got into their house and rolled around the top of the stove, sink, and kitchen cabinet. "Smelling hot, looking for somewhere to land. May said it was looking for [them]." That was when they "got smart" and decided to sit in their car. In their desire, they act out a psychic economy in which *no one* "has" the phallus. But they cannot help noticing that in the world of "reality" most people believe that this phallus belongs to men, and that men, who are psychically enjoined, doomed perhaps, to attempt constantly to represent it, seize the women where they believe the phallus is embodied.

So May and June keep their guns loaded. June does not divide May by zero. Instead, she ends the performance with this fantasy: "I'd love to watch her *really* kill somebody . . . Kill somebody by the railroad tracks in the wind while the trains went by, somebody with a beard of thorns and a crotch as soft and bitter as an unripe raspberry. Y'all know anybody like that?" Who might this "somebody" be? Let us hope that it is not someone who merely resembles the One.

May and June know that they are the false claimants, the sensual souls who introduce doubt into the conception of models and their copies. They know that they are "fallen women," but they like where they have landed. They reinhabit the "femme fatale" with a difference. The performance opens with a lip-sync parody of the classic film noir *Deception*: Shaw's Claude Raines is taken by surprise by Weaver's Bette Davis, who confronts him with the gun he bought her for protection. He treats her like a child, or a hysterical woman, and demands that she hand over the gun: "Give me that nonsensical object! I've seen this kind of thing before. Give it to me!" Failing to secure the promise that she wants from him—"I'll swear nothing! I'll do what I please, see whom I please, say what I please"—May kills him.

The "nonsensical" object can indeed change hands. Becoming the phallus, in this case, fulfills its threatening potential. In making woman embody the phallus man wagers that he might be either reassured or murdered. *Lesbians Who Kill* both reminds him of that bargain's perils and hopes for a place to play that is indifferent to it.

Notes

Preface

1. Michel Foucault, "Prison Talk," in *Power/Knowledge: Selected Interviews and Other Writings 1972–1977*, ed. Colin Gordon, trans. Colin Gordan et al. (New York: Pantheon Books, 1980), p. 40.

2. Roland Barthes, *The Pleasure of the Text*, trans. Richard Miller (New York: Hill and Wang, 1975), p. 32.

3. Diana Fuss, "Introduction," in *Inside/Out: Lesbian Theories, Gay Theories* (New York: Routledge, 1991), pp. 3 and 6.

4. Judith Butler, *Gender Trouble: Feminism and the Subversion of Identity* (New York: Routledge, 1990), p. x.

5. Mary Ann Doane, *Femmes Fatales: Feminism, Film Theory, Psychoanalysis* (London: Routledge, 1991), p. 270.

6. Julia Kristeva, "About Chinese Women," in *The Kristeva Reader*, ed. Toril Moi (New York: Columbia University Press, 1986), p. 149.

7. Teresa de Lauretis, "Film and the Visible," in *How Do I Look? Queer Film and Video*, ed. Bad Object-Choices (Seattle: Bay Press, 1991), pp. 223–276. Quotation is on p. 254.

8. Radicalesbians, "The Woman Identified Woman," in *Radical Feminism*, ed. Anne Koedt, Ellen Levine, and Anita Rapone (New York: Quadrangle, 1973), p. 240.

Chapter 1
Introduction: The Paradox of Prohibition

1. Cited by Jeffrey Weeks, in *Sex, Politics and Society: The Regulation of Sexuality since 1800* (London: Longman, 1981), p. 105.

2. Ibid.

3. Havelock Ellis, "Sexual Inversion in Women," in *Studies in the Psychology of Sex*, vol. 2 (Philadelphia: F. A. Davis Company, 1904), p. 124. Ellis's documentation of homosexuality among women in non-European countries is extensive. Indeed a large proportion of his text and footnotes are given over to reporting instances of homosexuality among women outside the circle of white, European patriarchy. Although Ellis's ostensible purpose in these citations is to point out that lesbianism is not abnormal but rather a common and frequent practice worldwide, this documentation effectively produces a racially marked image of the lesbian as distinctly nonwhite.

4. Lillian Faderman, *Surpassing the Love of Men: Romantic Friendship and Love between Women from the Renaissance to the Present* (New York: William Morrow and Company, 1981), p. 154.

5. Weeks, *Sex, Politics and Society*, p. 105.

6. David F. Greenberg, *The Construction of Homosexuality* (Chicago: University of Chicago Press, 1988), p. 16.

7. Weeks, *Sex, Politics and Society*, p. 105.

8. Louis Crompton, "The Myth of Lesbian Impunity," *Journal of Homosexuality* 6, nos. 1–2 (1980–1981): 11–25.

9. Ruthann Robson, *Lesbian (Out)law: Survival under the Rule of Law* (Ithaca, N.Y.: Firebrand Books, 1992), pp. 31–32.

10. Ibid., p. 41.

11. Ellis, "Sexual Inversion," pp. 121–122.

12. The notion that women are vacant, self-absorbed, undifferentiated, and therefore deceptive and dangerous is legion in Western discourses. This conception of women crosses over a number of historical periods. See, for example, Eva C. Keuls, *The Reign of the Phallus: Sexual Politics in Ancient Athens* (New York: Harper and Row, 1985); Ian Maclean, *The Renaissance Notion of Woman* (Cambridge: Cambridge University Press, 1985); Bram Dijkstra, *Idols of Perversity: Fantasies of Feminine Evil in Fin-de-Siècle Culture* (New York: Oxford University Press, 1986); Nina Auerbach, *Woman and the Demon: The Life of a Victorian Myth* (Cambridge: Harvard University Press, 1982); Otto Weininger, *Sex and Character* (New York: G. P. Putnam's Sons, 1906), for different readings of fantasies of feminine evil.

13. Ellis, "Sexual Inversion," p. 122.

14. Ibid., p. 134.

15. Luce Irigaray, *Speculum of the Other Woman*, trans. Gillian C. Gill (Ithaca: Cornell University Press, 1985), p. 27.

16. Monique Wittig, "One Is Not Born a Woman," in *The Straight Mind and Other Essays* (Boston: Beacon, 1992), p. 12.

17. Simone de Beauvoir, *The Second Sex*, trans. and ed. H. M. Parshley (New York: Random House, 1952).

18. George Chauncey, Jr., "From Sexual Inversion to Homosexuality: Medicine and the Changing Conception of Female Deviance," *Salmagundi* 58–59 (Fall 1982–Winter 1983): 132.

19. Crompton, "Myth of Lesbian Impunity," p. 20.

20. Luce Irigaray, *This Sex Which Is Not One*, trans. Catherine Porter (Ithaca: Cornell University Press, 1985), p. 69.

21. Marilyn Frye, *The Politics of Reality: Essays in Feminist Theory* (Freedom, Calif.: The Crossing Press, 1983), p. 173.

22. In "God and the *Jouissance* of The Woman"(in *Feminine Sexuality: Jacques Lacan and the école freudienne*, ed. Juliet Mitchell and Jacqueline Rose, trans. Jacqueline Rose [London: Macmillan, 1982]), Lacan explains that the "not all" of Woman "means that when any speaking being whatever lines up under the banner of women it is by being constituted as not all that they are placed within the phallic function. It is this that defines the . . . the what?—the woman precisely, except that *The* Woman can only be written with *The* crossed through. There is no such thing as *The* Woman, where the definite article stands for the universal. There is no such thing as *The* Woman since of her essence—having already risked the term, why think twice about it?—of her essence, she is not all" (p. 144).

23. Slavoj Žižek, *The Sublime Object of Ideology* (London: Verso, 1989), p. 75.

24. Chauncey, "From Sexual Inversion to Homosexuality," p. 119.

25. Ibid., p. 122. Chauncey is here citing J.F.W. Meagher, "Homosexuality: Its Psychobiological and Pathological Significance," *Urologic and Cutaneous Review* 33 (1929): 513.

26. Faderman, *Surpassing the Love of Men*, passim.

27. See Jeffrey Weeks, *Coming Out: Homosexual Politics in Britain from the Nineteenth Century to the Present* (London: Quartet Press, 1977), pp. 57–67.

28. Ellis, "Sexual Inversion," p. 119.

29. Robert G. Leger, "Lesbianism among Women Prisoners: Participants and Non-Participants," *Criminal Justice and Behavior* 14, no. 4 (1987): 462.

30. Ibid., p. 464.

31. Barbara Babcock, *The Reversible World: Symbolic Inversion in Art and Society* (Ithaca: Cornell University Press, 1978), pp. 15–16.

32. Ibid., p. 16.

33. Caesar Lombroso, *The Female Offender* (New York: D. Appleton and Co., 1895), p. 2.

34. Ann Jones, *Women Who Kill* (New York: Fawcett Columbine, 1980), p. 6.

35. Lombroso, *Female Offender*, p. 74.

36. Ibid., pp. 74 and 108.

37. Ibid., p. 107.

38. Ibid., p. 151.

39. Ibid., p. 153.

40. Ibid., p. 159.

41. Ibid., p. 161.

42. Ngaire Naffine, *Female Crime: The Construction of Women in Criminology* (Boston: Allen and Unwin), p. 43.

43. Sigmund Freud, "On Fetishism," in *The Standard Edition of the Complete Psychological Works of Sigmund Freud* (hereafter *SE*), ed. James Strachey, 24 vols. (London: The Hogarth Press, 1953–1974), 21:149–157.

44. Žižek, *Sublime Object of Ideology*, p. 162.

45. Anthony Wilden, "Lacan and the Discourse of the Other," in *Speech and Language in Psychoanalysis* by Jacques Lacan, trans. with notes and commentary by Anthony Wilden (Baltimore: Johns Hopkins University Press, 1968), p. 281.

46. Žižek, *Sublime Object of Ideology*, p. 162.

47. Chauncey, "From Sexual Inversion to Homosexuality," p. 133.

48. Frye, *Politics of Reality*, p. 171.

49. Eve Kosofsky Sedgwick, *Epistemology of the Closet* (Berkeley and Los Angeles: University of California Press, 1990), p. 80.

50. Ibid.

51. Jonathan Dollimore discusses the same perspective in Augustine's conception of evil as, "on the one hand, a foreign force or agency, at once alien, antithetic, and hostile; on the other as an inner deviation, the more insidious for having departed from the true, its point of departure from *within* the true being

also its point of contact for the perversion *of* the true. In the conflation of the two, evil becomes at once utterly alien and insidiously inherent" (*Sexual Dissidence: Augustine to Wilde, Freud to Foucault* [Oxford: Clarendon Press, 1991], p. 143).

52. If, as Leo Bersani has forcefully argued, sexuality is that which is "intolerable to the structured self" (*The Freudian Body: Psychoanalysis and Art* [New York: Columbia University Press, 1986], p. 38), then merely claiming one's identity as a sexual subject produces a radically destabilizing paradox.

53. As Catherine Clément explains, Lacan always defined the Real as "the impossible": it is "impossible to see, to speak, or to hear, since in any case it is 'always-already-there' " (*The Lives and Legends of Jacques Lacan*, trans. Arthur Goldhammer [New York: Columbia University Press, 1983], p. 168). See her chapter "Hopscotch and the Four Corners" in the same work for a brilliantly clear elucidation of the Real, the Imaginary, and the Symbolic. Also, Žižek's chapter "Which Subject of the Real?" (in *Sublime Object of Ideology*) further elaborates, expands, and applies Lacan's real-impossible.

54. Žižek, *Sublime Object of Ideology*, p. 65. If understood as a symptom that makes an appeal to a subject-supposed-to-know, the secret is a hysterical sign that appeals to the interpretive "cure." The historical narrative of desire between women as a secret ironically gave "lesbianism" a radical ontological status. For in the effort to repress desire between women, rather than bar it through official legislation, the makers of the law produced this impossible desire as a symptom. And the symptom is what gives support to being—the consistency of one's existence in the world. Žižek points out that "the only alternative to the symptom is nothing, pure autism, a psychic suicide, surrender to the death drive even to the total destruction of the universe" (p. 75).

55. Sarah Kofman, *Freud and the Enigma of Woman: Woman in Freud's Writings*, trans. Catherine Porter (Ithaca: Cornell University Press, 1985), p. 65.

56. Ibid., p. 66.

57. Jean Laplanche, *Life and Death in Psychoanalysis*, trans. Jeffrey Mehlman (Baltimore: Johns Hopkins University Press, 1976), p. 67.

58. Ibid.

59. Sigmund Freud, "On Narcissism, an Introduction," *SE*, 14:88.

60. Lacan discusses this most accessibly in "God and the *Jouissance* of The Woman," in *Feminine Sexuality*. I will take this point up at length later in the chapter.

61. Irigaray, *Speculum*, p. 90.

62. Kofman, *Freud and the Enigma of Woman*, p. 52.

63. Freud, "On Narcissism," *SE*, 14:89.

64. Kofman, *Freud and the Enigma of Woman*, p. 52.

65. Jacques Lacan, *The Seminar of Jacques Lacan: Book I, Freud's Papers on Technique 1953–1954*, ed. Jacques-Alain Miller, trans. John Forrester (New York: W. W. Norton and Co., 1991), p. 131.

66. Ibid.

67. For a brilliant reading of psychoanalysis's relationship to the "Supreme Being" and the impossibility of love, see Luce Irigaray, "Cosi Fan Tutti," in *This Sex Which Is Not One*.

68. Lacan, *Book I*, p. 113.
69. Ibid.
70. Lacan, "God and the *Jouissance* of The Woman," in *Feminine Sexuality*, p. 141.
71. Clément, *Lives and Legends*, p. 131.
72. Lacan, *Feminine Sexuality*, p. 157.
73. Ibid.
74. Ibid., p. 155.
75. For a fascinating discussion of Augustine's "lust," the "privative theory of evil," and the perversions, see chapter 9, "Augustine: Perversion and Privation," in Dollimore, *Sexual Dissidence*.
76. Louis Mackey, "Eros into Logos: The Rhetoric of Courtly Love," in *The Philosophy of (Erotic) Love*, ed. Robert C. Solomon and Kathleen M. Higgins (Lawrence: University Press of Kansas, 1991), p. 338.
77. Ibid.
78. Lacan, *Feminine Sexuality*, p. 154.
79. Mackey, "Eros into Logos," p. 341.
80. Ibid., p. 343.
81. Ibid., p. 349.
82. Lacan, *Feminine Sexuality*, p. 154.
83. Michel Foucault, *This Is Not a Pipe* (Berkeley and Los Angeles: University of California Press, 1982), p. 9.
84. Lacan, *Feminine Sexuality*, p. 157.
85. Ibid., p. 158.
86. Ibid.
87. Ibid., p. 157.
88. Laplanche, *Life and Death*, p. 75.
89. Freud, "On Narcissism," *SE*, 14:90.
90. Lacan, *Feminine Sexuality*, p. 156.
91. Kofman, *Freud and the Enigma of Woman*, p. 57.
92. Lombroso, *Female Offender*, p. 224.
93. Ibid., p. 195.
94. Kofman, *Freud and the Enigma of Woman*, p. 67.
95. Ibid.
96. Ibid., p. 68, citing Freud's "The Taboo of Virginity" ("Contributions to the Psychology of Love," III), II: 193–208 (1918 [1917]): "Woman is different from man, for ever incomprehensible and mysterious, strange and therefore apparently hostile" (p. 198).
97. Kofman, *Freud and the Enigma of Woman*, p. 69.
98. Ibid., p. 70.
99. Dollimore, *Sexual Dissidence*, p. 141.
100. Sigmund Freud, "Some Psychical Consequences of the Anatomical Distinction between the Sexes," *SE*, 19:257.
101. Sigmund Freud, "Femininity," *SE*, 22:129.
102. Freud, "Anatomical Distinction," *SE*, 19:258.
103. The notion that the "militant" feminist is likely to be a lesbian has been

a constant strategy for threatening, ostracizing, and dividing women. One finds it continually in right-wing rhetoric that resorts to accusations of lesbianism to frighten women away from activism. See my discussion in chapter 6, "Race and Reproduction," for an elaboration of this theme. Ellis alludes to the progression from women's independence to homosexuality—"a tendency develops for women to carry this independence still farther and to find love where they find work" ("Sexual Inversion," p. 262, cited in Chauncey, "From Sexual Inversion to Homosexuality"). Chauncey discusses how this idea became, for some medical people, "a literally organic relationship" (p. 141). He quotes James Kiernan on "Bisexuality," who stops just short of suggesting that every suffragist is an invert. Degeneracy theory tended to abolish finer distinctions made by the sexologists; and since the "sexual pervert" was on the lower end of this sliding scale of degeneracy, feminists were duly warned.

104. Sigmund Freud, "The Ego and the Super-Ego," SE, 19:35.
105. Ibid., p. 34.
106. Ibid., p. 37.
107. Sigmund Freud, "Criminals from a Sense of Guilt," SE, 14:333.
108. Havelock Ellis, The Criminal (New York: AMS Press, 1972), p. 1.
109. Cited by Ellis in ibid., p. 1.
110. Ibid., p. 2.
111. Bram Dijkstra, Idols of Perversity, chapter 5.
112. Ibid., p. 136.
113. Ibid., p. 137.
114. Cited in ibid., p. 147.

Chapter 2
The Victorian Villainess and the Patriarchal Unconscious

1. Jones, Women Who Kill, p. 6.
2. Mrs. Henry Woods, East Lynne (New Brunswick: Rutgers University Press, 1984), p. 237.
3. I am alluding here to Joanna Russ, How to Suppress Women's Writing (Austin: University of Texas Press, 1983).
4. Doane, Femmes Fatales, p. 2.
5. Elaine Showalter, A Literature of Their Own: British Women Novelists from Brontë to Lessing (Princeton: Princeton University Press, 1977), p. 180.
6. Martha Vicinus, "'Helpless and Unfriended': Nineteenth-Century Domestic Melodrama," in When They Weren't Doing Shakespeare: Essays on Nineteenth-Century British and American Theatre, ed. Judith L. Fisher and Stephen Watt (Athens: University of Georgia Press, 1989), pp. 184–185.
7. Showalter, A Literature of Their Own, p. 165. The novel went through eight editions in the first year and stayed in print throughout Braddon's lifetime. The stage version was also immensely popular. Hazelwood's adaptation is probably the best known, but the novel was also adapted for the stage by several other lesser-known nineteenth-century playwrights.

8. Vicinus, " 'Helpless and Unfriended,' " p. 183.

9. Jacqueline Rose, *Sexuality in the Field of Vision* (London: Verso, 1986), p. 117.

10. Ibid., p. 116.

11. Mary Elizabeth Braddon, *Lady Audley's Secret* (New York: Dover, 1974), p. 21.

12. Ibid.

13. Ibid., p. 22.

14. Ibid., pp. 37–38.

15. Ibid., p. 86.

16. Ibid.

17. Sedgwick, *Epistemology of the Closet*, p. 189.

18. Braddon, *Lady Audley's Secret*, p. 105.

19. Irigaray, *This Sex Which Is Not One*, p. 172.

20. Braddon, *Lady Audley's Secret*, p. 132.

21. Ibid., p. 137.

22. Ibid., p. 170.

23. Ibid., p. 245.

24. Irigaray, *This Sex Which Is Not One*, p. 178.

25. Braddon, *Lady Audley's Secret*, p. 167. Freud argues that the hypochondriac withdraws libidinal interest from his love-objects and is thus dependent on ego-libido, like the narcissist ("On Narcissism," *SE*, 14:82–85). Robert's fear that he will become a hypochondriachal old *bachelor* would indicate that he is referring to a projected period of celibacy rather than the popular notion of hypochondria as psychosomatic illness.

26. Braddon, *Lady Audley's Secret*, p. 126.

27. Auerbach, *Woman and the Demon*, pp. 7–8.

28. Braddon, *Lady Audley's Secret*, p. 168.

29. Ibid., p. 181.

30. Michael Booth, *English Melodrama* (London: Herbert Jenkins, 1965), p. 157.

31. Sigmund Freud, "The Uncanny," *SE*, 17:226.

32. Ibid., p. 241.

33. Doane, *Femmes Fatales*, p. 1.

34. Elizabeth Grosz, *Jacques Lacan: A Feminist Introduction* (New York: Routledge, 1990), pp. 6–7.

35. Mikkel Borch-Jacobsen, *Lacan: The Absolute Master*, trans. Douglas Brick (Stanford: Stanford University Press, 1991), p. 24.

36. C. H. Hazelwood, *Lady Audley's Secret*, in *Nineteenth-Century Plays*, ed. George Rowell (Oxford: Oxford University Press, 1972), p. 266.

37. Braddon, *Lady Audley's Secret*, p. 248.

38. Ibid., p. 249.

39. Ibid., p. 187.

40. Ibid.

41. Irigaray, *This Sex Which Is Not One*, p. 171.

42. W. Fraser Rae considers Lady Audley "fantastic" ("Sensation Novelists: Miss Braddon," *North British Review* 43 [September 1865]: 97); the reviewer for *Fraser's Magazine* 68 (1863) found her "scarcely a human being" (p. 259). Natalie Schroeder notes that "so depraved and devilish [a woman] as Lady Audley [struck reviewers as] an impossibility" ("Feminine Sensationalism, Eroticism, and Self-Assertion: M. E. Braddon and Ouida," *Tulsa Studies in Women's Literature* 7, no. 1 [1988]: 100).

43. Sigmund Freud, "On the Mechanism of Paranoia," *SE*, 12:59.

44. Freud, "On Narcissism," *SE*, 14:88–89.

45. Mikkel Borch-Jacobsen, *The Freudian Subject*, trans. Catherine Porter (Stanford: Stanford University Press, 1988), pp. 105–106.

46. Ibid., p. 106.

47. In "Some Neurotic Mechanisms in Jealousy, Paranoia, and Homosexuality," *SE*, 18:232, Freud repeats this myth of homosexual "superiority": "It is well-known that a good number of homosexuals are characterized by special development of their social instinctual impulses and by their devotion to the interests of the community."

48. Freud, "Mechanism of Paranoia," *SE*, 12:62.

49. Ibid., p. 63.

50. Ibid., p. 72.

51. Mary Ann Doane, *The Desire to Desire: The Woman's Film of the 1940s* (Bloomington: Indiana University Press, 1987), p. 129.

52. Freud, "On Narcissism," *SE*, 14:88.

53. Borch-Jacobsen, *Lacan*, p. 24.

54. Ibid., p. 25.

55. Jacques Lacan, *Écrits*, trans. Alan Sheridan (New York: W. W. Norton and Co., 1977), pp. 16, 22.

56. Schroeder, "Feminine Sensationalism," p. 91.

57. Braddon, *Lady Audley's Secret*, p. 233.

58. Schroeder, "Feminine Sensationalism," p. 89.

59. Mary Hartman, *Victorian Murderesses* (New York: Schocken Books, 1977), p. 48.

60. Ibid., p. 84.

61. Richard Altick, *Victorian Studies in Scarlet* (New York: Norton and Norton, 1970), p. 42.

62. Ibid.

63. Hartman, *Victorian Murderesses*, p. 64.

64. Rae, "Sensation Novelists," p. 104.

65. Ibid., p. 96.

66. Braddon, *Lady Audley's Secret*, p. 39.

67. Ibid., p. 70.

68. Ibid., p. 17.

69. Ibid., p. 70.

70. Ibid., p. 71.

71. Ibid., p. 74.

NOTES TO CHAPTER 3

Chapter 3
Enter the Invert: Frank Wedekind's Lulu Plays

1. Barry Paris, *Louise Brooks* (New York: Alfred A. Knopf, 1989), p. 305.
2. Frank Wedekind, *The Lulu Plays and Other Sex Tragedies*, trans. Stephen Spender (New York: Riverrun Press, 1978), p. 103.
3. Ibid., pp. 103–104.
4. Ibid.
5. Ibid., p. 105.
6. Ibid., p. 104.
7. For a full discussion of the Scientific Humanitarians and the Uranian movement in regard to lesbians in Germany, see Lillian Faderman and Brigitte Ericksson, *Lesbians in Germany: 1890's–1920's* (Tallahassee, Fla.: The Naiad Press, 1990). The historical information in this chapter on the subject is taken from this work.
8. Louise Brooks, *Lulu in Hollywood* (New York: Alfred A. Knopf, 1982), p. 97.
9. Dijkstra, *Idols of Perversity*, p. 153.
10. As Jacqueline Rose points out: "The voyeur is not . . . in a position of pure manipulation of an object . . . but is always threatened by the potential exteriorisation of his own function. That function is challenged three times over: first, by the fact that the subject cannot see what it wants to see . . . ; secondly, by the fact that it is not the only one looking; thirdly, that the reciprocity implied in this is immediately challenged, since the subject can never see its look from the point at which the other is looking at it" (*Sexuality in the Field of Vision*, p. 194).
11. Bernard S. Talmey, *Woman: A Treatise on the Normal and Pathological Emotions of Feminine Love* (1904; 6th enl. and rev. ed., New York: Practitioners Publishing Co., 1910), p. 123.
12. Ibid., p. 147.
13. Dijkstra's analysis of the visual arts addresses these paintings and others in which the resemblance between the women, which he reads as suggestive of lesbianism as an extension of autoeroticism, is strained to a breaking point.
14. Kofman, *Freud and the Enigma of Woman*, p. 141.
15. M. Valabrega makes this connection in *The Seminar of Jacques Lacan: Book II, The Ego in Freud's Theory and in the Technique of Psychoanalysis, 1954–1955*, ed. Jacques-Alain Miller, trans. Sylvana Tomaselli (New York: W. W. Norton and Co., 1991). The desire to sleep "is both one of the initial and one of the final motives for the dream. Freud never speaks of secondary work, the only work there is is in the dream in the present, the narrated dream. And then, to terminate, there is the desire to sleep, which is one of the final meanings of the dream. Consequently, the fulfillment of desire at one end, and desire to sleep at the other. I think that more modern interpretations, which are only alluded to in the *Traumdeutung*, or in other later texts, the interpretation of the desire to sleep as narcissistic desire, clearly tend in this direction" (p. 212). Havelock Ellis cites Freud at the end of his *Lectures* on the narcissism of dreams: "In the sleeper the primal state of the libido distribution is again reproduced, that of absolute Narcis-

sism, in which libido and ego-instincts dwell together still, unified and indistinguishable in the self-sufficient Self" (in *Studies in the Psychology of Sex*, vol. 7
[Philadelphia: F. A. Davis Company, 1928], p. 359).

16. Ellis, *Studies*, 7:355.

17. Ibid., pp. 357–367.

18. Ibid., p. 348n.

19. Ibid., p. 348.

20. John Milton, *Paradise Lost*, bk. 4, in *The Poetical Works of John Milton*,
ed. Sir Egerton Brydges (Boston: Crosby, Nichols, Lee & Company, 1861),
pp. 205–206.

21. Wedekind, *Lulu Plays*, p. 90.

22. Gail Finney, *Women in Modern Drama: Freud, Feminism, and European
Theater at the Turn of the Century* (Ithaca: Cornell University Press, 1989),
p. 95.

23. Dijkstra, *Idols of Perversity*, p. 151.

24. Doane, *Femmes Fatales*, p. 153.

25. Wedekind, *Lulu Plays*, pp. 169–170.

26. Ibid., p. 125.

27. In his discussion of Genet, Jean-Paul Sartre explains this binary birth:
"Thus are born spontaneously the myth of the criminal, that is, the projection
upon others of the qualities which the others have attributed to him, and the
dichotomic conception of outcast humanity which will be the major theme of this
poetry: 'the eternal couple of the criminal and the saint' " (*Saint Genet: Actor and
Martyr*, trans. Bernard Frechtman [New York: Braziller, 1963], p. 86).

28. Wedekind, *Lulu Plays*, p. 137.

29. Sigmund Freud, "Group Psychology and the Analysis of the Ego," *SE*,
18:105.

30. Rose, *Sexuality in the Field of Vision*, p. 182.

31. Ibid., p. 181n.

32. Sartre, *Saint Genet*, p. 108.

33. Wedekind, *Lulu Plays*, p. 136.

34. Ibid., p. 126.

35. Ibid., p. 169.

36. Ibid., p. 175.

37. Sigmund Freud, "The Psychogenesis of a Case of Homosexuality in a
Woman," *SE*, 18:154.

38. Doane, *Femmes Fatales*, p. 152.

39. Ibid., p. 154.

40. Wedekind, *Lulu Plays*, p. 35.

41. Ibid., p. 95.

42. Ibid., p. 127.

43. Ibid., p. 165.

44. Ibid., p. 138.

45. Kofman, *Freud and the Enigma of Woman*, p. 146.

46. Wedekind, *Lulu Plays*, p. 13.

47. Ibid., p. 21.

48. Kofman, *Freud and the Enigma of Woman*, p. 223.

49. Rose, *Sexuality in the Field of Vision*, p. 173.

50. Wedekind, *Lulu Plays*, p. 164.

51. Ibid.

52. Ibid., p. 77.

53. Lacan, *Book II*, p. 89.

54. Ibid.

55. Ibid., p. 90.

56. Ibid., p. 84.

57. Ibid.

58. Freud, "On Narcissism," p. 88.

59. Ibid., p. 89.

60. Kofman, *Freud and the Enigma of Woman*, p. 89.

61. Ibid., p. 193.

62. Ibid., p. 194.

63. Ibid., p. 187.

64. Irigaray, *Speculum*, p. 27.

65. Paris, *Louise Brooks*, p. 297.

66. Freud, "Three Essays on the Theory of Sexuality," *SE*, 7:145–146.

67. Wedekind, *Lulu Plays*, p. 38.

68. Ibid., pp. 82–83.

69. Laura Mulvey, *Visual and Other Pleasures* (Bloomington: Indiana University Press, 1989), p. 22.

70. Rose, *Sexuality in the Field of Vision*, p. 194.

71. Wedekind, *Lulu Plays*, p. 10.

72. Borch-Jacobsen, *The Freudian Subject*, p. 40.

73. Judith Walkowitz, "Jack the Ripper and the Myth of Male Violence," *Feminist Studies* 8, no. 3 (1982): 546.

74. Jane Caputi, *The Age of Sex Crime* (Bowling Green, Ohio: Bowling Green State University Press, 1987), p. 23.

75. Ibid., pp. 5–6.

76. Ibid., p. 7.

Chapter 4
Chloe Liked Olivia: Death, Desire, and Detection in the Female Buddy Film

1. Hélène Cixous, "The Laugh of the Medusa," in *New French Feminisms*, ed. Elaine Marks and Isabelle de Courtivron (New York: Schocken Books, 1981), p. 248.

2. Virginia Woolf, *A Room of One's Own* (London: Granada, 1977), pp. 85–86.

3. Ibid., p. 86.

4. Ibid., p. 88.

5. D. A. Miller, "Anal Rope," in *Inside/Out: Lesbian Theories, Gay Theories*, ed. Diana Fuss (New York: Routledge, 1991), pp. 124–125.

6. Roland Barthes, *S/Z*, trans. Richard Miller (New York: Farrar, Straus and Giroux, 1974), pp. 7–8.

7. Ibid., p. 9.

8. Ibid.

9. Miller, "Anal Rope," p. 125.

10. Barthes, *S/Z*, pp. 5–6.

11. Julie Baumgold, "Killer Women: Here Come the Hardbodies," *New York*, July 29, 1991, p. 28.

12. Cynthia J. Fuchs, "The Buddy Politic," in *Screening the Male: Exploring Masculinities in Hollywood Cinema*, ed. Steven Cohan and Ina Rae Hark (London: Routledge, 1993), p. 195.

13. For a lucid introduction to Lacan and his relationship to feminism, see Grosz, *Jacques Lacan*.

14. Doane, *The Desire to Desire*.

15. Robin Wood, *Hollywood from Vietnam to Reagan* (New York: Columbia University Press, 1986), pp. 222–245.

16. Ibid., pp. 228–229.

17. Tania Modleski, *Feminism without Women: Culture and Criticism in a "Postfeminist" Age* (New York: Routledge, 1991), p. 145.

18. Alice Cross, "The Bimbo and the Mystery Woman: Should We Go Along for the Ride? A Critical Symposium on *Thelma and Louise*," *Cineaste* 18, no. 4 (1991): 33.

19. Richard Schickel, "A Postcard from the Edge," *Time*, May 27, 1991, p. 64.

20. David Denby, "Road Warriors," *New York*, June 10, 1991, p. 56.

21. Margaret Carlson, "Is This What Feminism Is All About?" *Time*, June 24, 1991, p. 57.

22. Slavoj Žižek defines Lacan's Real as "the lack around which the symbolic order is structured . . . the void, the emptiness created, encircled by the symbolic structure" (*Sublime Object of Ideology*, p. 170). Catherine Clément points out that since the Real is a concept that cannot exist without the barrier of the Symbolic, when the Real "really does rear its head, the subject is terrified" (*Lives and Legends*, p. 168).

23. Kofman, *Freud and the Enigma of Woman*, p. 66 and passim.

24. Shoshana Felman, "Rereading Femininity," *Yale French Studies*, no. 62 (1981): 19 and 21.

25. Teresa de Lauretis, *Alice Doesn't: Feminism, Semiotics, Cinema* (Bloomington: Indiana University Press, 1984), p. 121.

26. Barthes, *Pleasure of the Text*, p. 10.

27. De Lauretis, *Alice Doesn't*, p. 134.

28. Carlson, "Is This What Feminism Is All About?" p. 57.

29. Richard A. Blake, "The Deadlier of the Species," *America*, June 29, 1991, p. 683.

30. Denby, "Road Warriors," p. 55.

31. "Why *Thelma and Louise* Strikes a Nerve," *Time*, June 24, 1991, pp. 53–54.

32. Ibid., p. 55.

33. Ruth Walker, "Why We Cheered *Thelma and Louise*," *Christian Science Monitor*, July 17, 1991, p. 18.

34. Denby, "Road Warriors," p. 55.

35. In the *Time* cover story ("Why *Thelma and Louise* Strikes a Nerve"), Khouri is quoted as saying, "I certainly don't hate men," and to confirm it we are told in the same sentence that she "celebrates her first year of marriage to writer and producer David Warfield this month" (p. 55). In "Lost in America," Carl Wayne Arrington tells us that Davis recently filed for divorce, but Susan Sarandon's "companion, Tim Robbins, visits frequently, as do their son and daughter" (*Premiere*, April 1991, p. 108). Davis is profiled in a *People* cover story ("Riding Shotgun," June 24, 1991), by Jim Jerome, that occupies much space filling in the details of her divorce from Jeff Goldblum while at the same time documenting her prior marriage and heterosexual romances. Of course it is common for actresses' private lives to be profiled in these ways (though not usually screenwriters'). Nevertheless, there is an unusual emphasis on the women's heterosexuality in the coverage of this film that I think can be attributed to accusations that *Thelma and Louise* is a "man-hating" movie. The cultural equation of "man-hater" and "lesbian" has been a powerful ideological strategy for discouraging women from expressing their anger. The effort to keep these usually conflated terms distinct in this reception rhetoric produces a provocative paradox. For, on the one hand, defenders of the film assert the women's heterosexuality in order to allay the public's discrediting of it. On the other hand, relinquishing this displacement makes women's aggression more threatening since it can no longer be contained with the "lesbian."

36. Denby, "Road Warriors," p. 55.

37. Joan Juliet Buck, *Vogue*, May 1991, pp. 161–162.

38. Margaret Carlson notes that Thelma's sexual encounter with J.D. reinforces the myth that "the only thing an unhappy woman needs is good sex" ("Is This What Feminism Is All About?" p. 57); Richard Schickel notes that "literalists criticize Thelma's erotic awakening because, they say, it could not happen so soon after the trauma of near rape" ("A Postcard from the Edge," p. 55).

39. Caroline Sheldon, "Lesbians and Film: Some Thoughts," in *Gays and Film*, ed. Richard Dyer (New York: Zoetrope, 1977), pp. 6 and 12.

40. In box-office hits such as *Fatal Attraction* and its derivatives like *The Hand That Rocks the Cradle*, a notable feature is their eroticized spectacles of mortal combat between two women, one of whom at first appears to be "normal" but turns out to be pathological. The good women in such films assume the cultural function of eliminating their deviant counterparts. Thus they reinforce the division of women through displacement of their aggression onto the woman whose sexuality is "deviant." The immense popularity of these films could be understood as a displacement of desire between women, which is, of course, enormously popular in heterosexual pornography. In mainstream cinema, the women can only be shown hacking each other to death.

41. Cixous, "Laugh of the Medusa," p. 255.

42. It is interesting to note that the only person of color who appears in the

film is the black male bicyclist, who blows marijuana smoke into the holes that Thelma shoots into the trunk of the state trooper's car. He is thus immediately allied with the white women's criminality. Since the state trooper represents the epitome of white male supremacy (Louise says he looks like a Nazi), spectators who identify against the white man's law from any number of perspectives are invited to take pleasure in this scene.

43. Valerie Traub, "The Ambiguities of 'Lesbian' Viewing Pleasure: The (Dis)articulations of *Black Widow*," in *Body Guards*, ed. Julia Epstein and Kristina Straub (New York: Routledge, 1992), pp. 305–328.

44. Another note about the film's "incoherent geography": Thelma and Louise are not really at the Grand Canyon. They misrecognize the space.

45. Slavoj Žižek offers Kasimer Malevich's painting *The Naked Unframed Icon of My Time*, which depicts a black square inside a white background, to exemplify this relationship. The white background, "the open space in which objects can appear[,] maintains its consistency only by means of the 'black hole' in its center (the Lacanian *das Ding*, the Thing that gives body to the substance of enjoyment), i.e. by the exclusion of the real, by the change of the status of the real into that of a central lack" (*Looking Awry: An Introduction to Jacques Lacan through Popular Culture* [Cambridge: MIT Press, 1991], p. 19).

46. Tzvetan Todorov, *The Poetics of Prose*, trans. Richard Howard (Ithaca: Cornell University Press, 1977), p. 46.

47. Barthes, *S/Z*, p. 17.

48. Freud, cited by Žižek in *Sublime Object of Ideology*, p. 14.

49. Barthes, *S/Z*, p. 21.

50. Sigmund Freud, "Psycho-analysis and the Establishment of the Facts in Legal Proceedings," *SE*, 9:108.

51. Ibid., 112.

52. Žižek, *Sublime Object of Ideology*, p. 42.

53. Freud, "Legal Proceedings," *SE*, 9:112.

54. Richard Alleva, "Lethal Smooches: *Kiss* and *Mortal Thoughts*," *Commonweal*, June 14, 1991, p. 407.

55. Ibid.

Chapter 5
Reconsidering Homophobia: Karen Finley's Indiscretions

1. Karen Finley, interview in *Angry Women*, ed. Andrea Juno and V. Vale (San Francisco: RE/SEARCH, 1991), pp. 41 and 44.

2. C. Carr, "The Sexual Politics of Censorship: War on Art," *Village Voice*, June 5, 1990, p. 28.

3. The antiobscenity clause was replaced by a statement requiring works of art to meet "general standards of decency and respect for the diverse beliefs of the American public," a requisite that could prove equally or more problematic.

4. David Leavitt, "The Fears That Haunt a Scrubbed Nation," *New York Times*, August 19, 1990, sec. 2, p. 1.

5. Simon Watney, *Policing Desire: Pornography, AIDS, and the Media* (Minneapolis: University of Minnesota Press, 1987), p. 16.

6. A special issue of *October* (61 [Summer 1992]), "The Identity in Question," indicates the persistent difficulties of these debates.

7. Linda Alcoff, "Cultural Feminism versus Post-Structuralism: The Identity Crisis in Feminist Theory," in *Reconstructing the Academy: Women's Education and Women's Studies*, ed. Elizabeth Minnich, Jean O'Barr, and Rachel Rosenfeld (Chicago: University of Chicago Press, 1988), p. 269.

8. Gayatri Spivak, "Subaltern Studies: Deconstructing Historiography," in *In Other Worlds: Essays in Cultural Politics* (New York: Methuen, 1987), p. 205.

9. Leavitt, "Fears," p. 1.

10. Ibid.

11. Joseph Neisen, "Heterosexism or Homophobia?" *Out/Look* 10 (Fall 1990): 36–37.

12. Jonathan Dollimore, "Masculine Sexuality—1: Homophobia and Sexual Difference," *Oxford Literary Review* 8, nos. 1–2 (1986): 9.

13. Peggy Phelan, "Serrano, Mapplethorpe, the NEA, and You: 'Money Talks,'" *Drama Review* 34, no. 1 (1990): 14.

14. Homi K. Bhabha, "Signs Taken for Wonders: Questions of Ambivalence and Authority under a Tree outside Delhi, May 1817," in *Race, Writing and Difference*, ed. Henry Louis Gates, Jr. (Chicago: University of Chicago Press, 1986), pp. 168–172.

15. I take the phrase "eccentric subject" from Teresa de Lauretis's "Eccentric Subjects: Feminist Theory and Historical Consciousness," *Feminist Studies* 16, no. 1 (1990): 115–150.

16. C. Carr, "Unspeakable Practices, Unnatural Acts: The Taboo Art of Karen Finley," *Village Voice*, July 24, 1986, pp. 17–18, 86. This article is reprinted in *Acting Out: Feminist Performances*, ed. Lynda Hart and Peggy Phelan (Ann Arbor: University of Michigan Press, 1993).

17. "Letters: The Yam Became a Hot Potato," *Village Voice*, July 15, 1986, pp. 4–6.

18. Eve Kosofsky Sedgwick, "A Poem Is Being Written," *Representations* 17 (Winter 1987): 129.

19. Guy Hocquenghem, "Family, Capitalism, Anus," *Semiotext(e): Anti-Oedipus* 2, no. 3 (1977): 157.

20. Lauren Berlant, "The Female Complaint," *Socialtext* 19–20 (1988): 242.

21. Catherine Schuler, "Spectator Response and Comprehension: The Problem of Karen Finley's *Constant State of Desire*," *Drama Review* 32 (Spring 1988): 135.

22. Finley was dubbed the "nude chocolate-smeared young woman" by Rowland Evans and Robert Novack, in "The NEA's Suicide Charge," *Washington Post*, May 11, 1990, p. A27.

23. Julia Kristeva, *Powers of Horror: An Essay on Abjection*, trans. Leon S. Roudiez (New York: Columbia University Press, 1982), p. 3.

24. Ibid., p. 4.

25. Mary Douglas, *Purity and Danger: An Analysis of Concepts of Pollution and Taboo* (London: Routledge, 1966), p. 5.

26. Elin Diamond, "Brechtian Theory/Feminist Theory," *Drama Review* 32, no. 1 (1988): 90.

27. The published version, in *Shock Treatment* (San Francisco: City Lights, 1990), reads slightly differently and does not indicate that Finley is gesturing over the wedding cake. I base my reading on a performance in Philadelphia at The Painted Bride in the spring of 1989. I use quotation marks to indicate transcription from notes I took during the performance. It should be kept in mind that some degree of improvisation is at work in Finley's performances and thus her words and gestures vary.

28. *The Theory of Total Blame* is unpublished. My notes are based on the performance at The Kitchen, New York City, 1989. For a fuller discussion of this play see my "Motherhood According to Karen Finley: *The Theory of Total Blame*," *Drama Review* 36, no. 1 (1991): 124–134.

29. Juliet Mitchell, "Introduction I," in *Feminine Sexuality*, p. 23.

30. Hélène Cixous and Catherine Clément, *The Newly Born Woman*, trans. Betsy Wing (Minneapolis: University of Minnesota Press, 1986), p. xii.

31. Quoted in ibid., p. 4.

32. Ibid., pp. 36–39.

33. Leo Bersani, "Is the Rectum a Grave?" in *AIDS: Cultural Analysis, Cultural Activism*, ed. Douglas Crimp (Cambridge: MIT Press, 1988), p. 211.

Chapter 6
Race and Reproduction: *Single* White *Female*

1. Ekua Omosupe, "Black/Lesbian/Bulldagger," *differences* 3, no. 2 (1991): 108.

2. Richard Dyer, "White," *Screen* 29, no. 4 (1988): 64.

3. Nietzsche, *Beyond Good and Evil*, excerpt in *The Philosophy of Erotic Love*, ed. Robert C. Solomon and Kathleen M. Higgins (Lawrence: University Press of Kansas, 1991), p. 150.

4. De Lauretis, "Film and the Visible," p. 264.

5. Ada Griffin, *How Do I Look?*, ed. Bad Object-Choices (Seattle: Bay Press, 1991), p. 268.

6. De Lauretis, "Film and the Visible," p. 225.

7. Anthony Wilden explains that when there is "nowhere for 'the return of the repressed' (the symptom) to return to (as it returns to the subject's 'history' in normal neurosis) . . . then what was wrongly rejected (expulsed), that is to say what never 'came to the light of the Symbolic,' *must logically appear in the Real* (the domain outside symbolization). In Freud's words: 'what was abolished internally returns from without.'" Anthony Wilden, "Lacan and the Discourse of the Other," in *Speech and Language in Psychonanalysis*, by Jacques Lacan, translated with notes and commentary by Anthony Wilden (Baltimore: Johns Hopkins University Press, 1968), pp. 280–281.

8. De Lauretis argues that the "lesbian subject position" in this film is constituted by the interaction of Jo and Agatha. Diegetically, Agatha is "the spectator
who occupies or is addressed in that position . . . sitting at the cutting table,
watching Jo's film, and reacting with intense participation because the film has
something to do with her life. And she, the filmmaker, who enunciates that sub-
ject-position, is represented in Jo, who is also sitting there, watching the words
and images she's put together into a *figure of her desire* for Agatha" ("Film and
the Visible," p. 228).

9. Ibid., p. 225.

10. Ibid., p. 253.

11. Ibid., p. 223.

12. Jane Gaines, "White Privilege and Looking Relations: Race and Gender in
Feminist Film Theory," *Screen* 29, no. 4 (1988): 12. An earlier version of this
essay appeared in *Cultural Critique* 4 (Fall 1986): 59–79.

13. Doane, *Femmes Fatales*, p. 216. It is interesting to notice that when Doane
turns her attention to the "dark continent" in psychoanalysis and to the ways in
which female sexuality is racially inscribed, the ostensible subject of her book—
the "femme fatale"—does *not* make an appearance in this chapter.

14. Gaines, "White Privilege," p. 15.

15. Sue-Ellen Case, "Toward a Butch-Femme Aesthetic," in *Making a Spectacle: Feminist Essays on Contemporary Women's Theatre*, ed. Lynda Hart (Ann
Arbor: University of Michigan Press, 1989), pp. 283–284.

16. Victor L. Streib, "Death Penalty for Female Offenders," *University of Cincinnati Law Review* 58, no. 3 (1990): 878–889. Ronald Flowers points out that
"official data do not record race and social class of female criminals, an unfortu-
nate omission when one considers the biases and assumptions so pervasive in
official interpretation of criminality. Equally, national statistics do not provide
the racial breakdown of women offenders." Individual studies, however, repeatedly indicate the race and class bias of arrests. Flowers cites studies showing that
black female criminals are closer in numbers to black male criminals than white
females are to white males; that although black women constitute only 10 percent
of the adult female population, they account for half of those incarcerated; that
black women are more than twice as likely as white women to be perceived as
criminals. But these studies, Flowers says, "fail to interpret what this means."
Ronald Barri Flowers, *Women and Criminality* (New York: Greenwood Press,
1987), pp. 76–77.

17. Homi K. Bhabha. "The Other Question: Difference, Discrimination and
the Discourse of Colonialism," in *Literature, Politics, Theory: Papers from the
Essex Conference, 1976–1984*, ed. Francis Barker et al. (London: Methuen,
1986), p. 151.

18. Ibid.

19. Ibid., citing Mark Cousins, "The Logic of Deconstruction," *Oxford Literary Review* 3, no. 2 (1978): 76.

20. Irigaray, *Speculum*.

21. Bhabha, "The Other Question," p. 151.

22. Ibid.

23. Ibid., pp. 165–166.

24. Dyer, "White," p. 45.

25. Ibid., p. 46.

26. Ibid.

27. Ibid., p. 47.

28. Patricia J. Williams, "Attack of the 50-Ft. First Lady: The Demonization of Hillary Clinton," *Village Voice*, January 26, 1993, pp. 35–39.

29. Promotional copy for video, *Attack of the 50-Ft. Woman*, Allied Artists Pictures Corporation, produced by Bernard Woolner, directed by Nathan Hertz (1958).

30. Williams, "Attack," p. 37.

31. Ibid.

32. Ibid.

33. Ibid.

34. Ibid.

35. Ibid.

36. The most notorious example of this inscription in recent American history is *The Moynihan Report*, which labeled the "matriarchal structure" of the "Negro community" as a "tangle of pathology." This "pathology" was attributed to "the often reversed roles of husband and wife" (Lee Rainwater and William L. Yancey, *The Moynihan Report and the Politics of Controversy* [Cambridge: MIT Press, 1967], p. 76), the transmission of culture by the women, the perpetuation of a "mother-centered pattern by [Negro mothers] taking a greater interest in their daughters than their sons" (p. 80). The report found, at the "root of the problem" that African-American women, significantly often together—"two women in charge" (p. 65)—dominated the Negro family structure.

37. Williams writes: "One reason I found the advertisement so terrifying was for the simple straightforwardness of the racial boundary and gender terrorization encoded in it" ("Attack," p. 37). But Williams does not notice that the ad itself in the film drops the request for a "white" roommate.

38. Hal Hinson, "*Single White Female*: Double Trouble," *Washington Post*, August 14, 1992, p. C6.

39. Cited in Williams, "Attack," p. 37.

40. Ibid., pp. 37–38.

41. Ibid.

42. Carroll Smith-Rosenberg, "The Abortion Movement and the AMA, 1850–1880," in *Disorderly Conduct* (Oxford: Oxford University Press, 1985), pp. 226–227. Smith-Rosenberg also argues that the AMA "in effect created a new Oedipal triangle, linking the male physician with the male fetus against the mother" (p. 242). This is powerful support for Phelan's argument. If the medical men of the nineteenth century figured themselves, as one spokesman put it, as "guardians of the rights of infants" (Smith-Rosenberg, "Abortion Movement," p. 242), the men of Operation Rescue are their heirs. For more discussion of race suicide, see Linda Gordon, *Woman's Body, Woman's Rights: A Social History of Birth Control in America* (New York: Grossman, 1976), pp. 136–158.

43. *Single White Female*, produced and directed by Barbet Schroeder, Columbia Pictures (1992).

44. Rosalind Pollack Petchesky, *Abortion and Woman's Choice: The State, Sexuality, and Reproductive Freedom* (New York: Longman, 1984), p. 160.

45. "Lesbians Coming Out Strong," *Newsweek*, June 21, 1993, p. 56.

46. Peggy Phelan, "White men and pregnancy: discovering the body to be rescued," in *Unmarked: The Politics of Performance* (New York: Routledge, 1993), p. 131.

47. Ibid., citing Frances Wilkinson, "The Gospel According to Randall Terry," *Rolling Stone*, October 5, 1989, pp. 85–89.

48. Ibid.

49. Demonstrators overheard at an anti-abortion demonstration in Queens, New York, 1992. I have not seen such statements documented anywhere; certainly one would not expect such rhetoric to be actually printed in antiabortionist literature. However, given the well-documented history of racism in the movements opposing abortion and birth control, I do not think that this statement was an aberration, but rather a passionate outburst that made the right-to-life agenda patent. The best discussion of racism in the fight against reproductive freedom is still Angela Davis, "Racism, Birth Control and Reproductive Rights," in *Women, Race and Class* (New York: Random House, 1981), pp. 202–221.

50. Phelan, "White men and pregnancy," p. 134.

51. Ibid., p. 144.

52. Sander L. Gilman, "Black Bodies, White Bodies: Toward an Iconography of Female Sexuality in Late Nineteenth-Century Art, Medicine, and Literature," *Critical Inquiry* 12 (Autumn 1985): 229.

53. Ibid., p. 218.

54. Ibid., p. 226.

55. Ibid., p. 234.

56. Ibid., p. 235.

57. Ibid., p. 237.

58. Dyer, "White," p. 48.

59. Ibid., p. 59.

60. Ibid., pp. 62–63.

61. Gilman, "Black Bodies, White Bodies," p. 237.

62. Dyer, "White," p. 63.

63. Ibid., pp. 63–64.

64. Ibid., p. 64.

65. Ibid.

66. Doane, *Femmes Fatales*, p. 211.

67. Andreas Capellanus, *The Art of Courtly Love*, trans. John Jay Parry (New York: Frederick Ungar, 1959), p. 150.

68. Mackey, "Eros into Logos," p. 341.

69. James Hillman, "Notes on White Supremacy: Essaying an Archetypal Account of Historical Events," *Spring* (1986): 38–39.

70. Bhabha, "The Other Question," p. 159.

Chapter 7
Why The Woman Did It: *Basic Instinct* and Its Vicissitudes

1. Jacques Lacan, "A Love Letter," in *Feminine Sexuality*, p. 158.

2. *Inside Basic Instinct*, trailer interview following the video release of the uncut (uncensored) version of the film. Verhoeven explains that all the evidence found in Beth's house has been set up by Catherine in the last couple of days. But he does not explain *how* Catherine could have managed such extraordinary feats. And despite his certainty that the film tells us Catherine did it, later in the interview, he concedes that he shot the final scene with the ice pick "two ways," for the ice pick under the bed is definitively Catherine's steel one, but the killer always used cheap ice picks with wooden handles. At this point Verhoeven seems perplexed by his own contradictions and makes an interesting segue into discussing ice picks, phallic symbols, and Freud, while denying that he had any intention of making such connections.

3. Among the media coverage concerning the "homosexual" controversy, see Curtis Rist, "Gays Find Movie's Instincts All Wrong," *Newsday*, March 21, 1992, p. 4; George Papajohn, *Chicago Tribune*, May 19, 1992, p. 1; Iain Johnstone, "Emotional Cop-out," *Sunday Times*, May 10, 1992; Margaret Russell, "What's behind All This Legal Reelism," *Legal Times*, April 13, 1992, p. 54; Matthew Gilbert, "Cashing In on Bad Publicity," *Boston Globe*, April 5, 1992, p. B29; David Sterritt, "*Basic Instinct*: Specimen of a Sorry Breed of Movie," *Christian Science Monitor*, March 30, 1992, p. 11; "Steaming Up the Screen: Michael Douglas Explains His Craft," *Maclean's*, March 30, 1992; Lewis Beale, "Gays vs. Hollywood," *Chicago Tribune*, March 29, 1992, p. 10; Harold von Kursk, "Accusations of Gay Bashing Rankle Douglas," *Toronto Star*, March 23, 1992, p. C5.

4. Richard Schickel, "Lots of Skin, but No Heart," *Time*, March 23, 1992, p. 65.

5. Ibid.

6. Ibid.

7. Verhoeven, interviewed in *Inside Basic Instinct*.

8. Todorov, *The Poetics of Prose*, p. 44. Todorov is quoting George Burton, "the author of many murder mysteries." He does not document this quotation.

9. Ibid., p. 47.

10. Ibid.

11. Ibid. The thriller may even then reverse the dynamic of identification so that our sympathies are as much or more with the "first murderer" (the classic perpetrator) who may stand falsely accused. And if there must always be a subject-supposed-to-know, if it is not the detective in the thriller then perhaps it is the first "murderer" himself/herself, who, by the thriller's generic conventions, can always only be the one who does indeed *know* the "truth," even though he/she fails to reveal it. This is a very different structure of the "secret." In the whodunit, the secret has an inner kernel of truth, awaiting disclosure by the penetrating gaze of the detective. In the thriller, the secret is merely a formal device; it has no essence, no "truth" to be told.

12. Lacan, "God and the *Jouissance* of The Woman," in *Feminine Sexuality*, p. 138.

13. Ibid., p. 139.

14. Georges Bataille, *Erotism: Death and Sensuality*, trans. Mary Dalwood (San Francisco: City Lights Books, 1986).

15. Lacan, "God and the *Jouissance* of The Woman," in *Feminine Sexuality*, p. 139.

16. I am thinking here simply of the obvious point that in order for Catherine to be presented convincingly as a "lesbian," it is important that her allegiance to "women" (not merely to *one* woman, Roxy) is demonstrated. However, this point also suggests that it takes at least two women, maybe more, to represent "a lesbian." I remind readers here of Teresa de Lauretis's article, "Film and the Visible," in which she argues that it is the sharing of "a common fantasy, a lesbian fantasy," that constitutes the two women in Sheila McLaughlin's film *She Must Be Seeing Things* as "a lesbian subject. Not the least implication of which is that it takes two women, not one, to make a lesbian" (p. 232). While I am certainly not arguing that any of the women in *Basic Instinct*, coupled or uncoupled, are lesbian subjects, I am suggesting that in a masculine imaginary The Woman is a doubled figure (not a "coupled" one in de Lauretis's sense); and that one-half of this double (the shadow side) is "lesbian" in the terms in which that figure has been historically constructed by men. The difference between my reading of *Basic Instinct*, in which it takes two women to make The Woman of the masculine imaginary, and de Lauretis's coupled lesbian subject position, can perhaps be thought of as the difference between bisexuality and lesbianism. Here I am in complete agreement with de Lauretis, who warns her readers that she will advance a thesis likely to be "unpopular in feminist circles": that "the notion of female sexuality as fluid, diffuse, polymorphously perverse, or mobile and unbounded, is applicable to lesbian sexuality only if the above qualifiers are not, as they usually are, taken to be equivalent to bisexual" (p. 237).

17. *Basic Instinct*, screenplay by Joe Eszterhas, directed by Paul Verhoeven (1992).

18. Sigmund Freud, "Instincts and Their Vicissitudes," *SE*, 14:117.

19. Ibid.

20. Ibid.

21. Jacques Lacan, "Of the Subject Who Is Supposed to Know," in *The Four Fundamental Concepts of Psycho-Analysis*, trans. Alan Sheridan (New York: W. W. Norton and Co., 1981), p. 232.

22. Freud, "Instincts," *SE*, 14:133.

23. Ibid.

24. Ibid.

25. Freud, "On Narcissism," *SE*, 14:88.

26. Freud, "Instincts," *SE*, 14:139.

27. Ibid.

28. Lacan, "God and the *Jouissance* of The Woman," in *Feminine Sexuality*, p. 140.

29. Ibid., p. 141.

30. *The Fourth Man*, directed by Paul Verhoeven.

Chapter 8
Surpassing the Word: Aileen Wuornos

1. Aileen Carol Wuornos, "In Her Own Words," testimony in self-defense in the Mallory trial. Reprinted in Phyllis Chesler, "Sex, Death and the Double Standard," *On the Issues*, Summer 1992, p. 31. Even this reproduction of Wuornos's "own words" has been censored for publication. In the trial transcripts, she quotes Mallory saying, "I'm going to kill you now and fuck you after you're dead." She apologizes for using "street language" on the witness stand. It should be noted that it is the man who was raping her who is protected by this "cleaning up," censoring, of *his* words in her testimony. Excerpts from Wuornos's testimony are included in Nick Broomfield's documentary *Aileen Wuornos: The Selling of a Serial Killer* (1993), hereafter cited as Broomfield.

2. For a full account of Richard Mallory's criminal history and how it was "overlooked" by both the defense and the prosecution, see Michele Gillen's "Dateline" interview, November 10, 1992. State prosecutor John Tanner, when confronted with Mallory's history of sexual assaults against women, responded that his office was careless in checking out Mallory's past. Tanner allowed that the newly uncovered evidence was aggravating, because "we may have to try the case again. It may be reversed on appeal and we'd have to try her all over again" (p. 11).

3. Dori Laub, M.D., "Bearing Witness or the Vicissitudes of Listening," in Shoshana Felman and Dori Laub, M.D., *Testimony: Crises of Witnessing in Literature, Psychoanalysis, and History* (New York: Routledge, 1992), pp. 70–71.

4. Dawn (who prefers not to be further identified), cited in James S. Kunen et al., "Florida Cops Say Seven Men Met Death on the Highway When They Picked Up Accused Serial Killer Aileen Wuornos," *People*, February 25, 1991, p. 48.

5. Steven A. Egger, "A Working Definition of Serial Murder and the Reduction of Linkage Blindness," *Journal of Police Science and Administration* 12, no. 3 (1984): 350.

6. Jane Caputi, "The New Founding Fathers: The Lore and Lure of the Serial Killer in Contemporary Culture," *Journal of American Culture* 13, no. 3 (1990): 1–12.

7. Kate Millett, *Sexual Politics* (New York: Ballantine Books, 1970), pp. 59–60.

8. Slavoj Žižek, *Enjoy Your Symptom! Jacques Lacan in Hollywood and Out* (New York: Routledge, 1992), p. 57.

9. Ibid., pp. 39–40.

10. Ibid., pp. 52–53.

11. Ibid., p. 46.

12. Cixous and Clément, *The Newly Born Woman*, p. 17.

13. Robert K. Ressler and Tom Shachtman, *Whoever Fights Monsters: My Twenty Years Tracking Serial Killers for the F.B.I.* (New York: St. Martin's Press, 1992), p. 33.

14. Mike Clary, "A Mother's Love," *Los Angeles Times*, December 17, 1991, pp. E1–2.

15. Doane, *Femmes Fatales*, pp. 2–3.

16. "Dateline NBC," August 25, 1992, p. 11.

17. Ibid., pp. 8–9:

GILLEN [voice-over]: You understand now that for many people, because you were a prostitute, they don't understand how a prostitute can be raped.

Ms. WUORNOS: I don't understand how nobody can understand how a prostitute can be raped. Because when a man rapes a woman, he assaults your whole body. He puts his . . . [censored by network] . . . down your throat, cramming it down your throat. He tears your hair out of your head. He—beats your face in. He—he rips your . . . [censored by network] . . . wide open.

Notice the slide from the interviewer's "prostitute" to Wuornos's "woman." Wuornos responds to Gillen's question with a graphic, literal description of *how* she was raped. What she does not understand here (nor does Michele Gillen, the woman interviewing her) is that a "prostitute" is *not* a "woman" who *can* be raped in a patriarchal symbolic.

18. Ibid., p. 23.

19. Ibid., page missing in transcript. (Quotation is verbatim from videotape of the broadcast.)

20. Ibid.

21. "Geraldo. Profile of Aileen Wuornos: The Woman behind the Murders," March 23, 1993, pp. 19–20.

22. Jeffner Allen, *Lesbian Philosophy: Explorations* (Palo Alto, Calif.: Institute of Lesbian Studies, 1986), p. 38.

23. "Dateline NBC," August 25, 1992, pp. 7 and 13.

24. "Geraldo," p. 18.

25. Žižek, *Looking Awry*, p. 39.

26. Ibid., pp. 40–41.

27. Ibid., p. 57.

28. René Girard, *Violence and the Sacred*, trans. Patrick Gregory (Baltimore: Johns Hopkins University Press, 1977), p. 51.

29. Ibid., p. 5.

30. Ibid., p. 35.

31. Ibid., p. 36.

32. Jacques Lacan, "Motifs du Crime Paranoïaque: Le Crime des Soeurs Papin," *Minotaure: Revue Artistique et Litteraire*, February 15, 1933, pp. 26–27 (my translation).

33. Clément, *Lives and Legends*, p. 72.

34. Ibid., pp. 76–78.

35. Ibid., p. 78.

36. Jacques Lacan, "The Mirror Stage as Formative of the Function of the I," in *Écrits*.

37. Clément, *Lives and Legends*, p. 91.

38. "The Maids of Le Mans," in *Infamous Murderers* (London: Verdict Press, 1975), p. 112.

39. Clément, *Lives and Legends*, p. 56.

40. Elisabeth Roudinesco, *Jacques Lacan & Co.: A History of Psychoanalysis in France, 1925–1985*, trans. Jeffrey Mehlman (Chicago: University of Chicago Press, 1990), p. 113.

41. Clément, *Lives and Legends*, p. 57.

42. Roudinesco, *Jacques Lacan & Co.*, p. 113.

43. Ibid.

44. Clément, *Lives and Legends*, p. 72.

45. Lynda Hart, " 'They Don't Even Look Like Maids Anymore': Wendy Kesselman's *My Sister in This House*," in *Making a Spectacle: Feminist Essays on Contemporary Women's Theatre*, ed. Lynda Hart (Ann Arbor: University of Michigan Press, 1989), pp. 131–146.

46. Clément, *Lives and Legends*, p. 73.

47. Lacan, "God and the *Jouissance* of The Woman," in *Feminine Sexuality*, pp. 137–161.

48. Žižek, *Looking Awry*, p. 32.

49. Ibid., p. 33.

50. Clément, *Lives and Legends*, pp. 73–74.

51. Ibid., p. 79.

52. Ibid.

53. Arlene Pralle, quoted in Mark MacNamara, "Kiss and Kill," *Vanity Fair* 54 (September 1991): 104.

54. Implicitly or explicitly, Wuornos's lesbianism has been a major concern for the media, the courts, and the criminal and psychiatric "experts." The question of whether she "hated men," which is an all-too-obvious euphemism for lesbianism, comes up in every interview. The fact that she is repeatedly labeled the *first* "female" serial killer, when even the same reports acknowledge that this is technically inaccurate, points to the persistent confusion of her sexuality with her criminality. What can be deduced from the substitutions and deletions is that Wuornos is the first "real" female serial killer (i.e., *real* because she fits the male serial killer's profile more closely than any other woman in history) *because* she is a lesbian. Conversely, because she is a lesbian she has been made to fit the profile of the male serial killer. The feminist, lesbian, and gay communities have not been quick to respond to the obvious homophobia that is running the course of Wuornos's case. There have, however, been a few good commentaries on this issue. See Lindsy Van Gelder, "Attack of the 'Killer Lesbians,' " *Ms.*, January/February 1992, pp. 80–82; Victoria A. Brownworth, "Crime and Punishment," *QW*, October 25, 1992, pp. 24–26; and Donald Suggs, "Did the Media Exploit the 'Lesbian Serial Killer' Story?" *Advocate*, March 10, 1992, p. 98. Without any critical commentary, Susan Edmiston reports the FBI agent Robert Ressler's opinion: "There may be an intrinsic hatred of males here, as well as an identification with male violence which helped push her across the line into what has been considered a 'male' crime." And a Dr. Morall who opines: "You might not expect

a woman of clear sexual identity to do this. I see her as a woman whose sexual identity is distorted. If this woman's makeup is such that she takes pride in being masculine, her motivation would be a psychological challenge to the male—'I'm more masculine than you.'" Quoted in "The First Woman Serial Killer?" *Glamour*, September 1991, p. 325.

55. Arlene Pralle, quoted in MacNamara, "Kiss and Kill," p. 106.

56. Aileen Wuornos, "Dateline NBC," November 10, 1992, p. 12.

57. Phyllis Chesler, quoted in *Los Angeles Times*, December 17, 1991, p. E3.

58. Brownworth, "Crime and Punishment," p. 27.

59. Wuornos, "Dateline NBC," August 25, 1992, p. 10. Under pressure from Gillen, Wuornos admits that she "didn't like [her] childhood," but that she "didn't dwell on it. It didn't mess [her] life up." I am not trying to argue that Wuornos, or anyone, can just "take [their] past and . . . [throw] it in the river." But what is alarming in this case is how the "trauma theory" has been swiftly mobilized to *condemn* her. While Wuornos has insisted all along that in *each* incident she was being raped or threatened (two of the men did rape her; five tried, she said), the impact of evidence about the first "victim," Richard Mallory, concerning his history of sexual assault has served to fuel the theory that Wuornos was repeating an early trauma. Even those who seem to agree that Mallory probably was raping her have simply substituted the Mallory rape for an earlier sexual violation—by her father, grandfather, brother, or the unidentified man who got her pregnant when she was fourteen. Wuornos is intelligent enough to surmise that the trauma theory is not working in her defense.

60. Peggy Phelan, "Anita Hill and Clarence Thomas: Law, Psychoanalysis, and Sexual/ized Rumors" (Paper delivered at the 108th Convention of the Modern Language Association of America, New York, December 30, 1992).

61. Broomfield documentary.

62. Cixous and Clément, *The Newly Born Woman*, p. 53.

63. The association between lesbians and prostitutes, and the tendency of the judicial system to conflate them, is discussed by Joan Nestle in *A Restricted Country* (Ithaca, N.Y.: Firebrand Books, 1987) and by Robson in *Lesbian (Out)law*.

Chapter 9
Afterword: Zero Degree Deviancy—*Lesbians Who Kill*

1. Michel Foucault, ed., *I, Pierre Rivière, having slaughtered my mother, my sister, and my brother . . . : A Case of Parricide in the Nineteenth Century*, trans. Frank Jellinek (New York: Pantheon Books, 1975), pp. 205–206.

2. Deb Margolin, *Lesbians Who Kill*. All quotations are taken from an unpublished manuscript generously made available to me by Margolin.

3. Foucault, *Pipe*, p. 46.

4. Gilles Deleuze, "Plato and the Simulacrum," trans. Rosalind Krauss, *October* 27 (Winter 1983): 45.

5. Ibid.

6. Ibid.

7. Ibid., p. 47.

8. Ibid., p. 48.

9. Ibid.

10. Ibid., p. 54.

11. Lacan, *Four Fundamental Concepts*, p. 252.

12. Peggy Phelan, "Broken symmetries: memory, sight, love," in *Unmarked*, p. 24.

13. Lacan, *Four Fundamental Concepts*, p. 252.

14. Ibid., p. 250.

Works Cited

Alcoff, Linda. "Cultural Feminism versus Post-Structuralism: The Identity Crisis in Feminist Theory." In *Reconstructing the Academy: Women's Education and Women's Studies*, edited by Elizabeth Minnich, Jean O'Barr, and Rachel Rosenfeld. Chicago: University of Chicago Press, 1988.

Allen, Jeffner. *Lesbian Philosophy: Explorations*. Palo Alto, Calif.: Institute of Lesbian Studies, 1986.

Alleva, Richard. "Lethal Smooches: *Kiss* and *Mortal Thoughts*." *Commonweal*, June 14, 1991, pp. 406–407.

Altick, Richard. *Victorian Studies in Scarlet*. New York: Norton and Norton, 1970.

Arrington, Wayne. "Lost in America." *Premiere*, April 1991, pp. 104–108.

Auerbach, Nina. *Woman and the Demon: The Life of a Victorian Myth*. Cambridge: Harvard University Press, 1982.

Babcock, Barbara. *The Reversible World: Symbolic Inversion in Art and Society*. Ithaca: Cornell University Press, 1978.

Bad Object-Choices, eds. *How Do I Look? Queer Film and Video*. Seattle: Bay Press, 1991.

Barthes, Roland. *The Pleasure of the Text*. Translated by Richard Miller. New York: Hill and Wang, 1975.

———. *S/Z*. Translated by Richard Miller. New York: Farrar, Straus and Giroux, 1974.

Bataille, Georges. *Erotism: Death and Sensuality*. Translated by Mary Dalwood. San Francisco: City Lights Books, 1986.

Baumgold, Julie. "Killer Women: Here Come the Hardbodies." *New York*, July 29, 1991, pp. 24–29.

Beale, Lewis. "Gays vs. Hollywood." *Chicago Tribune*, March 29, 1992, p. 10.

Beauvoir, Simone de. *The Second Sex*. Translated and edited by H. M. Parshley. New York: Random House, 1952.

Berlant, Lauren. "The Female Complaint." *Socialtext* 19–20 (1988): 237–259.

Bersani, Leo. *The Freudian Body: Psychoanalysis and Art*. New York: Columbia University Press, 1986.

———. "Is the Rectum a Grave?" In *AIDS: Cultural Analysis, Cultural Activism*, edited by Douglas Crimp. Cambridge: MIT Press, 1988.

Bhabha, Homi K. "The Other Question: Difference, Discrimination and the Discourse of Colonialism." In *Literature, Politics, Theory: Papers from the Essex Conference, 1976–1984*, edited by Francis Barker, Peter Hulme, Margaret Iversen, and Diana Loxley. London: Methuen, 1986.

———. "Signs Taken for Wonders: Questions of Ambivalence and Authority under a Tree outside Delhi, May 1817." In *Race, Writing and Difference*, edited by Henry Louis Gates, Jr. Chicago: University of Chicago Press, 1986.

188

Blake, Richard A. "The Deadlier of the Species." *America*, June 29, 1991, p. 683.

Booth, Michael. *English Melodrama*. London: Herbert Jenkins, 1965.

Borch-Jacobsen, Mikkel. *The Freudian Subject*. Translated by Catherine Porter. Stanford: Stanford University Press, 1988.

———. *Lacan: The Absolute Master*. Translated by Douglas Brick. Stanford: Stanford University Press, 1991.

Braddon, Mary Elizabeth. *Lady Audley's Secret*. New York: Dover, 1974.

Brooks, Louise. *Lulu in Hollywood*. New York: Alfred A. Knopf, 1982.

Broomfield, Nick. *Aileen Wuornos: The Selling of a Serial Killer*. Documentary. 1993.

Brownworth, Victoria A. "Crime and Punishment." *QW*, October 25, 1992, pp. 24–26.

Buck, Joan Juliet. *Vogue*, May 1991, pp. 161–162.

Butler, Judith. *Gender Trouble: Feminism and the Subversion of Identity*. New York: Routledge, 1990.

Capellanus, Andreas. *The Art of Courtly Love*. Translated by John Jay Parry. New York: Frederick Ungar, 1959.

Caputi, Jane. *The Age of Sex Crime*. Bowling Green, Ohio: Bowling Green State University Press, 1987.

———. "The New Founding Fathers: The Lore and Lure of the Serial Killer in Contemporary Culture." *Journal of American Culture* 13, no. 3 (1990): 1–12.

Carlson, Margaret. "Is This What Feminism Is All About?" *Time*, June 24, 1991, p. 57.

Carr, C. "The Sexual Politics of Censorship: War on Art." *Village Voice*, June 5, 1990, p. 28.

———. "Unspeakable Practices, Unnatural Acts: The Taboo Art of Karen Finley." *Village Voice*, June 24, 1986, pp. 17–18, 86.

Case, Sue-Ellen. "Toward a Butch-Femme Aesthetic." In *Making a Spectacle: Feminist Essays on Contemporary Women's Theatre*, edited by Lynda Hart. Ann Arbor: University of Michigan Press, 1989.

Chauncey, George, Jr. "From Sexual Inversion to Homosexuality: Medicine and the Changing Conception of Female Deviance." *Salmagundi* 58–59 (Fall 1982–Winter 1983): 114–146.

Chesler, Phyllis. "Sex, Death and the Double Standard." *On the Issues*, Summer 1992, pp. 28–31.

Cixous, Hélène. "The Laugh of the Medusa." In *New French Feminisms*, edited by Elaine Marks and Isabelle de Courtivron. New York: Schocken Books, 1981.

Cixous, Hélène, and Catherine Clément. *The Newly Born Woman*. Translated by Betsy Wing. Minneapolis: University of Minnesota Press, 1986.

Clary, Mike. "A Mother's Love." *Los Angeles Times*, December 17, 1991, pp. E1–2.

Clément, Catherine. *The Lives and Legends of Jacques Lacan*. Translated by Arthur Goldhammer. New York: Columbia University Press, 1983.

Cousins, Mark. "The Logic of Deconstruction." *Oxford Literary Review* 3, no. 2 (1978): 70–78.

Crompton, Louis. "The Myth of Lesbian Impunity." *Journal of Homosexuality* 6, nos. 1–2 (1980–1981): 11–25.

Cross, Alice. "The Bimbo and the Mystery Woman: Should We Go Along for the Ride? A Critical Symposium on *Thelma and Louise*." *Cineaste* 28, no. 4 (1991): 28–36.

"Dateline NBC" (transcript produced by Burrelle's Information Services, Livingston, N.J.). August 25, 1992.

"Dateline NBC" (transcript produced by Burrelle's Information Services, Livingston, N.J.). November 10, 1992.

Davis, Angela. "Racism, Birth Control and Reproductive Rights." In *Women, Race and Class*. New York: Random House, 1981.

Davy, Kate. "From *Lady Dick* to Ladylike: The Work of Holly Hughes." In *Acting Out: Feminist Performances*, edited by Lynda Hart and Peggy Phelan. Ann Arbor: University of Michigan Press, 1993.

de Lauretis, Teresa. *Alice Doesn't: Feminism, Semiotics, Cinema*. Bloomington: Indiana University Press, 1984.

———. "Eccentric Subjects: Feminist Theory and Historical Consciousness." *Feminist Studies* 16, no. 1 (1990): 115–150.

———. "Film and the Visible." In *How Do I Look? Queer Film and Video*, edited by Bad Object-Choices. Seattle: Bay Press, 1991.

Deleuze, Gilles. "Plato and the Simulacrum." Translated by Rosalind Krauss. *October* 27 (Winter 1983): 45–56.

Denby, David. "Road Warriors." *New York*, June 10, 1991, pp. 55–56.

Diamond, Elin. "Brechtian Theory/Feminist Theory." *Drama Review* 32, no. 1 (1988): 82–94.

Dijkstra, Bram. *Idols of Perversity: Fantasies of Feminine Evil in Fin-de-Siècle Culture*. New York: Oxford University Press, 1986.

Doane, Mary Ann. *The Desire to Desire: The Woman's Film of the 1940s*. Bloomington: Indiana University Press, 1987.

———. *Femmes Fatales: Feminism, Film Theory, Psychoanalysis*. London: Routledge, 1991.

Dollimore, Jonathan. "Masculine Sexuality—1: Homophobia and Sexual Difference." *Oxford Literary Review* 8, nos. 1–2 (1986): 5–11.

———. *Sexual Dissidence: Augustine to Wilde, Freud to Foucault*. Oxford: Clarendon Press, 1991.

Douglas, Mary. *Purity and Danger: An Analysis of Concepts of Pollution and Taboo*. London: Routledge, 1966.

Dyer, Richard. "White." *Screen* 29, no. 4 (1988): 44–64.

Edmiston, Susan. "The First Woman Serial Killer?" *Glamour*, September 1991, pp. 302–325.

Egger, Steven A. "A Working Definition of Serial Murder and the Reduction of Linkage Blindness." *Journal of Police Science and Administration* 12, no. 3 (1984): 348–357.

Ellis, Havelock. *The Criminal*. New York: AMS Press, 1972.

———. "Sexual Inversion in Women." In *Studies in the Psychology of Sex*. Vol. 2. Philadelphia: F. A. Davis Company, 1904.

Ellis, Havelock. *Studies in the Psychology of Sex*. Vol. 7. Philadelphia: F. A. Davis Company, 1928.

Evans, Rowland, and Robert Novack. "The NEA's Suicide Charge." *Washington Post*, May 11, 1990, p. A27.

Faderman, Lillian. *Surpassing the Love of Men: Romantic Friendship and Love between Women from the Renaissance to the Present*. New York: William Morrow and Company, 1981.

Faderman, Lillian, and Brigitte Eriksson. *Lesbians in Germany: 1890's–1920's*. Tallahassee, Fla.: The Naiad Press, 1990.

Felman, Shoshana. "Rereading Femininity." *Yale French Studies*, no. 62 (1981): 19–44.

Felman, Shoshana, and Dori Laub, M.D. *Testimony: Crises of Witnessing in Literature, Psychoanalysis, and History*. New York: Routledge, 1992.

Finley, Karen. *Shock Treatment*. San Francisco: City Lights, 1990.

Finney, Gail. *Women in Modern Drama: Freud, Feminism, and European Theater at the Turn of the Century*. Ithaca: Cornell University Press, 1989.

Flowers, Ronald Barri. *Women and Criminality*. New York: Greenwood Press, 1987.

Foucault, Michel. *The History of Sexuality*. Vol. 1. New York: Vintage Books, 1980.

———. *Power/Knowledge: Selected Interviews and Other Writings 1972–1977*. Edited by Colin Gordon. Translated by Colin Gordon, Leo Marshall, John Mepham, and Kate Soper. New York: Pantheon Books, 1980.

———. *This Is Not a Pipe*. Berkeley and Los Angeles: University of California Press, 1982.

———, ed. *I, Pierre Riviere, having slaughtered my mother, my sister, and my brother . . . : A Case of Parricide in the Nineteenth Century*. Translated by Frank Jellinek. New York: Pantheon Books, 1975.

Freud, Sigmund. *The Standard Edition of the Complete Psychological Works of Sigmund Freud*. Edited by James Strachey. 24 vols. London: The Hogarth Press, 1953–1974. Hereafter *SE*.

———. "Criminals from a Sense of Guilt" (1916). *SE*, 14:332–333.

———. "The Ego and the Id" (1923). *SE*, 19:19–27.

———. "The Ego and the Super-Ego (Ego Ideal)" (1923). *SE*, 19:28–39.

———. "Femininity" (1933). *SE*, 22:112–135.

———. "Group Psychology and the Analysis of the Ego" (1921). *SE*, 18:67–143.

———. "Instincts and Their Vicissitudes" (1915). *SE*, 14:117–140.

———. "On Fetishism" (1927). *SE*, 21:149–157.

———. "On the Mechanism of Paranoia" (1911). *SE*, 12:59–79.

———. "On Narcissism, an Introduction" (1914). *SE*, 14:73–102.

———. "Psycho-analysis and the Establishment of the Facts in Legal Proceedings" (1906). *SE*, 9:103–114.

———. "The Psychogenesis of a Case of Homosexuality in a Woman" (1920). *SE*, 18:145–172.

———. "Some Neurotic Mechanisms in Jealousy, Paranoia, and Homosexuality" (1921). *SE*, 18:223–232.

————. "Some Psychical Consequences of the Anatomical Distinction between the Sexes" (1925). *SE*, 19:243–258.

————. "Three Essays on the Theory of Sexuality" (1905). *SE*, 7:125–243.

————. "The Uncanny" (1919). *SE*, 17:219–252.

Frye, Marilyn. *The Politics of Reality: Essays in Feminist Theory*. Freedom, Calif.: The Crossing Press, 1983.

Fuchs, Cynthia J. "The Buddy Politic." In *Screening the Male: Exploring Masculinities in Hollywood Cinema*, edited by Steven Cohan and Ina Rae Hark. London: Routledge, 1993.

Fuss, Diana, ed. *Inside/Out: Lesbian Theories, Gay Theories*. New York: Routledge, 1991.

Gaines, Jane. "White Privilege and Looking Relations: Race and Gender in Feminist Film Theory." *Screen* 29, no. 4 (1988): 12–27.

"Geraldo. Profile of Aileen Wuornos: The Woman behind the Murders" (transcript). March 23, 1993.

Gilbert, Matthew. "Cashing In on Bad Publicity." *Boston Globe*, April 5, 1992, p. B29.

Gilman, Sander L. "Black Bodies, White Bodies: Toward an Iconography of Female Sexuality in Late Nineteenth-Century Art, Medicine, and Literature." *Critical Inquiry* 12 (Autumn 1985): 205–242.

Girard, René. *Violence and the Sacred*. Translated by Patrick Gregory. Baltimore: Johns Hopkins University Press, 1977.

Gordon, Linda. *Woman's Body, Woman's Rights: A Social History of Birth Control in America*. New York: Grossman, 1976.

Greenberg, David F. *The Construction of Homosexuality*. Chicago: University of Chicago Press, 1988.

Grosz, Elizabeth. *Jacques Lacan: A Feminist Introduction*. New York: Routledge, 1990.

Hart, Lynda. "Motherhood According to Karen Finley: *The Theory of Total Blame*." *Drama Review* 36, no. 1 (1991): 124–134.

————. " 'They Don't Even Look Like Maids Anymore': Wendy Kesselman's *My Sister in This House*." In *Making a Spectacle: Feminist Essays on Contemporary Women's Theatre*, edited by Lynda Hart. Ann Arbor: University of Michigan Press, 1989.

Hart, Lynda, and Peggy Phelan, eds. *Acting Out: Feminist Performances*. Ann Arbor: University of Michigan Press, 1993.

Hartman, Mary. *Victorian Murderesses*. New York: Schocken Books, 1977.

Hazelwood, C. H. *Lady Audley's Secret*. In *Nineteenth-Century Plays*, edited by George Rowell. Oxford: Oxford University Press, 1972.

Hillman, James. "Notes on White Supremacy: Essaying an Archetypal Account of Historical Events." *Spring* (1986): 29–58.

Hinson, Hal. "*Single White Female*: Double Trouble." *Washington Post*, August 14, 1992, p. C6.

Hocquenghem, Guy. "Family, Capitalism, Anus." *Semiotext(e): Anti-Oedipus* 2, no. 3 (1977): 148–158.

Hughes, Holly. "You Have a Gal in Kalamazoo." *Performance Journal* 1, no. 1 (1990): 10.

Hughes, Holly, and Richard Elovich. "Homophobia at the N.E.A." *New York Times*, July 28, 1990, p. 21.

Infamous Murderers. London: Verdict Press, 1975.

Irigaray, Luce. *Speculum of the Other Woman*. Translated by Gillian C. Gill. Ithaca: Cornell University Press, 1985.

———. *This Sex Which Is Not One*. Translated by Catherine Porter. Ithaca: Cornell University Press, 1985.

Jerome, Jim. "Riding Shotgun." *People*, June 24, 1991.

Johnstone, Iain. "Emotional Cop-out." *Sunday Times*, May 10, 1992.

Jones, Ann. *Women Who Kill*. New York: Fawcett Columbine, 1980.

Juno, Andrea, and V. Vale, eds. *Angry Women*. San Francisco: RE/SEARCH, 1991.

Keuls, Eva C. *The Reign of the Phallus: Sexual Politics in Ancient Athens*. New York: Harper and Row, 1985.

Koedt, Anne, Ellen Levine, and Anita Rapone, eds. *Radical Feminism*. New York: Quadrangle, 1973.

Kofman, Sarah. *Freud and the Enigma of Woman: Woman in Freud's Writings*. Translated by Catherine Porter. Ithaca: Cornell University Press, 1985.

Kristeva, Julia. "About Chinese Women." In *The Kristeva Reader*, edited by Toril Moi. New York: Columbia University Press, 1986.

———. *Powers of Horror: An Essay on Abjection*. Translated by Leon S. Roudiez. New York: Columbia University Press, 1982.

Kunen, James S., Meg Grant, Cindy Dampier, and Sara Gay Dommann. "Florida Cops Say Seven Men Met Death on the Highway When They Picked Up Accused Serial Killer Aileen Wuornos." *People*, February 25, 1991.

Lacan, Jacques. *Écrits*. Translated by Alan Sheridan. New York: W. W. Norton and Co., 1977.

———. *Feminine Sexuality: Jacques Lacan and the école freudienne*. Edited by Juliet Mitchell and Jacqueline Rose. Translated by Jaqueline Rose. London: Macmillan, 1982.

———. *The Four Fundamental Concepts of Psycho-Analysis*. Translated by Alan Sheridan. New York: W. W. Norton and Co., 1981.

———. "Motifs du Crime Paranoïaque: Le Crime des Soeurs Papin." *Minotaure: Revue Artistique et Litteraire*, February 15, 1933, pp. 25–28.

———. *The Seminar of Jacques Lacan: Book I, Freud's Papers on Technique, 1953–1954*. Edited by Jacques-Alain Miller. Translated by John Forrester. New York: W. W. Norton and Co., 1991.

———. *The Seminar of Jacques Lacan: Book II, The Ego in Freud's Theory and in the Technique of Psychoanalysis, 1954–1955*. Edited by Jacques-Alain Miller. Translated by Sylvana Tomaselli. New York: W. W. Norton and Co., 1991.

Laplanche, Jean. *Life and Death in Psychoanalysis*. Translated by Jeffrey Mehlman. Baltimore: Johns Hopkins University Press, 1976.

Leavitt, David. "The Fears That Haunt a Scrubbed Nation." *New York Times*, August 19, 1990, sec. 2, p. 1.

Leger, Robert G. "Lesbianism among Women Prisoners: Participants and Non-Participants." *Criminal Justice and Behavior* 14, no. 4 (1987): 448–467.

"Lesbians Coming Out Strong." *Newsweek*, June 21, 1993, pp. 54–60.

"Letters: The Yam Became a Hot Potato." *Village Voice*, July 15, 1986, pp. 4–6.

Lombroso, Caesar. *The Female Offender*. New York: D. Appleton and Co., 1895.

Mackey, Louis. "Eros into Logos: The Rhetoric of Courtly Love." In *The Philosophy of (Erotic) Love*, edited by Robert C. Solomon and Kathleen M. Higgins. Lawrence: University Press of Kansas, 1991.

Maclean, Ian. *The Renaissance Notion of Woman*. Cambridge: Cambridge University Press, 1980.

MacNamara, Mark. "Kiss and Kill." *Vanity Fair* 54 (September 1991): 90–106.

Margolin, Deb. *Lesbians Who Kill*. Manuscript. 1992.

Miller, D. A. "Anal Rope." In *Inside/Out: Lesbian Theories, Gay Theories*, edited by Diana Fuss. New York: Routledge, 1991.

Millett, Kate. *Sexual Politics*. New York: Ballantine Books, 1970.

Milton, John. *Paradise Lost*. In *The Poetical Works of John Milton*, edited by Sir Egerton Brydges. Boston: Crosby, Nichols, Lee & Company, 1861.

Modleski, Tania. *Feminism without Women: Culture and Criticism in a "Postfeminist" Age*. New York: Routledge, 1991.

Mulvey, Laura. *Visual and Other Pleasures*. Bloomington: Indiana University Press, 1989.

Naffine, Ngaire. *Female Crime: The Construction of Women in Criminology*. Boston: Allen and Unwin, 1987.

Neisen, Joseph. "Heterosexism or Homophobia?" *Out/Look* 10 (Fall 1990): 36–37.

Nestle, Joan. *A Restricted Country*. Ithaca, N.Y.: Firebrand Books, 1987.

Nietzsche, Friedrich. *Beyond Good and Evil*. Translated by Walter Kaufmann. New York: Random House, 1966.

Omosupe, Ekua. "Black/Lesbian/Bulldagger." *differences* 3, no. 2 (1991): 101–111.

Papajohn, George. *Chicago Tribune*, May 19, 1992, p. 1.

Paris, Barry. *Louise Brooks*. New York: Alfred A. Knopf, 1989.

Petchesky, Rosalind Pollack. *Abortion and Woman's Choice: The State, Sexuality, and Reproductive Freedom*. New York: Longman, 1984.

Phelan, Peggy. "Anita Hill and Clarence Thomas: Law, Psychoanalysis, and Sexual/ized Rumors." Paper delivered at the 108th Convention of the Modern Language Association of America, New York, December 30, 1992.

———. "Serrano, Mapplethorpe, the NEA, and You: 'Money Talks.' " *Drama Review* 34, no. 1 (1990): 4–15.

———. *Unmarked: The Politics of Performance*. New York: Routledge, 1993.

Rae, W. Fraser. "Sensation Novelists: Miss Braddon." *North British Review* 43 (September 1865).

Rainwater, Lee, and William L. Yancey. *The Moynihan Report and the Politics of Controversy*. Cambridge: MIT Press, 1967.

Ressler, Robert K., and Tom Shachtman. *Whoever Fights Monsters: My Twenty Years Tracking Serial Killers for the F.B.I.* New York: St. Martin's Press, 1992.

Rist, Curtis. "Gays Find Movie's Instincts All Wrong." *Newsday*, March 21, 1992, p. 4.

Robson, Ruthann. *Lesbian (Out)law: Survival under the Rule of Law*. Ithaca, N.Y.: Firebrand Books, 1992.

Roof, Judith. *The Lure of Knowledge*. New York: Columbia University Press, 1992.

Rose, Jacqueline. *Sexuality in the Field of Vision*. London: Verso, 1986.

Roudinesco, Elisabeth. *Jacques Lacan & Co.: A History of Psychoanalysis in France, 1925–1985*. Translated by Jeffrey Mehlman. Chicago: University of Chicago Press, 1990.

Russ, Joanna. *How to Suppress Women's Writing*. Austin: University of Texas Press, 1983.

Russell, Margaret. "What's behind All This Legal Reelism." *Legal Times*, April 13, 1992, p. 54.

Sartre, Jean-Paul. *Saint Genet: Actor and Martyr*. Translated by Bernard Frechtman. New York: Braziller, 1963.

Schickel, Richard. "Lots of Skin, but No Heart." *Time*, March 23, 1992, p. 65.
———. "A Postcard from the Edge." *Time*, May 27, 1991, p. 64.

Schroeder, Natalie. "Feminine Sensationalism, Eroticism, and Self-Assertion: M. E. Braddon and Ouida." *Tulsa Studies in Women's Literature* 7, no. 1 (1988): 87–103.

Schuler, Catherine. "Spectator Response and Comprehension: The Problem of Karen Finley's *Constant State of Desire*." *Drama Review* 32 (Spring 1988): 131–145.

Sedgwick, Eve Kosofsky. *Epistemology of the Closet*. Berkeley and Los Angeles: University of California Press, 1990.
———. "A Poem Is Being Written." *Representations* 17 (Winter 1987): 110–143.

Sheldon, Caroline. "Lesbians and Film: Some Thoughts." In *Gays and Film*, edited by Richard Dyer. New York: Zoetrope, 1977.

Showalter, Elaine. *A Literature of Their Own: British Women Novelists from Brontë to Lessing*. Princeton: Princeton University Press, 1977.

Smith-Rosenberg, Carroll. "The Abortion Movement and the AMA, 1850–1880." In *Disorderly Conduct*. Oxford: Oxford University Press, 1985.

Solomon, Robert C., and Kathleen M. Higgins, eds. *The Philosophy of (Erotic) Love*. Lawrence: University Press of Kansas, 1991.

Spivak, Gayatri. "Subaltern Studies: Deconstructing Historiography." In *In Other Worlds: Essays in Cultural Politics*. New York: Methuen, 1987.

Sterritt, David. "*Basic Instinct*: Specimen of a Sorry Breed of Movie." *Christian Science Monitor*, March 30, 1992, p. 11.

Streib, Victor L. "Death Penalty for Female Offenders." *University of Cincinnati Law Review* 58, no. 3 (1990): 878–889.

Suggs, Donald. "Did the Media Exploit the 'Lesbian Serial Killer' Story?" *Advocate*, March 10, 1992, p. 98.

Talmey, Bernard S. *Woman: A Treatise on the Normal and Pathological Emotions of Feminine Love*. 1904. 6th enl. and rev. ed. New York: Practitioners Publishing Co., 1910.

Todorov, Tzvetan. *The Poetics of Prose*. Translated by Richard Howard. Ithaca: Cornell University Press, 1977.

Traub, Valerie. "The Ambiguities of 'Lesbian' Viewing Pleasure: The (Dis)articulations of *Black Widow*." In *Body Guards*, edited by Julia Epstein and Kristina Straub. New York: Routledge, 1992.

Van Gelder, Lindsy. "Attack of the 'Killer Lesbians.' " *Ms.*, January/February 1992, pp. 80–82.

Vicinus, Martha. " 'Helpless and Unfriended': Nineteenth-Century Domestic Melodrama." In *When They Weren't Doing Shakespeare: Essays on Nineteenth-Century British and American Theatre*, edited by Judith L. Fisher and Stephen Watt. Athens: University of Georgia Press, 1989.

von Kursk, Harold. "Accusations of Gay Bashing Rankle Douglas." *Toronto Star*, March 23, 1992, p. C5.

Walker, Ruth. "Why We Cheered *Thelma and Louise*." *Christian Science Monitor*, July 17, 1991, p. 18.

Walkowitz, Judith. "Jack the Ripper and the Myth of Male Violence." *Feminist Studies* 8, no. 3 (1982): 543–574.

Watney, Simon. *Policing Desire: Pornography, AIDS, and the Media*. Minneapolis: University of Minnesota Press, 1987.

Wedekind, Frank. *The Lulu Plays and Other Sex Tragedies*. Translated by Stephen Spender. New York: Riverrun Press, 1978.

Weeks, Jeffrey. *Coming Out: Homosexual Politics in Britain from the Nineteenth Century to the Present*. London: Quartet Press, 1977.

———. *Sex, Politics and Society: The Regulation of Sexuality since 1800*. London: Longman, 1981.

Weininger, Otto. *Sex and Character*. New York: G. P. Putnam's Sons, 1906.

Wilden, Anthony. "Lacan and the Discourse of the Other." In *Speech and Language in Psychoanalysis*, by Jacques Lacan, translated with notes and commentary by Anthony Wilden. Baltimore: Johns Hopkins University Press, 1968.

Wilkinson, Frances. "The Gospel According to Randall Terry." *Rolling Stone*, October 5, 1989, pp. 85–89.

Williams, Patricia J. "Attack of the 50-Ft. First Lady: The Demonization of Hillary Clinton." *Village Voice*, January 26, 1993, pp. 35–39.

Wittig, Monique. *The Straight Mind and Other Essays*. Boston: Beacon, 1992.

Wood, Robin. *Hollywood from Vietnam to Reagan*. New York: Columbia University Press, 1986.

Woods, Mrs. Henry. *East Lynne*. New Brunswick: Rutgers University Press, 1984.

Woolf, Virginia. *A Room of One's Own*. London: Granada, 1977.

Žižek, Slavoj. *Enjoy Your Symptom! Jacques Lacan in Hollywood and Out*. New York: Routledge, 1992.

———. *Looking Awry: An Introduction to Jacques Lacan through Popular Culture*. Cambridge: MIT Press, 1991.

———. *The Sublime Object of Ideology*. London: Verso, 1989.

Index